Bob Silverman

Bob Silverman
The Impossible Hero
John Symon and Stéphane Desjardins

University of Ottawa Press 2025

Les **Presses** de l'Université d'Ottawa
University of Ottawa **Press**

Les Presses de l'Université d'Ottawa / University of Ottawa Press (PUO-UOP) is North America's flagship bilingual university press, affiliated to one of Canada's top research universities. PUO-UOP enriches the intellectual and cultural discourse of our increasingly knowledge-based and globalized world with peer-reviewed, award-winning books.

www.Press.uOttawa.ca

Library and Archives Canada Cataloguing in Publication

Title: Bob Silverman : the impossible hero / John Symon and Stéphane Desjardins.
Names: Symon, John, author. | Desjardins, Stéphane, 1962- author.
Description: Includes bibliographical references.
Identifiers: Canadiana (print) 20250213427 | Canadiana (ebook) 20250213397 | ISBN 9780776641782 (hardcover) | ISBN 9780776641799 (softcover) | ISBN 9780776641874 (PDF) | ISBN 9780776641881 (EPUB)
Subjects: LCSH: Silverman, Robert, 1933-2022. | LCSH: Political activists—Québec (Province)—Montréal—Biography. | LCSH: Bicycle commuting—Québec (Province)—Montréal—History—20th century. | LCSH: Bicycle trails—Québec (Province)—Montréal—History—20th century. | LCSH: Monde à bicyclette (Association)—History. | LCGFT: Biographies.
Classification: LCC HE5739.C3 S96 2025 | DDC j388.3/47209714—dc23

Legal Deposit: Fourth Quarter 2025
Library and Archives Canada

© University of Ottawa Press 2025
All rights reserved

No part of this publication may be reproduced or transmitted in any form or by any means, or stored in a database and retrieval system, without prior permission.

Production Team

Copy editing	Céline Parent
Proofreading	Robbie McCaw
Typesetting	Édiscript enr.
Cover design	Benoit Deneault

Cover Image
Le Monde à bicyclette archive

uOttawa

PUO-UOP gratefully acknowledges the funding support of the University of Ottawa, the Government of Canada, the Canada Council for the Arts, the Ontario Arts Council and the Government of Ontario.

Table of Contents

List of Figures		vii
List of Acronyms		ix
List of People Featured in this Book		xiii
Acknowledgements		xxiii
Foreword	A Prophet before His Time	xxv
Chapter 1	Killed by a Car, Reborn on a Bicycle	1
Chapter 2	The Seven Steps Bookstore	11
Chapter 3	Arriving in Castro's Cuba	21
Chapter 4	Back in Montreal, Protesting against the Vietnam War	29
Chapter 5	Meeting His Second Wife at an Israeli Kibbutz	35
Chapter 6	The Save Montreal Movement	43
Chapter 7	Le Monde à Bicyclette	53
Chapter 8	The First Demonstration	61
Chapter 9	Storming the Metro	75
Chapter 10	The Battle for Bike Lanes	87
Chapter 11	Convincing Drapeau to Do the Right Thing	93
Chapter 12	A Brief History of Montreal Bike Paths	99
Chapter 13	One Million Cyclists Trapped on Montreal Island	103
Chapter 14	A Bike-Friendly Mayor Is Elected	111
Chapter 15	Protesting the Auto Show	121
Chapter 16	The Philadelphia Bicycle Coalition and International Connections	127
Chapter 17	MàB and Vélo Québec: Allies or Rivals?	135
Chapter 18	Participatory Volleyball, Good Volleyball Is like Good Sex	143
Chapter 19	The Handbook of How to Run a Vélorution	149
Chapter 20	Vietnam and Cuba	157
Chapter 21	Silverman and Politics	163
Chapter 22	Milton Park Days	181
Chapter 23	A Jew in Support of Palestinians	187
Chapter 24	Moving to Val-David	191
Chapter 25	Nearing the Finish Line	197
Chapter 26	Epilogue and Homages	199

Annex	205
Notes	221
Bibliography	231

List of Figures

	Bob Silverman in a gas mask with his bike	xxii
Figure 1.1	Bob at summer camp in 1945	2
Figure 1.2.	Bob and his sister skiing	3
Figure 1.3.	The house on Roslyn	4
Figure 1.4.	Bert, Florence, and Bob Silverman at Continental Divide	5
Figure 2.1.	A facsimile of the ad in *The Montreal Star* announcing performances by Bob Dylan at the Potpourri	13
Figure 2.2.	Leonard Cohen mural in Montreal	14
Figure 2.3.	Portrait of Silverman by Godfrey Stephens	17
Figure 2.4.	TSS as a Subway restaurant	19
Figure 6.1.	Silverman on his bike, October 1976	51
Figure 8.1.	Richard "Tooker" Gomberg	70
Figure 8.2.	Procession of cyclists on a downtown street	71
Figure 8.3.	The "die in" protest by MàB	72
Figure 9.1.	Members of MàB with Bob and Claire in the centre	76
Figure 9.2.	Police Arresting an Elephant	78
Figure 10.1.	We want bike lanes now!	88
Figure 10.2.	MàB members clandestinely painting unofficial bike lanes	89
Figure 10.3.	Enthusiastic MàB supporters at inauguration of unofficial bike lane	90
Figure 11.1.	Silverman participating in a "die-in" holding a volleyball	96
Figure 11.2.	1,200 cars per hour is too many!	97
Figure 12.1.	Map showing bike lanes in Montreal from 1897	100
Figure 12.2.	Silverman prepares for the spatial protest	102
Figure 14.1.	André Lavallée and Jean Doré	112
Figure 16.1.	John Dowlin, in Philadelphia, on his cargo bike in 2019	127
Figure 16.2.	MàB Logo	131
Figure 18.1.	Silverman with Regan at the volleyball courts	145
Figure 20.1.	Silverman in Vietnam	158
Figure 24.1.	FRAPRU protest	192
Figure 24.2.	Jacques Desjardins and Bob Silverman in 2015	196
Figure 24.3.	Carlton Reid and Bob Silverman	196

Figure 26.1. Unofficially naming Saint-Denis Street REV after Silverman   200
Figure A.1. John Symon with Silverman   220

List of Acronyms

ADHD   Attention deficit hyperactivity disorder
AIDS   Acquired immunodeficiency syndrome
AMT   Agence métropolitaine de transport, a transit authority now known as Exo
BC   British Columbia
BIXI   Montreal's public rental bikes; the name combines bicycle and taxi
CBC   Canadian Broadcasting Corporation (Radio Canada in French)
CCF   Co-operative Commonwealth Federation
CCNR   Canadian Coalition for Nuclear Responsibility
CEO   Chief executive officer
CHMP   Cooperative Housing Milton-Parc
CHSLD   Centre d'hébergement de soins de longue durée (long-term care centre)
CIA   Central Intelligence Agency (of the US)
CLSC   Centre Local de Services Communautaires
CMHC   Canada Mortgage and Housing Corporation
CNS   Cyclo Nord-Sud, a charity that sends bicycles to the Third World
CoC   Citizens on Cycles, the English name for le Monde à bicyclette
COFI   Centre d'orientation et de formation des immigrants
CRTC   Canadian Radio-Television and Telecommunications Commission
CTCUM   Commission de transport de la Communauté urbaine de Montréal: former acronym for Montreal's transit authority, now the STM
CUCND   Combined Universities Campaign for Nuclear Disarmament
DC   District of Columbia, where the US capital is located
EBC   Edmonton Bicycle Commuters
EI   Employment Insurance
ELRT   Edmonton Light Rail Transit
EMAB   Encore du Monde à bicyclette (a group continuing some of MàB's work)
FDA   US Food and Drug Administration
FLQ   Front de libération du Québec: a militant separatist group
FQSC   Fédération québécoise des sports cyclistes
FRAP   Front d'action politique (a former political party in Montreal)

FRAPRU	Front d'action populaire en réaménagement urbain (tenants' advocacy group)
GHG	Greenhouse gasses
GM	General Motors Company
GPC	Green Party of Canada
GPCQM	Grands Prix cyclistes de Québec et de Montréal (elite bicycle races)
ICBM	Intercontinental Ballistic Missile
IJV	Independent Jewish Voices
JCCB	Jacques Cartier and Champlain Bridges Incorporated (bridge authority)
LGBTQ	Lesbian, gay, bisexual, transgender and queer
LIP	Local Initiatives Program, a defunct federal work-creation program
LSD	Lysergic acid diethylamide
MàB	Monde à bicyclette
MCM	Montreal Citizens' Movement, a defunct political party in Montreal
MIT	Massachusetts Institute of Technology
MNA	Member of Quebec's National Assembly, equivalent of MPP, MLA or state legislator
MP	Member of Parliament
MUC	Montreal Urban Community
NATO	North Atlantic Treaty Organization
NDG	Notre-Dame-de-Grâce (a west-end Montreal neighbourhood)
NDP	New Democratic Party
NORAD	North American Aerospace Defense Command
PAE	Physician-Administered Euthanasia
PAJU	Palestinians and Jews United
PAS	Physician-Assisted Suicide
PAVN	Peoples' Army of Vietnam
PBC	Philadelphia Bicycle Coalition (now the Bicycle Coalition of Greater Philadelphia)
PLO	Palestinian Liberation Organization
PQ	Parti Québécois: a separatist political party in Quebec
PVQ	Parti vert du Québec or Québec Green Party
PTSD	Post-traumatic stress disorder
RCM	French acronym for the MCM
RCMP	Royal Canadian Mounted Police
RCP	Revolutionary Communist Party, a Trotskyite party in Canada
REM	Réseau express métropolitain (a train and new component of Montreal's transit system)
REV	Réseau express vélo or "bicycle boulevard" in English
RIN	Rassemblement pour l'indépendance nationale
SAAQ	Société de l'assurance automobile du Québec

STM	Société de transport de Montréal, the Montreal transit authority
STOP	Save Tomorrow, Oppose Pollution, an environmental group
SVP	Société pour vaincre la pollution an environmental group
TESL	Teaching English as a Second Language (certificate)
TSS	The Seven Steps
TTS	Text-to-Speech
TV	Television
UCI	Union cycliste internationale (governing body for competitive cycling worldwide)
UCLA	University of California (Los Angeles)
UI	Unemployment Insurance (now Employment Insurance or EI)
USSR	Union of Soviet Socialist Republics: transcontinental federal state under a Communist regime grouping some twenty socialist republics, including Russia and Ukraine, created in 1918 and dissolved in 1991
VQ	Vélo Québec
WHO	World Health Organization
YMCA	Young Men's Christian Association

List of People Featured in this Book

Saul Alinsky: Author who wrote *Rules for Radicals* about how to accomplish social change. Silverman never met Alinsky but was deeply influenced by his ideas while with le Monde à bicyclette.

Yasser Arafat: Former leader of the Palestinian Liberation Organization (PLO) with whom Silverman met and spoke during a visit to Israel in 2000.

Angela Bischoff: Angela Bischoff is Gomberg's widow. She wrote the following on social media to commemorate Silverman's eighty-eighth birthday in 2021:

> Robert, Beautiful Bicycle Bob, Happy Birthday! You changed my life and so many others. You brought the concept of 'cyclists' rights' to Canada. You trained so many activists the skill of using the media to further our goals, and we followed your lead around the country. A poet, you created vocabulary to represent our needs: a true Vélorutionary. You brought the joy of cooperative volleyball to us, the appreciation of revolutionary Vietnam, and the potential of vision improvement with concerted exercise […] I think of you often, old friend! Sending love and peace… xoxo

Today, Bischoff works with the Clean Air Alliance in Ontario, a group that works toward phasing out polluting energies and advancing renewable energy.

Nick Auf der Maur: Primarily known as a columnist for the *Gazette* and as a maverick municipal politician. Silverman hired an adolescent Auf der Maur to work at the Seven Steps Bookstore.

Dida Berku: A young lawyer in the 1980s, Berku represented MàB members in their case against the CTCUM. Today she is a politician.

Fidel Castro: Leader of the 1959 Cuban revolution who became the long-time president of Cuba. He was a hero to Silverman although the two never met.

Gordon Cohen: Next door neighbour and skiing buddy of Silverman's in the 1950s. Also the cousin of Leonard Cohen.

Leonard Cohen: Often compared to Bob Dylan, the Canadian folk-pop singer and songwriter was a novelist and poet in the early 1960s. He and Silverman were friends.

John Dowlin: Philadelphia-based bike advocate, custodian of cycling information, and unofficial liaison officer for putting 1970s bike movements in touch with each other. "A real poetico-Vélorutionary," according to Silverman. As with Silverman in Montreal, Dowlin's childhood home (in Detroit) was demolished to make way for a highway.

Bob Dylan: A relatively unknown musician from New York when he played what was presumably his first international venue at the Potpourri in Montreal in 1962. Silverman did not meet Dylan, but suspects his wife facilitated that 1962 visit.

Jacques Desjardins: Former employee of Vélo Québec and co-founder of the MàB. Today a member of the group that succeeded MàB, Encore du Monde à bicyclette.

Stéphane Desjardins: Activist with MàB in the late 1970s and early 1980s; today a journalist and co-author of this book.

Jean Doré: Reformist mayor who served from 1986 to 1994. Silverman was a member of Doré's party, the Montreal Citizens' Movement (MCM), also known as the Rassemblement des citoyens et des citoyennes de Montréal (RCM).

Jean Drapeau: Mayor of Montreal 1954–1957 and 1960–1986, espousing a conservative, populist, federalist ideology and very autocratic style. His ideas on urban planning and transportation apparently included wanting to demolish much of the downtown and favouring car travel. But Drapeau also brought the metro (subway) to Montreal.

Louis Dudek: Canadian poet, McGill professor, and the author of over two dozen books. He was photographed with Silverman at the Seven Steps Bookstore.

Morris Feinstein: Business associate who took over the Seven Steps Bookstore and Ember Coffee Shop in early 1962, renaming it the Potpourri. During Feinstein's tenure, Bob Dylan played at the Potpourri.

Michael Fish: Architect who co-founded Save Montreal, a community group often opposed to Mayor Drapeau to which Silverman belonged.

List of People Featured in this Book xv

Dr. Gilberto Fleites: Cuban oncologist befriended by Silverman in the 1990s.

Rob Ford: Mayor of Toronto from–2014 who was controversial for many reasons, among them that he was a staunch opponent of bicycle infrastructure and he denigrated cyclists. While Silverman never met him, Ford's comments probably vocalize the unstated opinions of many who are fiercely opposed to urban bicycling. Silverman might have said Ford suffered from cyclophobia.

Josh Freed: Journalist, cyclist, friend, and neighbour of Silverman's on Esplanade Street.

John Gardiner: MCM politician, sometimes served as a spokesperson for MàB.

Tooker Gomberg: An early member of MàB who was described as "Silverman's protégé" and eventually carried this ideology to other cities. He was a city councillor in Edmonton from 1992 until 1996, later moving to Toronto where he finished second in the 2000 mayoralty race.

Ernesto "Che" Guevara: Fidel Castro's second-in-command during the Cuban Revolution. His image is a global icon of rebellion. Silverman met Guevara while cutting sugarcane in the early 1960s.

Bernard Hallé: Co-founder of the bike group Roue Libre from Québec City. Silverman visited this group and Hallé quickly became very influenced by Silverman's way of thinking. Militants in Québec City then began plotting car accidents with cyclists or pedestrians on a map. They were shocked to find a huge cluster of such accidents at the intersection of the Dufferin-Montmorency Highway (now Honoré-Mercier Avenue) and St-Jean Street.

> The pedestrian light at this intersection only lasted a few seconds and hundreds of pedestrians had been injured by cars there, explains Hallé. With Bob and about fifty other cyclists, we did a die-in [demonstration] and blocked the intersection for five minutes. One motorist panicked and deliberately drove into the cyclists, crushing a bicycle, but fortunately not causing any serious injuries. After that demonstration, the pedestrian light was extended, making the intersection much safer.

Hallé soon made it a habit of staying at Silverman's place when visiting Montreal. He also recounts going to New York twice with Silverman, once to attend a bike advocacy group convention there. "I lost touch with Bob for almost forty years. In part this was because I moved to the countryside and had to buy a car. I was too embarrassed to tell Bob."

Lawrence Hanigan: Former municipal councillor for Mayor Jean Drapeau's Civic Party, he became director and president of the Montreal transit authority, then known as the CTCUM (today the STM). Hanigan was one of Silverman's greatest foes.

Ivan Illich: Author whose ideas formed a central part of Silverman's ideology. Silverman, an avid reader, has described Illich as his favourite author.

Michel Labrecque: President of Vélo Québec in the 1970s and an ally in MàB's struggles. Labrecque later became the CEO of the STM (Montreal transit authority).

Yvon Lamarre: Former politician with Jean Drapeau's Civic Party and once touted as a possible successor to Drapeau.

Suzanne Lareau: Director of Vélo Québec until 2020 and employee of that organization since the late 1970s.

André Lavallée: Strong Quebec nationalist, former FLQ member, and early ally of MàB. Later elected to city council, he became vice-president of the executive committee of the City of Montreal, responsible for the first urban plan of Montreal (1992) and the first transport plan for the agglomeration (2008), and ultimately the political father of the BIXI collective bicycle program.

Irving Layton: Notable Canadian poet and associate of Silverman's during the Seven Steps Bookstore days.

Max Layton: Musician and son of Irving Layton. Layton learned guitar from Leonard Cohen. Like Auf der Maur, Layton was an adolescent hired to work at Silverman's Seven Steps Bookstore.

Jack Layton: Best known as a federal NDP leader and leader of the opposition in 2011. (No relation to either Irving or Max Layton.) Silverman claimed that Layton was an early member of MàB, but Layton moved from Montreal to Toronto in 1970, five years before MàB was founded. Silverman probably had a loose definition of "membership" in MàB. In a 2008 interview with *La Presse*, Layton confirmed: "I was campaigning for bike paths with Bob Silverman in Montreal in 1970!"[1] Layton certainly followed Silverman's lead on this issue. Layton was elected to Toronto council in 1982, soon becoming known as a strong cycling advocate. In the 1980s, Layton created the city's first cycling committee; he had some role devising the Post and Ring park-and-lock bike stand. Like Silverman, he renounced driving his car for urban travel, instead using his bike. In 1987, Layton—on a bike— won a six-kilometre race in downtown traffic against two other councillors, one driving a car and the other using public transit. This race was presumably inspired by Silverman's similar race in Montreal in 1975. Layton's widow, Olivia Chow, was elected to be the 66th mayor of Toronto in 2023.

France Lebeau: France Lebeau worked for MàB during "the sad years" as the organization was nearing the end. This was just after Lebeau moved to Montreal in 1993, making her part of "MàB's fifth generation." She is often referred to as "the group's archivist."

"I wouldn't say that I was an archivist, it was more like I cleaned up the files. I also got rid of a lot of irrelevant stuff that was taking up a lot of space."

Lebeau worked part-time at MàB; she was actually one of two employees sharing one salary.

"There were perhaps only fifteen members left at the end; Claire [Morissette] was busy with Cyclo Nord-Sud (CNS) and perhaps also with Communauto. Her last article in the MàB newsletter was about CNS."

After leaving her paid position with MàB, Lebeau stayed in touch with the people there. In 2003, Lebeau was involved when Silverman and Morissette worked with the cycling group Critical Mass.

"I contacted Bob and Claire to organize a die-in after a cop voluntarily opened his car door into cyclists and gave tickets to them." Opening a door into oncoming cyclists, which is very dangerous, is referred to as "dooring" and a violation of the traffic code in many jurisdictions.

Zvi Leve: Bike advocate originally from Israel, now living in Montreal who maintained close ties with Silverman.

René Lévesque: Leader of the centre-left and separatist Parti Québécois (PQ). Lévesque became premier of Quebec in 1976. Under his mandate, many social changes were initiated and Quebec's language laws were strengthened, officially establishing French as the dominant language. Lévesque also promised a referendum on whether Quebec should secede from Canada. Although the "non" side ultimately prevailed in that referendum, much of Montreal's anglophone elite and many corporate head offices left the province. Other factors were also involved, but within fifteen years, some two hundred thousand anglophones left Montreal. Toronto usurped Montreal's place to become Canada's largest city and most important business centre. This same exodus was also pivotal in helping to spread Silverman's ideology to the rest of Canada, pedalling the philosophy of bike advocacy across the land.

Gabriel Lupien: Former priest who, in 1967, founded what eventually became Vélo Québec. His original aim was apparently to promote recreational cycling. Silverman never met Lupien.

Peter McQueen: Member of MàB in the 1980s who travelled to Cuba with Silverman in the 1990s. McQueen was elected to Montreal City Council in 2009 with Projet Montréal and today rides his bike widely.

Claire Morissette: The "organizer" at MàB who complemented Silverman's creative talents. She was an articulate eco-feminist and editor of the MàB's newsletter.

Norman Nawrocki: Vancouver-based anarchist reporter who interviewed Silverman, then later moved to Montreal, living in the same housing co-op as Silverman.

Alex Norris: Municipal politician in Montreal and former journalist.

Nick Peck: American Vietnam War resistor and bike activist based in Massachusetts who travelled to Cuba and to Europe with Silverman in the 1990s.

Terrence Regan: Worked with Silverman to establish outdoor volleyball in Jeanne-Mance Park and longtime confidante of Silverman's.

Edith Rosenkranz: Silverman's first wife, who helped him organize some events at the Ember Coffee Shop and joined him in Cuba from 1962 to 1964. The two married in 1961 and divorced in 1964.

Dimitri Roussopoulos: Prominent Montreal anarchist, leader of anti-nuclear missile demonstrations in 1959, who accompanied Silverman to Cuba in 1962. He was also founder of Montreal Ecology Party in 1980s.

Guy Rouleau: Former director with Vélo Québec who joined with Silverman et al. in the 1970s, demanding more bicycle facilities in Montreal.

Louise Roy: Former administrator with Vélo Québec. Another person of the same name succeeded Lawrence Hanigan to head the STM.

Vicki Schmolka: Silverman describes Schmolka as "the co-founder of (MàB)," while twenty people were at the founding meeting. Schmolka was a prominent Montreal bike advocate in the mid-1970s before moving to Ontario.

Ruth Schou: Danish woman whom Silverman met in 1967 at an Israeli kibbutz and whom he later married. She assisted at many early MàB meetings at their Esplanade Street apartment before leaving Silverman and moving to New York.

Frank Scott: Canadian poet, McGill professor, and constitutional scholar who helped found the New Democratic Party (NDP). An opponent of Maurice Duplessis, he challenged his "padlock law" in court. Scott won a Governor General's Literary Award in 1977. Leonard Cohen sang Scott's poem "A Villanelle for Our Time" on his 2004 album *Dear Heather*.

Godfrey Stephens: Prominent painter today living in Victoria, BC. In the early 1960s, Stephens was hitchhiking through Montreal when Silverman befriended him and found him a place to stay.

Snavely: Python that, for some mysterious reason, lived in the Seven Steps Bookstore.

John Symon: Freelance journalist, author and friend of Silverman, meeting through playing volleyball.

Armand Vaillancourt: Prodigious sculptor, Quebec nationalist, MàB supporter, and long-time friend of Silverman's since the bookstore days. The two were close neighbours when Silverman lived on Esplanade Street.

Scott Weinstein: MàB member arrested with Silverman and Morissette for illegally painting bike lanes. All three were found guilty and opted for jail rather than paying a twenty-five dollar fine. Weinstein is a member of Independent Jewish Voices-Montreal, an organization that fights racism and promotes peace in Israel and Palestine. He was a spokesperson for the pro-Palestinian McGill University encampment during the 2023-2025 war between Israel and Hamas.

Dedicated to Robert "Bicycle Bob" Silverman
1933–2022

*Unless otherwise noted,
all poems in this volume
are by Bob Silverman.*

Bob Silverman in a gas mask with his bike.
Source: Tooker Gomberg, courtesy of Angela Bischoff.

Acknowledgements

BELOW IS A LIST OF PEOPLE who have helped me along this path, with apologies to all those possibly omitted: Magali Bebronne, Lorri Benedik, Dida Berku, Angela Bischoff, George Bliss, Alain Brunet, Michel Camus, Gordon Cohen, Hedy Dab, Gerard Dab, Jacques Desjardins, Stéphane Desjardins, Yvon Dinel, Debby Dowlin, John Dowlin, Gordon Edwards, Peter Feldstein, Michael Fish, Anna Louise Fontaine, Josh Freed, Marianne Giguère, Ray Gottlieb, Bernard Halles, Pierre Hamel, Douglas Jack, Charles Komanoff, Michel Labrecque, Suzanne Lareau, Diane Larsen, André Lavallée, Max Layton, France Lebeau, Marie-Josée Legault, Raymond Lemieux, Isabelle Lesens, Zvi Leve, Jeff Mapes, Maureen Marovitch, Peter McQueen, Serge Mongeau, Guy Montpetit, Laurence Amelie Montpetit, Christian Morissette, Norman Nawrocki, Alex Norris, Nick Peck, Jean-François Pronovost, Carlton Reid, Terry Regan, Josee Riopel, Mary Robinson, Sheindl Rothman, Reesa Roumel, Dimitri Roussopoulos, Glenn Rubenstein, Jack Rudnicki, Vicki Schmolka, Godfrey Stephens, Stuart Anthony Stilitz, Steve Stollman, Anna Symon, Elizabeth Symon, Gail Tedstone, Alex Tyrrell, Armand Vaillancourt, Scott Weinstein, Abraham Weizfeld, and Richard Wutzke.

We also reached out to Silverman's sister, Rona Klein, but, unfortunately, she did not contribute to the telling of Robert's story. We do gratefully acknowledge, however, her permission to reproduce some of Robert's poems and some family photographs. We owe a similar thank you to the Morissette family for allowing us to reproduce one of Claire's poems.

The authors thank the many people who agreed to be interviewed, but whose contribution is not included here due to space limitations. The authors also thank the people at Cyclo Nord-Sud and at Encore du Monde à bicyclette for help and especially Josée Riopel for her help in research with this project.

Last, but not least, the authors give special thanks to their respective spouses, Liza Mintz and Lucie Hortie, for their exceptional patience and support on this project.

Since both authors were at times involved in the events recounted in this book and knew Bob Silverman personally, they are identified as sources in certain passages.

Foreword
A Prophet before His Time

THEY MUST HAVE LOOKED RIDICULOUS, this ragtag band of Montreal cyclists with cardboard wings strapped to their backs, riding along in a small group in July 1980. They were protesting the lack of bicycle access around their city; their wings symbolizing how it was impossible for them to cross the river. The day was warm as they rode through bucolic parkland on Saint Helen's Island. Then, unexpectedly, Mayor Jean Drapeau drove by in the other direction. Drapeau had ruled autocratically over Canada's second-largest city for almost three decades with essentially no opposition. There was probably little that Drapeau was afraid of but the mayor must have just seen something that terrified him.

Suddenly, the cyclists were in hot pursuit of Drapeau, furiously flapping their wings as they pedalled hard to catch the fleeing mayor. And catch him they did when the mayor changed vehicles, at which point Drapeau was showered with pamphlets. A watching journalist found the scene hilarious, writing: "Cyclists wear the wings but the mayor takes flight."[1]

Who were these cyclists and why were they so able to intimidate the long-time mayor of Montreal? This is the incredible story of "Bicycle Bob" Silverman and his merry band, le Monde à bicyclette (MàB). The MàB was the most militant bicycling group in Canada or perhaps anywhere. Lacking money, the group creatively employed guerrilla street theatre, irony, humour, and research. With these tactics, MàB invariably forced the most resolute adversaries to bend. For some two decades, that is exactly what MàB did, completely transforming Montreal in the process.

Now considered the foremost city in the Americas for bicycling, in the mid-1970s, Montreal actually lagged New York, Toronto, and Ottawa in urban bicycle facilities.

Journalist Josh Freed explains that this incredible change happened because "early cycling zealots like Bicycle Bob Silverman and the MàB used guerrilla tactics to demand bicycle rights. They laid down in rush-hour traffic covered in fake blood to protest the 'auto-cracy.'"

André Lavallée, a prominent politician, bureaucrat, and consultant in Montreal, echoed Freed's line of thinking about Silverman: "As a long-time player in the development of Montreal, I have witnessed the countless poetic-militant actions deployed by le *Monde à bicyclette* to promote a new vision of the movement of people in the city. If Montreal is now one of the great urban cycling metropolises, it is thanks to the work of these pioneers." Lavallée concluded that "Bob was the spark that made it all happen."[2]

In fact, Silverman's influence extends far beyond Montreal: he has been called the "granddaddy of the bike movement in Canada," and the ideology and tactics that he developed were adopted across the country. This is also a story about how citizens can stand up to authority, make themselves heard, and refuse to take *no* for an answer. It can also be an instruction manual of how you, too, can improve the world in the face of seemingly impossible odds. You might even have fun in the process!

There was also a lot more to "Bicycle Bob" than just bicycles. His life story features such figures as Leonard Cohen, Bob Dylan, Che Guevara, Ivan Illich, Jack Layton, Armand Vaillancourt, and Yasser Arafat, among many others. Silverman was quick to call out injustices; dabbled in poetry; actively opposed the Vietnam War; was largely responsible for bringing outdoor volleyball to Montreal's parks; loudly advocated for Palestinian rights alongside fellow Jews; and was an evangelist for unconventional vision-improvement techniques. Friends and foes alike sometimes used the term "exasperating" to describe him.

We will probably never see someone like Robert Silverman again.

★★★

Robert Silverman was a loser in many ways: he failed his high school French and English exams; flunked out of preparatory school and two universities; was fired from his father's firm; bankrupted his own business; was alienated from his family; and saw two marriages dissolve. He even failed to take his own life at age twenty-one. But when Silverman discovered community activism, it gave him a *raison d'être*. He gained a new name, "Bicycle Bob," and a new persona who opposed the "Juggernaut," of the 1970s, which including a car-dominated culture; the war machine that was attacking Vietnam; the interrelated car and oil industries; as well as Big Pharma and the medical establishment. Like his father, they put profits before people or concern for the planet.

It seemed impossible to fight the Juggernaut, but just when all seemed lost, a modern-day Don Quixote came riding—on two wheels—to the rescue. Despite, or perhaps because of, his wacky and unconventional methods, Silverman proved astonishingly effective. In contrast to many other famous people, most of the things that brought Silverman greatness were done as a volunteer. Therein is perhaps a lesson that we are not dependent on our professions to achieve fame or change the world. Silverman once half-joked to the *Gazette* that he preferred attempting the impossible because simply achieving the possible was boring.³ And he often succeeded.

A Poem to Silverman

Claire Morissette, who also belonged to the MàB group, wrote a poem for Silverman in French. We have translated an excerpt here:

> To Bicycle Bob
> Ah! Bob Silverman!
> The disturber! The wacky one! The fanatic!
> Bicycle Bob Silverman!
> The curious one! The exhausting one! The exasperating one!

★★★

> Without a Bible or quarterly plan
> He knows how to get to the point,
> This fearless questioner.

> He gives the villains their pill
> Of paradox, of ridicule,
> This mocking orator.

★★★

> Two wheels, pedals, a handlebar,
> A bunch of dreams near his futon,
> A typewriter, a telephone,
> Here is the inventory of this visionary.

> Bridges, bike routes, métro, car parks,
> All will be cyclable at his command!
> What a magician
> Nothing in his pockets, nothing in his hands!

> By tens, hundreds, thousands,
> People are proud to pedal.
> Bob Silverman, look at all your fans!

★★★

You make our dreams come true
Thanks to you, we can breathe,
And even better, we can hope!

You, we, together we are capable,
Victory is inevitable!
Bob Silverman, we love you.[4]

Killed by a Car, Reborn on a Bicycle

TALENT FOR THE ABSTRACT
My mother did not see me;
my father, even less;
what could I do?
mental chess![1]

STEPHEN ROBERT SILVERMAN was born on November 30, 1933, in Montreal and was variously known as "Bob," "Robert," or "Bobby." He was the only son of Berthold "Bert" and Florence (née Horlick) Silverman, a Jewish couple living on Iona Street in the Snowdon neighbourhood. A younger sister, Rona, joined the family in 1936.

The Silvermans had lived in Montreal for two generations; his paternal grandparents were from the former Austro-Hungarian Empire. Silverman's mother was born in Cincinnati to parents originally from Russia. The Silvermans were not particularly religious, typically visiting the synagogue just three times a year and had "middle-class values." Silverman remembered the four members of his family arguing a lot as well as long periods of silence.

Learning Problems at School

Young Robert had a learning disability that hindered his ability to write in cursive, making what he wrote illegible to anyone else. His attempts to write compositions in school ran into ridicule from teachers and classmates. While he had a bicycle, Silverman did not think anything special of it. He was also afraid of playing baseball, a competitive game popular among his peers.

Bert Silverman was a successful businessman, working with Max Seigler in real estate and insurance. For various reasons discussed later in the book, Bert Silverman never really accepted his son. The son's poetry speaks of a father who "came home tired every night," and of little communication between the two.

In 1950, Silverman graduated from the High School of Montreal (today the FACE school occupies this building) on University Street, but failed his English and French final exams.[2] This school primarily served the "Golden Square Mile"

Figure 1.1. Bob at summer camp in 1945.
Source: Silverman family collection.

district of Montreal where many of Canada's prominent families lived at that time.³ Although both girls and boys attended this school, they were kept largely apart until the 1960s. He later attended the boys-only Clark Preparatory School in Hanover, New Hampshire. The plans of Silverman's parents for their son were probably echoed in the creed of the prep school: "to prepare a boy adequately and thoroughly for College or Business, and to inculcate in him those basic principles and high ideals which tend toward the development of a manly character."⁴

This excerpt suggests that his parents expected their son to get a respectable university degree or to succeed in business. That their son so notably did neither no doubt later contributed to his parents' disappointment and Silverman's eventual estrangement from his family. Silverman's transcript from Clark in spring 1952 shows grades in academic subjects ranging from F in Physical Education to Bs in English and History. By fall 1952 his marks were Fs in Accounting, Economics, Trigonometry, and Art Appreciation, with a D in Recent World History. A notation at the bottom of his transcript reads: "dismissed for scholastic deficiency."

Despite his dismal record at Clark, Silverman was somehow accepted for a commerce program at the University of Connecticut in Mansfield. He later started liberal arts at Sir George Williams University (now Concordia University) in Montreal. He did not complete either program. At some point, the Silvermans left Iona Street for 4960 Roslyn Avenue, a two-storey house near Queen Mary Street, and were living there by 1955. While Silverman was having problems academically, his part of Montreal was having traffic circulation problems. The proposed solution was to build the Decarie Expressway. That highway, which opened in 1967, was built in a massive trench, cutting the Snowdon neighbourhood in two.⁵ As such, cars were responsible for the destruction of Silverman's childhood home on Iona Street, demolished in the 1960s to make way for this new highway. "A cousin in Hampstead said how convenient the new highway was for getting downtown; it was disgusting," recalled Silverman in 2020. By 1969, a similar highway project in Toronto sparked widespread protests against the Spadina Expressway—notably involving activist Jane Jacobs—and that project was never completed. But such opposition was lacking in Montreal in the early 1960s. A backyard neighbour, Gordon Cohen, made friends with Silverman while he lived on Roslyn and the two often skied together. Gordon also had a cousin, Leonard, but more on that later.

Gordon Cohen describes Silverman as "easy to get along with, but not known for his technique on the ski slopes. He compensated with strength and guts."

As a young man, he rented ski houses with friends in the Laurentians or in Vermont. For such ski trips, Silverman often borrowed his mother's car, but preferred to have Cohen drive it, indicative of his growing dislike of cars.[6]

Figure 1.2. Bob and his sister skiing. *Source*: Rona Klein.

"I was once a good skier, but eventually gave it up as it required a car," Silverman recounted in 2020.

Silverman lived close to downtown, but never thought of cycling. Like many young men, he thought he "needed a car to meet girls and all that."[7]

(Nearly) Killed by a Car

Silverman had failed at or dropped out from three different post-secondary institutions; his father was no doubt beyond disappointed. Afterwards Silverman fell into a depression, and attempted to take his own life. In his twenty-first year, he attempted suicide by turning on a car in the family garage. His poem about being killed by the car refers in part to this. He awoke in a hospital room.

> MY LIFE
> Killed by a car
> reborn by a bike
> that's the story
> of my life.

Figure 1.3. The house on Roslyn.
Source: Monde à Bicyclette archives.

That rebirth on a bike would have to wait another fourteen years…

★★★

One rare photo shows an adolescent Silverman, standing close to his mother, who in turn is flanked by his father in what appears to be either Colorado or Wyoming. They are beside a wooden sign indicating "Continental Divide, 8312 feet." Over time, a similarly big divide developed between Silverman and his father.

> POEM TO MY FATHER
> Let us go,
> hand in hand,
> to greet the friend
> to meet the foe,
> old contradictions
> long forgot,
> together,
> we'll find
> life's "true" jackpot.

Silverman began working as a clerk and salesman at his father's company, but this only led to further friction and further deterioration of their relationship. Having Silverman do entry-level bookkeeping and perform other tedious mundane tasks would have seemed like torture to him. He also disapproved of some of his father's business practices, telling Gordon Cohen that these included the use of inside information to profit from municipal land developments. In one of Silverman's poems, "My Mother's Marriage," he writes that she was "lured to become a gangster's wife."

Figure 1.4. Bert, Florence, and Bob Silverman at Continental Divide. *Source:* MàB Archive.

Silverman's World of the Late 1950s and Early 1960s

The world was in a tumultuous state in the late 1950s and early 1960s when Silverman was in his early twenties. A wave of decolonization was sweeping the "Third World." The two superpowers, the United States and the Soviet Union, were pitted against each other in the Cold War.[8] While not in direct conflict, they both supported warring factions in various proxy wars. As many former colonies in the Third World were gaining independence, the United States often supported right-wing dictatorships fighting against Soviet-supported Communist insurgents. The 1959 overthrow of a US-backed dictator in Cuba by Fidel Castro was one Soviet victory.

A principal reason why there was no direct conflict between the two superpowers was the prospect of "Mutually Assured Destruction" due to the massive arsenals of nuclear weapons that both sides maintained. Appropriately, the acronym for this is MAD. Fears of nuclear annihilation prompted the ban the (nuclear) bomb movement. Meanwhile, the US civil rights movement was gaining prominence, notably led by Martin Luther King Jr. who preached a non-violent approach. The United States was also becoming embroiled in the Vietnam War. Then, in late 1963, the world was stunned by the traumatic assassination of US President John F. Kennedy.

Culturally, new music was coming into vogue in the West, along with new clothing and hairstyles. A sexual revolution was happening, and many youths were experimenting with select drugs. A relatively new invention, television, broadcast images into people's living rooms, showing protest marches, sometimes involving tens of thousands of people.

Meanwhile, in Montreal...

Montreal was a fascinating place from which to see all this; while not in the United States, it is just forty-five minutes north of the border and only a six-hour drive from New York City. Montreal was also seeing profound homegrown changes during this same period.

Two Solitudes, a 1945 novel by Hugh MacLennan, described the sharp linguistic and geographical divide between the English and French-speaking communities at this time. MacLennan, however, glossed over the occasional animosity between the two groups.

Frictions ran high between anglophones and francophones, evident in a referendum held during the Second World War, when Quebecers voted 72.9 percent against forced conscription while the rest of Canada voted 64.5 percent in favour. Camillien Houde, the mayor of Montreal, was imprisoned for opposing conscription and for publicly expressing admiration for the Fascist dictator of Italy, Benito Mussolini.

In March 1955, riots erupted in Montreal after National Hockey League president Clarence Campbell suspended popular Montréal Canadiens star Maurice Richard. Fans of Richard—who were mainly francophones—saw this as an exaggerated penalty for a fairly minor infraction. Those hockey riots may have initiated the modern nationalist movement in Quebec. The anglophone minority dominated business in Montreal—the fourth-largest French-speaking city in the world—often obligating francophone employees to speak English on the job and subordinating the French language.[9]

In 1962, the president of Montreal-based Canadian National Railroad, Donald Gordon, publicly declared what may have been common thinking among corporate bosses at that time. He explained the complete absence of francophone vice presidents at his company was because "no francophones had the necessary competencies to do the job."

Gordon's remarks led to public protests and also to the creation of the Royal Commission on Bilingualism and Biculturalism (Laurendeau-Dunton). This commission ultimately recommended that Canada officially become a bilingual country. Official bilingualism was not enough for many francophone Quebecers, angered by what they saw as longstanding injustices. Some called for the "decolonization of Quebec." The 1968 book *Nègres blancs d'Amérique* (*White Niggers of America*) by Pierre Vallières captures such anger. Today this title, including the "n" word, might seem offensive to many but Vallières contended that the situation of francophones in Quebec was then similar to that of the black community in the United States. While some today might consider this contention to be a great exaggeration, economist Pierre Fortin defends Vallières, using historical data from 1960.[10]

If the US civil rights movement was a model for Vallières, he was not following King's pacifist approach, but rather that of the Black Panthers. Vallières prescribed violent separation from Canada as the path to take, but the majority of Quebecers rejected this option.[11]

Vallières was a member of the *Front de libération du Québec* (FLQ), a militant group that followed his aggressive policy, setting off bombs and conducting some high-profile kidnappings. This all precipitated the October Crisis, when the federal government briefly declared martial law in 1970. Soldiers with machine guns then patrolled Montreal streets. Is it possible that Montreal narrowly avoided degenerating into the kind of sectarian violence later seen in Northern Ireland? Notably, René Lévesque, leader of the separatist Parti Québécois, was very quick to condemn the FLQ and its violent methods during the October Crisis.[12] As a journalist who experienced the Second World War, Lévesque had personally witnessed the damage that anti-democratic ideologies can cause.

The Jewish community living in Montreal through this period were a minority within the English minority. It was difficult to integrate into the francophone community because the Catholic Church, which operated most of Quebec's schools, excluded students who would not join their faith. Among anglophones, Jews were partially accepted, but notably faced barriers such as limited enrollment (quotas) at McGill University's faculties of law and of medicine.[13] Meanwhile, McGill's faculty of arts had more stringent admissions requirements for Jewish students than for non-Jews.[14]

From the Great Darkness to the Quiet Revolution

Apart from the uprising against English-speaking bosses, there were big changes happening within Quebec's francophone majority. Quebec during the 1950s was a very traditional place, dominated by the repressive Catholic Church and the conservative Union Nationale government. That government actively opposed trade unions while persecuting some minorities such as Jehovah's Witnesses and anyone perceived to be Communist. Political patronage and corruption were rife during what is referred to as the "Grande Noirceur" or "Great Darkness." Silverman also described the 1950s as a time of sexual repression. During this time, Quebec's birth rate was high among francophones, often encouraged by the church. Sex was a means of procreation rather than something done for pleasure. Then in the 1960s, the birth control pill, the church's fading influence, women entering the workforce, and divorce caused Quebec's birth rate to fall dramatically.[15]

In 1948, Paul-Émile Borduas and others from the artistic community authored the *Refus global* manifesto, challenging the Great Darkness. The call for change was gathering momentum and a huge change, called "The Quiet Revolution" was coming.

"The Quiet Revolution was the work of four ministers, twenty officials, twenty songwriters, and then some poets," once declared former Quebec premier Jacques Parizeau.[16] His list should also include painters and sculptors such as Borduas. Some suggest that Montreal's small Jewish community also played a pivotal role in facilitating the Quiet Revolution.[17] Quebec's Quiet Revolution officially began in 1960 with the election of the Liberals under Premier Jean Lesage, defeating Union Nationale. What followed, starting in the early 1960s, was a period of intense socio-political and socio-cultural change involving the secularization of government and creation of a welfare state. In a few short years, Quebec had dramatically shifted from being among the most religious and conservative provinces in Canada to being perhaps its most liberal, with the Montreal area becoming the most liberal within Quebec.

The Making of a Radical

Canada has never developed its own nuclear weapons. But, in 1958, the Conservative government of John Diefenbaker announced its intention to deploy US Bomarc anti-aircraft missiles in Canada, later confirming that these would be nuclear tipped.

Whether Canada should host US nuclear weaponry was hotly debated until 1970, when Canada officially withdrew from that role.[18] However, Canada is a military ally of the United States—a leading nuclear power—through both NATO and NORAD. Canada also allows US nuclear weapon-carrying naval vessels in its waters. In late 1959, Silverman had just been fired from his father's business. He was attracted to a meeting opposing deployment of Bomarcs in Canada. This meeting, at Sir George Williams University, was for the group that later became known as the Combined Universities Campaign for Nuclear Disarmament (CUCND).

CUCND organizer Dimitri Roussopoulos recalls that it was a "small but good meeting" and plans were made for a public protest. Roussopoulos described himself as a political activist, ecologist, writer, editor, publisher, community organizer, and public speaker.[19] That protest took place in Ottawa on Christmas Day 1959, with Silverman participating. Protesters walked around in the cold, chanting "we don't want to be nuclear!" Later recounting the experience, Silverman used the words "dealienation" and "solidarity" to describe his new-found connection with his fellow protestors.[20]

"I owe a lot to Dimitri," said Silverman, speaking of Roussopoulos. "He convinced me to become a radical. I had never gone to a demonstration before. It changed my life."

Silverman joined the group for a second demonstration a few weeks later in North Bay, Ontario. This was one of the proposed deployment sites for the Bomarcs. The other site for the Bomarcs was La Macaza, Quebec, and some of these same "peaceniks" also protested there.[21] The "Ban the bomb" movement was thus Silverman's initiation to public protest and to radicalism. This movement seems to have given Silverman new purpose in life and new energy; after his botched suicide attempt, he was ready for the next adventure.

> "I owe a lot to Dimitri," said Silverman, speaking of Roussopoulos. "He convinced me to become a radical. I had never gone to a demonstration before. It changed my life."

The Seven Steps Bookstore

IN JUNE 1960, despite having no previous experience in the book business, twenty-six-year-old Silverman opened a small independent bookstore. He explained this bold move to a reporter saying: "experience can sometimes be a hindrance to new ideas and trends."[1] Silverman's shop incorporated more than a few new ideas, for one, it was advertised as the only bookstore in Canada that was also a coffee house. The building was split in two; the back, or downstairs of the establishment was an air-conditioned coffee shop called Ember serving as a venue for poetry readings and music; the bookstore was upstairs.

The Seven Steps (TSS) was named for the seven steps leading up to this storefront in the heart of downtown at 1430 Stanley Street, a former house just a stone's throw from Sainte-Catherine Street.

The avant-garde City Lights Bookstore in San Francisco apparently served as inspiration for Silverman. Opened in 1953, City Lights was the first all-paperback bookstore in the United States and has been "associated from the outset with radical left-wing politics and issues of social justice."[2] Its founders, including poet Lawrence Ferlinghetti, envisioned "a 'Literary Meeting Place,' where writers and readers could congregate to share ideas about poetry, fiction, politics, and the arts." City Lights has been connected to beatnik culture, with poets Alan Ginsberg and Charles Bukowski as well as with LSD enthusiast Timothy Leary. There is no coffee shop under the roof of City Lights Bookstore in San Francisco, though just across Jack Kerouac Lane is the Vesuvio Café is, once a favourite haunt for the beatniks.

A Hangout for Beatniks

Silverman used $8,000 of his bar mitzvah money as startup capital to launch TSS. He chose the location on Stanley Street because "it harboured both intellectualism and nonconformity while being close to [McGill] University."[3]

"Bob" as he called himself then, would be wearing a white shirt, tie, and sporting a goatee, the epitome of a spiffy-looking, young, and chic businessman, spending most of his time in the bookstore section. Meanwhile, the downstairs coffee shop was filled with beatniks wearing black turtlenecks and wearing sunglasses even in the dim candlelight, and clicking their fingers to jazz music.

In front of TSS was a big abstract wooden sculpture by Robert Roussil that Silverman bought and placed there, although he had difficulty explaining what it was supposed to represent.[4] Roussil's work was often censored in those prudish times; some of his less-controversial sculptures still survive, such as *Girafes* on Saint Helen's Island.

The store opened with an exhibit about the horrors of nuclear war; the newspaper reporter had trouble understanding what that had to do with the theme of the bookstore. The store, of course, embodied Silverman's personality. His opposition to nuclear weaponry was a big part of who he was; it only made sense that the bookstore opened with this theme. There were magazines in the store and books: mostly paperbacks, which were just coming into vogue. The titles were influenced by his personal likes, and often hard to find elsewhere, such as Jack Kerouac's *On the Road*, an inspiration for the beat generation. There was also a "Commie Section" of books brought in from the Soviet Union, in English. Poetry was often placed centre stage and Silverman spoke idealistically about helping young Canadian poets to be published.[5] Some ads in local papers described the store as a "friendly" place where "odd and unusual" items could be found. For some bizarre reason, a python named Snavely lived in the Soviet section.[6] The name can mean "anything cunning, sneaky or underhand." Snavely was a gift from Silverman's friend "Gibby" Rosenberg, the owner of Gibby's, a popular restaurant. Silverman had trouble refusing the gift, which serendipitously proved useful in controlling the bookstore's mouse population. Snavely lived in a cage.

Silverman tried to bridge the dichotomy represented by both sections of TSS. He also tried to manage a private business while, as a Communist, advocated for the abolition of private property.

Marrying Edith Rosenkranz

Before opening TSS, Silverman met Edith Rosenkranz at a party. He described Edith to this author as "a very attractive" woman four years his junior. She was born in Austria and came to Canada after the Second World War.

Rosenkranz taught elementary students for what was then the Protestant School Board (today the English Montreal School Board). She also apparently later played a role in bringing musical talent to the Ember. Friends say that Silverman was "devoted to Edith."[7] There are indications, however, that this devotion was not reciprocal.

Rosenkranz held very left-wing political views; these apparently pulled Silverman towards Trotskyism. She certainly shared his views on the ban the bomb movement as per a letter she wrote to the editor of the *Gazette*.[8] One old friend from that time suggests that Rosenkranz was quite wealthy and drove an expensive car. The two were married on October 15, 1961.[9] "Edith did not want to have kids," Silverman later explained, without expanding.

Bob Dylan's Performance

A then-unknown folk singer from New York played in the coffee house for four evenings in June and July, 1962. Bob Dylan was only twenty-one years old when he performed in Montreal. The Ember had changed names by then, becoming the Potpourri. Dylan began to gain attention in 1963 after releasing his songs "Blowin' in the Wind" and "A Hard Rain's a-Gonna Fall."

An ad for the event, placed in the *Montreal Star*, gives more prominence to a Congo drummer named Leah Ananda. No door charge was indicated on the ad, suggesting that admission for both events could have been free if patrons ordered drinks once inside. Apparently, members of the audience walked out of Dylan's performances; his unusual vocals were not an immediate hit.[10] After playing at Potpourri, Dylan got another gig at Westmount's Finjan Club.[11] It seems that a one-hour recording of Dylan at Finjan in 1962 still survives, featuring early versions of some of his later famous songs.[12]

Silverman could not attend Dylan's performances, having already left for Cuba. Rosenkranz, however, probably played a role in bringing Dylan to Montreal. Silverman also suspected that she had an affair with Dylan at that time.

Figure 2.1. A facsimile of the ad in *The Montreal Star* announcing performances by Bob Dylan at the Potpourri, June 27 1962.
Source: Lisa Mintz.

Dylan's songs later became anthems for the civil rights and anti-war movements, highlighting his influence on social change in the United States during the 1960s. Dylan also greatly influenced many other musicians of his day, especially John Lennon of the Beatles.[13] The lyrics of Dylan's songs may be analyzed as poetry and tend to possess deeper meanings in a period when many other musicians wrote "nonsense lyrics." In 2016, he was awarded the Nobel Prize for Literature, which sparked a controversy. A *New York Times* editorial argued against conferring him this prize;[14] *Rolling Stone* countered that Dylan richly merited it.[15]

It is remarkable that Dylan thought it worthwhile to play at a small Montreal coffee house in 1962, initiated by Silverman. Dylan is an important footnote in this story, but he did not define the Potpourri. Despite some major issues with Silverman's management style, he did a brilliant job of creating a venue that attracted noteworthy people to his store and coffee shop. Below are some of those other noteworthy people.

Leonard Cohen and Silverman

Leonard Cohen is today proudly considered one of Montreal's favourite sons. The late singer and songwriter Leonard Cohen was a poet and novelist before launching his musical career in late 1967. He was also a bookseller, according to Silverman.

Figure 2.2. Leonard Cohen mural in Montreal. *Source*: Anna Symon.

Silverman recounted walking down the street once when somebody yelled out to him "Hey Bob!" He turned around, and asked who it was, "My name is Leonard Cohen," came the reply. Silverman later joked about not recognizing the man who afterwards became famous around the world, but Cohen recognized him.[16]

Cohen and Silverman had much in common. They were about the same age and both were "black sheep," marginalized within Montreal's Jewish community, noted for its conservative values and capitalist ethos. They grew up in the same general neighbourhood. Both were poets and frequented the McGill campus. Both spent time in Cuba in the early 1960s and travelled widely. Neither of them was any good at making money and both suffered from depression.[17] They also had numerous friends in common.

"Cohen had his own bookstore—also on Stanley Street—at the corner of Sherbrooke Street," said Silverman. "He lived in Montreal for about half of the year then." When in town, Cohen was also a regular in Silverman's bookstore, often buying books, sometimes giving poetry readings, and "always having polite arguments."[18]

When Cohen was once about to leave for Greece, Silverman was the one to sell him travel insurance, presumably while he was still working at his father's firm. Returning briefly to Bob Dylan, he greatly appreciated Leonard Cohen. *Rolling Stone* wrote that: "The two gifted songwriters are arguably two of the most literary lyricists of all time [...] The two artists share many similarities and, equally, held a great deal of affection and admiration for each other's work."[19]

Irving Layton, John Max, Robert Roussil, Frank Scott, and Armand Vaillancourt

A photo from a *Canadian Jewish Chronicle* article, published in 1960, shows Silverman standing in TSS surrounded by Henry Moscovitch, Irving Layton, Frank Scott, and Louis Dudek, all poets among other things.[20]

Irving Layton was a regular at TSS, using it as a venue for poetry readings.[21] Described as "outspoken and flamboyant," like with Roussil, his work may have been too sensual for its time. Nonetheless, Layton eventually won the Governor General's Award for Literature.[22] As a teacher at Herzliah High School, he became the "literary mentor, and later inspiration" for Leonard Cohen.

"I taught him how to dress; he taught me how to live forever," Cohen once remarked about Layton.[23] Irving Layton was also implicated with left-wing politics in the 1950s, causing him to be banned from travelling to the United States, accused of being a Communist. Surprisingly, Silverman escaped a similar ban, though he was refused entry once in 1984.

Frank Scott was a tall and imposing fellow who happened to be the dean of law at McGill University. He wrote poetry and helped found the first Canadian social democratic party, the Co-operative Commonwealth Federation (CCF), and its successor, the leftist New Democratic Party (NDP). Even more notably, he served on the Royal Commission on Bilingualism and Biculturalism whose recommendations led the federal government to enact the Official Languages Act in 1969.[24] At private parties, his favourite joke was to pull out his glass eye.[25] Louis Dudek was a Canadian poet, McGill professor, and the author of over two dozen books. His work had a strong influence on Canadian poetry. Dudek was also close to Leonard Cohen.[26] Not in the photo, Armand Vaillancourt, a prodigious sculptor and painter, was a close friend. Among his many works is the 61 m (200 foot) long "Vaillancourt Fountain / Québec libre!" statue in San Francisco, made of precast concrete. His wife Suzanne (née Verdal) was the inspiration for Leonard Cohen's song of the same name.[27] It may have been Silverman who introduced Cohen to Verdal...

"I've known Bob (Silverman) since the 1950s or 1960s," recalled a surprisingly spry ninety-two-year-old Vaillancourt in 2022. "I often dropped by his bookstore."

"I loved Bob, there was a solidarity between him and francophones. He knew I was a separatist and it didn't bother him for a second. I liked his attitude. Frankly, he was a good guy, a pearl."

"I knew him with Leonard Cohen; for a certain while (in the early 1960s), the three of us saw each other almost every week. Bob told me I looked like a giant," jokes Vaillancourt, who even today remains a towering character. "Cohen replied tit-for-tat: 'No, Vaillancourt IS a giant!'"

In 2020, Silverman recalled how Vaillancourt urged him to run for mayor of Montreal in the October 1962 election. Silverman, however, had made other plans.

"A Real Happening Place"
Silverman hired Irving Layton's teenage son Max to sweep the floors of the bookstore. "It was one of my first jobs. I can't remember how much I was paid or even if I was paid," the younger Layton explains. "TSS was a real happening place; I was only too eager to be part of that scene."

Max Layton also took guitar lessons from Leonard Cohen and soon became confident with his music. "A few years later, I played two gigs in the coffee house. While I was playing on stage, some guy was mingling in the audience, selling peace signs. Outside, you could sign petitions calling for unilateral nuclear disarmament. That's what kind of place it was." Today, Layton is a musician and a poet.

"Bob was running a business, but he was also anticapitalist and wanted to make the system more humane," adds Max Layton.

Notably, Silverman did not want his bookstore to become "too commercialized." Among the innovative features found at TSS were chairs and couches for customers to sit down on and read books.

Some thirty-five years after TSS went bankrupt, Chapters, a giant bookselling chain (it merged with rival, Indigo, in 2001), opened around the corner on Stanley Street and Sainte-Catherine Street West.[28] "Innovative" features at Chapters in the mid-1990s included comfortable chairs for customers to sit and read, as well as a Starbucks coffee shop on the second floor. Was Silverman three decades ahead of his time?

How Does a Communist Businessman Let Off Steam?

Godfrey Stephens is a well-known painter and sculptor, now living in Victoria, BC. In 1961, he was hitchhiking from New Orleans to Montreal—on his way to India—when Silverman befriended him. Silverman found Stephens an apartment near TSS. In return, Stephens provided artwork for TSS, including a portrait of Silverman.

Figure 2.3. Portrait of Silverman by Godfrey Stephens.
Source: Richard Wutzke.

This portrait shows a somewhat milky-eyed Silverman in an image seemingly held together by screws. When asked in 2022, Stephens no longer recalled why he painted screws on Silverman's portrait. Stephens does recall that Silverman, during his free time, spent evenings at the Poubelle nightclub with owner Tex Lecor who was also a singer, actor, and painter. Lecor's rendition of the song "Le Frigidaire" was a hit on the radio. Robert Roussil, the sculptor whose wooden abstract stood in front of TSS, was also part of Silverman's gang. Another member of the crowd was photographer John Max; some of his photos taken at Silverman's apartment appeared in a 1961 *Macleans* magazine article about Montreal entitled "The Last Bohemia."[29]

The examples above point to an artsy, quirky, and left-wing crowd frequenting TSS and Ember. Such a crowd probably indicates the selection of book titles at TSS. Silverman's entourage was also surprisingly inclusive during Montreal's *Two Solitudes* era. Stephens recounts learning his first words of (Quebecois) French during this period when the prevailing attitude among anglophones might have been that it was unnecessary—or even unbecoming—to learn Quebecois French. Stephens also recalls an unhappy Silverman "because he had to manage the bookstore." During his time off work, Silverman ran down the street in the dark, loudly yelling "revolution!" to anyone who might listen. How else is a Communist businessman to let off steam?

Curiously, six decades later, Stephens says that he "never remembered (Silverman as) having a wife. He was a loner and a bit of a Commie."

Bankrupting the Bookstore

Silverman also hired a young Nick Auf der Maur—later a prominent journalist for the *Gazette* and Montreal politician—to work at TSS.[30] Many years later, Auf der Maur wrote about how, when "Bob" came to work, he would whisper "is my accountant here?" This was all part of an effort to avoid the accountant who wanted to give Silverman "a stern lecture" on how to properly run a business.

Properly running a business, of course, meant encouraging customers to actually buy books, instead of "borrowing" books and "returning them a week later for free."

"That wasn't true except near the very end of the bookstore's existence," retorted Silverman who admitted that he might have "confused managing a bookstore with operating a library." He then qualified this by claiming to suffer from what he calls the "fear of making money." Clinically, this condition is known as *chrometophobia* or *chrematophobia*.

Silverman may have had his revenge on this accountant who, according to some accounts, was doing the books alone one evening at the bookstore when he looked up and was terrified to see a python staring down on him from a ceiling light fixture. Snavely, it seems, had escaped his cage.

"It is rumoured that Bob once caught a customer stealing a book. Silverman then declared if he wants it so badly, he should be allowed to keep the book," recounts Max Layton.[31]

Our parents tend to be important role models, usually to emulate. In Silverman's case, his father's role—the conventional successful businessman—was a model for how not to live. The father was an unabashed capitalist while the son became a Communist, environmentalist, and anarchist. Silverman shunned conventionality and excelled at "thinking outside of the box."

Working at his father's firm opened Silverman's eyes to how business practices can be unethical, putting profits before the community. An adverse reaction to that experience perhaps provoked his chrometophobia, subsequently he had difficulty asking customers to pay for books they wanted to buy. Instead, he seemed to crave a feeling of being of service to the community. Silverman displayed a flair for marketing, but also faced organizational challenges. If he had found a business partner whose strengths compensated for this weakness, would the bookstore have survived, or possibly even thrived?

In the 1980s, City Lights Bookstore similarly ran into financial difficulties. Luckily for Lawrence Ferlinghetti, the poet who co-founded that bookshop, he recruited a competent manager and it is still in business today.

"Running the bookstore wasn't much fun," said Silverman to summarize the end of his time with TSS, comparing himself to a zombie and using the term "catatonic." He added: "my father rejected me." This contrasts sharply with the upbeat tone Silverman used in 1960 to describe his parents' perceived silent approval of the bookstore project.[32]

On May 19, 1962, a small notice in the *Gazette* detailed how a bailiff would be holding an auction at Silverman's apartment on May 30 "to sell all goods and chattels of said defendant," to pay for the bookstore debts.[33] One of his associates, Morris Feinstein, ultimately took over the bookstore and coffee shop in early 1962, renaming it the Potpourri.

Figure 2.4. TSS as a Subway restaurant.
Source: Anna Symon.

From Potpourri to a Subway Sandwich Shop

"Feinstein tried running TSS as a coffee shop afterwards, but was not successful," recounted Silverman. After Feinstein, The Seven Steps name later reappeared as the Seven Steps Pub, but police ultimately shut down that bar after altercations with bikers.[34] There are also references to a shooting incident. Long after Silverman had left, TSS remained a "happening place" although not always in the way Silverman had imagined...

Subsequently, the Rainbow Bar & Grill operated out of this same address on Stanley Street. The location continued to be a venue for poetry readings up until 1968, where Leonard Cohen would read, as well as other poets.[35] Since then, the location has become a sandwich shop; the downstairs is occupied by a sustainable clothing store.

Arriving in Castro's Cuba

BY EARLY 1962, Silverman had put his bookstore into bankruptcy. He was broke "with nowhere to go," as he put it. Indeed, a bailiff was scheduled on May 30 to sell off all his worldly belongings, using Silverman's apartment as the auction venue.[1] Presumably, Silverman was either forbidden from returning to the family abode or too ashamed to ask. Then a student organization invited him to attend the May Day celebrations in Havana, Cuba. The invitation included plane fare, but no accommodation.

Three years earlier, while Quebec was undergoing its *Révolution tranquille*, another kind of revolution happened in Cuba. Fidel Castro had dramatically toppled Cuba's pro-American dictator, Fulgencio Batista. Castro quickly nationalized many US businesses on the island, ushered in radical reforms, as well as much closer relations with the Soviet Union. American conservatives warned of "Communists only 90 miles from our shores [the distance from Florida to Cuba]." The administration of President Eisenhower was openly hostile to Castro. With help from the US government, Cuban-American exiles in Florida plotted an invasion to overthrow Castro. But John F. Kennedy, who became president three months before the Bay of Pigs invasion in April 1961, ultimately withheld vital air force support for the invasion, after the initial assault. This lack of air support doomed the invasion attempt. Castro's hold on power was only strengthened by these events. Cuba had also become an important source of inspiration for left-wing thinkers in Montreal.[2]

After arriving by plane, Silverman ended up at the luxurious Riviera Hotel. The Riviera, which offers an ocean view from each of its 352 rooms, had been built in the 1950s—reputedly by the American mafia. Before Castro, Havana, with its sunshine, nightlife, and casinos was a popular destination for US tourists.

Dimitri Roussopoulos, a fellow Montrealer who was also attending the same 1962 May Day ceremonies, explains that Silverman had no place to stay: "Bob asked if he could come back to my hotel room and sleep on the floor. The hotel management later scolded me for lending space to Bob. I said it was fine with me; I knew him from Montreal and he needed a place to stay. Then Bob disappeared."

Finding a Job in the Workers' Paradise

Silverman speaks about how "Dimitri found me in his (hotel) room [...] I had just gone bankrupt." He also talks about "opportunistically" staying in Cuba after the May Day celebrations and finding work in a field where he had no experience:

"I got a job teaching English. Living in Cuba was easy. There was a colony of pro-Castro Americans living there, admirers of the revolution. Meanwhile, wealthy Cubans did not feel comfortable with the Castro regime; they were called *gusanos* (worms) and many of them were leaving."

"A lot of people spoke English, which was good; I didn't know any Spanish (then). Things were very disorganized there, but I managed to get an apartment. I may have reminded the lady in charge (of allocating apartments) of her son killed in the revolution. She found me an apartment in Havana."

Silverman also speaks about how teaching English in Cuba changed his life; it certainly gave him a lifelong vocation.

The tense diplomatic relations between the United States and Castro's Cuba deteriorated further. Castro turned to the Soviet Union for help and many Russians began coming to the Caribbean island.

The Cuban Missile Crisis Seen from Cuba, October 1962

Silverman was impressed by what he saw of the revolution, speaking almost fifty years later about how former prostitutes and chambermaids "had light in their eyes" under the new regime. Such women learned to type and became secretaries, gaining new dignity.

Castro's regime had domestic support, but was seeking both economic and military assistance abroad. Sugar was Cuba's main export to the world; after the United States stopped buying Cuban sugar, Castro turned to the Soviets for help. At the same time, Castro was fearful of another attempted American-led invasion of his island; he thought that Cuban-based Soviet missiles could provide a powerful deterrence against further US aggression. In those days, much of North America was too distant to potentially be hit by missiles based in Russia.

The "Cuban Missile Crisis," which lasted from October 16 to 28, 1962, was a thirteen-day confrontation between the United States and the Soviet Union initiated by the American discovery of Soviet ballistic missiles in Cuba. The United States and the Soviet Union had been engaged in a Cold War since the mid-1940s, but without being in direct conflict with each other. The Cuban Missile Crisis was the closest the two superpowers came to actual war, which would likely have involved a devastating exchange of nuclear missiles. Tens of millions of people would probably have died within hours. It also looked briefly as if the United States might invade Cuba.

"It was a scary time," recounts Silverman. "Couples were fucking for what they thought was the last time."

Despite being a Canadian, Silverman volunteered to defend Cuba. "I was recruited into the Cuban army for a few days. We marched a bit and I learned how to handle a gun. But it all ended in about a week."

In short time, US President John F. Kennedy and Soviet Premier Nikita Khrushchev reached a diplomatic solution, de-escalating tensions between the two nuclear superpowers. The Soviet Union agreed to remove missiles from Cuba while the United States promised not to invade the island.[3] Secretly, the United States also removed its missiles from Turkey.[4] Since this time, a hotline telephone has linked the White House and the Kremlin.

Silverman Has Visitors from Montreal

Soon after, Rosenkranz came to Havana. She was accompanied by her mother, along with Silverman's father. They stayed at the Hotel Nacional, an iconic hotel with 457 rooms offering commanding views of the sea and city. The Nacional infamously hosted a conference of American mobsters in 1946.

"Both my father and Edith's mom tried to convince me to return to Montreal. For my father, it was a pretense; he didn't really want me back. He was also a show-off and told Cubans that he was a capitalist. That was stupid."

This anecdote suggests that Silverman's father was quite brave, travelling to Communist Cuba shortly after the Missile Crisis, then saying: "I am a capitalist." Was the father also a show-off? Despite their animosity, it seems that Silverman acquired certain traits from his father.

Possibly, the real motive for his father's trip was genuine concern for the well-being of his son. But the younger Silverman did not perceive it as such and he had no desire to leave Cuba. The two older visitors returned to Montreal. Rosenkranz, forgiven for her infidelity, stayed on in Havana, sharing Silverman's apartment. Eventually, she also found work teaching English.

Meeting Che Guevara

Almost six decades later, Silverman remained an ardent defender of Castro's revolution, "A lot of people (in Canada) don't know about Cuba's successes in training doctors. That country has more doctors per capita than the USA; it sends doctors around the world." During his time in Cuba, Silverman eventually met the most famous doctor on the island.

Ernesto "Che" Guevara was Castro's second-in-command in the Cuban government. He is described as a Marxist revolutionary; guerrilla leader; medical doctor; author; diplomat; and brilliant military theorist. A controversial figure, Guevara's notoriety may have surpassed Castro's. In show of support for Castro's revolution, Silverman volunteered to help cut sugar cane—an arduous task. The Cuban economy still depended on the labour-intensive sugar harvest and city dwellers were encouraged to swing a machete out in the fields on weekends. Silverman was thus in the sugar fields in early 1963. "It was pretty bloody hard work. You had to bend low and hit low with the machete. There were a lot of volunteers cutting sugar cane and they took us there from the city in buses."

Apart from these volunteers, some of Cuba's leaders were also out there swinging a machete, looking for photo opportunities, and trying to boost the morale of their compatriots. "One day, in the fields, I met revolutionary leader Che Guevara, shaking hands with him. Later, the Cuban Ministry of Industry gave me a diploma for cutting sugar cane—it was the first post-secondary diploma that I received."

Their meeting was brief, but presumably had a huge impact on Silverman. On that occasion, Guevara would almost certainly have taken the opportunity to give a speech and effusively thank the *brigadistas* (foreigners in Cuba supportive of the revolution) present, probably singling them out for praise. Continuing this tradition, Fidel Castro spent Christmas Day 1969 cutting sugar cane with other such *brigadistas*.[5] To Silverman's ears, Guevara's words must have sounded like a hero's welcome, contrasting sharply with his father's disapproval over the years. He had bankrupted his bookstore, been fired from the family business, and dropped out of two universities, but earned praise from the world-renowned Guevara. Silverman said that the diploma "came from Guevara's ministry." Che Guevara was the Cuban minister of industry from

1961 to 1965. Silverman proudly displayed the diploma in his apartment almost six decades later. Guevara shone in many roles, but not in everything. Apparently, Castro once asked of his inner circle "who here is a good economist?" Guevara misheard the question as "who is a good Communist?" and put up his hand. He was thus appointed governor of Cuba's central bank, an appointment Castro later regretted.[6] Brilliant revolutionaries, it seems, are not always suited for mundane office jobs.

Today, Guevara's image has become a global symbol and icon of rebellion in popular culture. Silverman also had a Che Guevara poster hanging in his apartment more than half a century later. Despite a short and very busy career, Guevara somehow authored many books, notably writing a 1961 handbook on how to win revolutions using guerrilla warfare. Some of Guevara's advice, such as how the revolutionaries can create favourable conditions for themselves, might also have been applicable to a pacifist bike advocacy group.

Silverman has described Guevara among his favourite authors. Over the following decades, some articles about Silverman used the adjective "guerrilla" to describe him or his methods.

Another Happening Place

In some of his writings, Silverman claims that he was in Cuba for the 1961 Bay of Pigs invasion, apparently confusing this event with the 1962 Missile Crisis. Anecdotally, it seems others confuse these two events, which happened close together in time.

"After successfully fighting off the invaders, Havana became a cosmopolitan meeting ground for thousands of supporters including artists, students, and other activists who shared the political ideals of the 1960s. The Cuban Revolution quickly gained iconic status the world over," reads one article about this time period in Cuba.[7] Silverman, it seems, arrived on the island in a stimulating time.

And life was good after Rosenkranz arrived in Cuba:

"We had a big apartment on Calle 13 [13th Street] overlooking a square and paid rent to the government. Our

> And life was good after Rosenkranz arrived in Cuba.

rent was about half the cost it was before Castro took over Cuba. Those were good years." Silverman was even among the fortunate few to own a car, a Czech-built Skoda. "Fidel believed that everyone should buy a car," as Silverman later described it.

Expulsion from Castro's Cuba

Things started to sour one evening when, for unknown reasons, Silverman drove his car onto a quiet road and began dipping the headlights to signal a friend. Little did he realize that a military base was nearby. Nervous Cuban officials quickly picked Silverman up for interrogation.

"The Cubans let me go when they realized they had made a mistake," he explained. Technically, Silverman had not overstayed his visa because no visa had been issued to him, upon his arrival in 1962. Adding to his troubles, however, Silverman had brought many Trotskyite magazines with him to Cuba; these were seized by customs authorities on his arrival. When the authorities finally examined the magazines, they considered the material to be dangerous.

"I was kicked out of Cuba. They read all my magazines." The most dangerous material, in the eyes of the Cuban authorities, detailed conflicts between pro-Soviet forces and the guerrillas who won the Cuban revolution. Silverman also had brought *Revolution Betrayed* by Leon Trotsky.[8] Silverman's material must have struck a nerve within the Cuban government. About the same time, different factions within the regime were arguing for different paths that their revolution should take.

Guevara, a Marxist-Leninist and hero of the revolution, was openly criticizing the Soviet Union. Castro, on the other hand, depended on the Soviets for financial support and was eager not to offend Moscow. Guevara left Cuba to try and spread the revolution, first to the Congo in 1965, then to Bolivia in 1967. Bolivian soldiers, aided by the CIA, ultimately captured and killed him.

Silverman's deportation from the workers' paradise was unceremonious: "I didn't want to leave. The Cubans put me and Edith on a freighter bound for Montreal. At least, we obtained passage at no cost."

Losing Edith

Edith Rosenkranz left Silverman soon after their return from Cuba. Another man, a Trotskyite from France, stole her away. She then moved to Lyon, dying there in a car accident in 1972, apparently crashing her car into a boat that was being towed on a trailer. According to Silverman, the boat did not have a requisite flag to indicate it as a driving hazard.

Despite her having left him years before, Silverman was very shaken by Edith's death. Many years later, Hedy Dab was an acquaintance of Silverman's who often turned up at the same demonstrations. "When he saw me, I obviously made an impression on him. Bob didn't always seem to know who I was, but insisted that I wait for him while he spoke to the media," says Dab. "That would take a while and I usually drifted away. Only later did a mutual friend tell me how much I looked like Edith Rosenkranz."

Back in Montreal, Protesting against the Vietnam War

AFTER RETURNING TO MONTREAL in 1964, Silverman drove for Diamond Taxis; he also found work as a Spanish-English translator and as a research assistant for the Economics Department at Concordia University. Politically, he became involved in the Trotskyites' Fourth International movement, a Marxist faction that follows the ideology of Leon Trotsky (1879–1940). Trotsky, a Russian, tried to take over leadership of the Soviet Union but was defeated by Josef Stalin.

A painting of Silverman circa 1961 by Godfrey Stephens looks much like some photos of Trotsky circa 1930. Asked in 2020 about this resemblance, Silverman laughed and called it "a coincidence."

Silverman spoke about the animosity between Stalinists and Trotskyites persisting to this day. He also blamed Josef Stalin's poor leadership for allowing Adolf Hitler's Nazi Party to come to power in the 1932 German elections: "The workers' [parties] should have been united in Germany, but they were not and that is how the Nazis won."

Trotsky came from a bourgeois Jewish family and presented himself as an intellectual; Stalin on the other hand came from a peasant family and could come across as crude. Trotsky, an ideological purist, believed in spreading the revolution everywhere while Stalin pragmatically called for "socialism in one country," making him less alarming to capitalists and fascists. In the Second World War, despite the ideological differences, Stalin pragmatically worked first with Nazi Germany and then—only after Germany attacked the USSR—did Stalin switch sides to join with the Allies.

The Revolutionary Communist Party of Canada (RCP) espouses Trotskyist ideology and regularly runs candidates in federal elections. However, no RCP candidates have ever been elected or even obtained a sizable share of the vote. Members of the RCP must have tremendous perseverance for valiantly continuing against such daunting odds. There is also a long-standing joke that many of the RCP members are actually informants for the RCMP (police).

Learning to Give Speeches

"I benefited from time with the Trotskyites," recounted Silverman. "It was there that I learned to give speeches, to do research, organize parades, and write articles." Continuing to remark on the benefits, Silverman said that "some of the articles I wrote for the Trotskyite newspaper, *La Lutte Ouvrière*, were pretty good. One was entitled 'No compromise On Vietnam.'"

Speaking about Trotskyites selling their publications outside a Pete Seeger concert, Silverman said that they "made a strange impression, somewhat akin to that made by the Jehovah's Witnesses. They seemed very sincere, hopeless, and they presented themselves publicly with a kind of inspired, but pathetic dignity." Silverman wrote about the Trotskyites, saying that he was "ill at ease with their dogmatism and sectarianism."

The United States became embroiled in the Vietnam War in the early 1960s, aiding the South Vietnamese army fight against the Communist Vietnamese forces. By 1969, US military deployment in Vietnam peaked at over 500,000 personnel stationed there, assisted by units from South Korea, Australia, Thailand, and New Zealand. Martin Luther King was one of the earliest and most vocal opponents of the war, describing American aggression as a violation of the 1954 Geneva Accord. He also declared that the Vietnam War was "a blasphemy against all that America stands for."[1] Canada was officially neutral during the Vietnam War, serving as a haven for up to sixty thousand American draft dodgers. But the economies of Canada and the United States are highly integrated; many Canadian companies were supplying materials for the war effort. There were also criticisms that Canada—as part of the International Control Commission and ostensibly monitoring violations of the 1954 Geneva Accord—was actually covering up US atrocities in Vietnam.[2] The Liberal government of Lester B. Pearson and the Conservative opposition under John Diefenbaker both supported the war; the only anti-war voice in Parliament came from the NDP. Dimitri Roussopoulos's CUCND group was still active in the summer of 1964, calling for nuclear disarmament and holding a peaceful protest at the Bomarc missile deployment site in La Macaza, Quebec. A military policeman confronted the peaceniks, scolding them to say that Canada needed to be prepared in case of war. "I'd like to see you people go to Russia and try this," he taunted.

"I have been to Russia, my friend," Roussopoulos responded, recounting how he once handed out leaflets in Moscow's Red Square, calling for a bilateral end to nuclear testing. Russians countered that they couldn't trust the Americans, having the same stereotypes of Westerners as we have of the Russians. Roussopoulos added that he wanted to create a third force to at least get the two sides talking.³

The peaceniks withdrew from La Macaza promising that they would be back on Hiroshima Day (August 6). But the group chose another venue instead.

Canada's First Anti-Vietnam War Protest

Montreal was an important centre of anti-war activities in Canada despite more documentation being available about events in Toronto.⁴

The first documented Vietnam War protest in Canada occurred at the cenotaph in downtown Montreal on August 6, 1964, marking the nineteenth anniversary of the nuclear bombing of Hiroshima, Japan.⁵ Some one hundred protestors demonstrated peacefully, carrying placards reading "Remember Hiroshima! Stop the Dirty War in Vietnam."

Only four days earlier, the Gulf of Tonkin incident took place, where US forces alleged that an unprovoked attack took place on one of its navy ships. This led to a massive US escalation in the Vietnam War. Dimitri Roussopoulos, one of the protest organizers, today says that "Silverman was most likely at the Cenotaph protest."

The anti-war movement in the United States was enhanced by many high-profile personalities such as Muhammad Ali, Joan Baez, Jane Fonda, Abbie Hoffman, Martin Luther King, George McGovern, and Phil Ochs. In contrast, the Canadian anti-war movement had few highly recognizable public figures. One personality campaigning against the Vietnam War in the United States, who only became famous later was Petra Kelly, a young German-American woman. She subsequently returned to Germany to co-found the world's first Green Party.⁶ Montreal saw protest marches synchronized to be on the same day as the much larger marches in various cities both in the United States and internationally. "We had up to a thousand participants in Montreal, often going up to the American consulate, then located on Doctor Penfield Ave. at McGregor," said Silverman. The Trotskyites were among many groups in Canada protesting the Vietnam War. Silverman claimed that they were more vocal in their protests than the Communists. While Marxists were prominent in the anti-war movement, they were not alone. Also prominent in the movement were the New Democratic Party (NDP) and the separatist *Rassemblement pour l'Indépendance Nationale*. The Student Union for Peace Action, Student Nonviolent Coordinating Committee, church groups, feminists, and trade unions were also present. Silverman became active in this cause in 1964, serving as treasurer of an anti-war group in Montreal, the

Quebec Committee against the War in Indochina, also referred to as *le Comité québécois contre la guerre du Vietnam*.

"In April 1971, two thousand [veterans of the war], many on crutches and wheelchairs, marched on Washington and dumped the medals some had won at the Pentagon. Huge coordinated international days of protest against the war were held regularly. One in Washington attracted over a million people," wrote Silverman in a blog.[7]

Anti-War Protests Turn Violent

Silverman has written about the many US atrocities committed in Vietnam. He believed that the 1964 Gulf of Tonkin incident was fabricated. Other sources concur that at least part of that incident was a fabrication by US authorities.[8] The Montreal anti-war protests were not always peaceful; October 1967 saw demonstrators throw red paint on the US Consulate. Police responded by viciously attacking demonstrators, wounding twenty and arresting forty-six.[9]

October 1967 also saw an anti-war protest of about one hundred thousand demonstrators in Washington, DC, leading to a brutal confrontation with security forces. In that country, civil rights leader Martin Luther King spoke out against the war, sharply criticizing his former ally, President Lyndon Johnson. The following April, King was assassinated in Tennessee.

Protests were often violent; most notably in 1970 at Kent State in Ohio when national guardsmen fired sixty-seven rounds into the crowd, killing four unarmed demonstrators and wounding nine. The Vietnamese conflict was also the first war fought by the United States where images of the violence—and body bags containing dead US soldiers—were broadcast regularly onto TV screens as families sat around to watch the evening news. This literally brought home the horrors of that war, gave people much to talk about, and helped to turn public opinion against US involvement in the Vietnam conflict.

Give Peace a Chance

During the 1960s, anti-war songs became popular on the airwaves. Apart from the Bob Dylan, Joan Baez, and Phil Ochs songs, among the best known was "Give Peace a

Chance" recorded in 1969 by ex-Beatle John Lennon and Yoko Ono in Suite 1742 at Montreal's Queen Elizabeth Hotel.[10] The view from that suite window looks toward Silverman's former bookstore, though it is probably hidden from sight by higher buildings.

"Give Peace a Chance" was recorded on a mobile device by André Perry. The sound quality was horrible, but Perry worked magic in his Brossard studio, asking Robert Charlebois and Mouffe (Claudine Monfette) to be in a studio chorus. Ironically, Lennon never knew that Charlebois had his voice on that song, which became a worldwide hit. Perry was also the engineer behind Charlebois' iconic Lindberg record. He later created the famous Morin-Heights studio, where the Bee Gees, the Police, and many other bands recorded.[11]

There were many anti-war songs, and also chants used by protestors. The protests were big and loud and colourful. They took place in many countries around the world and were successful in reversing public opinion in the United States. They may also have had some unintended consequences.

The Anti-War Movement Boosts Environmentalism

The anti-Vietnam War movement was not a single-issue cause; Martin Luther King decried the disproportionate number of African Americans among new recruits and returning casualties. Furthermore, US forces were not only attacking Communist forces, but also the very environment of Vietnam, dropping toxic chemicals to target the flora and fauna of that country as a way to expose their enemy and poison the environment in which the Communists lived.[12] Civil rights activists and environmentalists increasingly saw common cause with anti-war protestors.

Anti-war activists were joined by "ban the bomb" activists at Canada's first anti-Vietnam war protest in Montreal in August, 1964; this association continued throughout the war. Activists notably protested the US development of nuclear weapons between 1965 and 1971 when three thermonuclear devices were tested on Amchitka Island, a wildlife preserve off the coast of Alaska. Fears that detonating powerful hydrogen bombs of up to five megatons on an earthquake fault line might set off a wave of tsunamis down the Pacific coast led to the formation of the environmental organization Don't Make a Wave Committee in Vancouver. This group later became known as Greenpeace, perhaps the best known international environmental organization today.[13]

Americans who fled to Canada—including draft dodgers—sometimes participated in anti-war events in Canada, but the majority were Canadian. At the same time, however, some Americans also became prominent in the nascent Canadian environmental movement, including Greenpeace co-founders Jim Bohlen, Gary Gallon, and Irving Stowe. Bohlen helped develop ICBM missile systems for the US military before moving to Canada to work with Greenpeace and the Green

Party of BC. Gallon later served with the UN Earthwatch in Nairobi, Kenya, and as president of the Canadian Institute for Business and the Environment in Montreal. Irving Stowe helped finance early Greenpeace expeditions with music concerts featuring Joni Mitchell, James Taylor, and Phil Ochs.[14]

A decade later, the first Green Party in North America was co-founded in BC by Paul George, also a US expatriate.[15] One of Silverman's favourite authors, Jane Jacobs, moved to Canada from the United States during the 1960s so that her sons would avoid the draft. While living in Toronto, Jacobs actively opposed the Spadina Expressway project, which was ultimately never completed.[16]

Meeting His Second Wife at an Israeli Kibbutz

IN 1967, Silverman travelled to Israel, where he worked at the Ein HaShofet agricultural kibbutz near Haifa.[1] The collective lifestyle such places offered must have attracted Silverman. It was also here that he met Ruth Schou, the Danish woman who eventually became Silverman's second wife.

"I started working as a truck driver but didn't like that so I became an agricultural worker, picking apples at night because of the heat. It was much harder work, but I liked it better. However, I only stayed six months."

After the kibbutz, Silverman found a hotel job in Jerusalem. "I was a desk clerk at the President Hotel in the Old City. A friend's father helped me get the job," explained Silverman, also mentioning a Moroccan connection. Moroccans often speak French because of the country's colonial past. "I was accused of addressing clients with the informal 'tu' instead of a more formal 'vous' and got fired," he says, suggesting that this was a pretext. Silverman and Schou next found their way to Ashkelon National Park, renowned for its numerous archeological sites dating back to the Bronze Age. The park is on the Mediterranean in southern Israel, near the Gaza Strip. "It was a great time we had in Ashkelon. The locals tended to hire Europeans for guards and we secured jobs there as night watchmen. We didn't have to do anything. The ruins there are impressive: Homeric Greeks, Crusaders, etc. There were beautiful sculptures, especially from the Greek period." Silverman mentioned living very frugally at this time, sometimes begging for food.

Silverman was in Israel during the Six-Day War (June 5–10, 1967) between Israel and three of its Arab neighbours: Egypt, Jordan, and Syria. His mother then told him to leave Israel while his father urged him to stay, which he did. The war ended in a decisive Israeli victory and its annexation of the West Bank, Gaza Strip, Sinai Peninsula, East Jerusalem, and Golan Heights. The Sinai was later returned to Egypt under the Camp David Accords in 1978. "I became pro-Palestinian after reading works by Jean-Paul Sartre and Maxime Rodinson," recalled Silverman. "Both of these authors wrote that the Israelis were practicing colonialism." Rodinson, a French Jew, compared the colonial mindset of Europeans in the late nineteenth century to that of Zionists. The debate about Israeli colonialism continues to this day.

The trip back to Montreal involved a car ride to France and train to Luxembourg. From there it was a cheap flight to New York, then Silverman and Schou took a connecting flight to Montreal where Silverman's parents met them at the airport.

A Green Card Marriage?

"Ruth and I married in Montreal," said Silverman. His second marriage lasted much longer than the first but may have lacked romance. Officiated in front of a notary, probably in December of 1970, Ruth did not apparently want to return to Denmark and may have seen marrying Silverman as a way to obtain Canadian citizenship. Unlike Silverman's first marriage, there was no public ceremony when they married. It is not even clear if Silverman informed his family of his marriage to Ruth Schou. When they ultimately parted, sometime after 1975, Ruth left quietly. It is unclear if there was a divorce or not. Ruth left Montreal for New York where there is no further trace of her.

Independent Jewish Voices Canada

"I also co-founded Jews & Palestinians Together in Montreal," related Silverman. While there is little documentation on that group, its aims were probably similar to that of Independent Jewish Voices Canada (IJV), described on its website as "a grassroots organization grounded in Jewish tradition that opposes all forms of racism and advocates for justice and peace for all in Israel-Palestine." Silverman in 2020 claimed to still be a member of IJV.

Picketing the Israeli consulate in Montreal—then also on MacGregor (now Docteur Penfield Avenue)—soon became part of Silverman's routine. That consulate, like the American one, eventually moved to a more secure location downtown.

Travels and Study in Europe

Despite living precariously, Silverman spent much of the late 1960s travelling and studying. He visited Amsterdam in 1967, meeting with a radical group there called the

Provo. The Provo—whose name could be interpreted as *the provokers*—are credited, among other things, as having originated the idea of a collective bicycle program—the forerunner to BIXI. They also developed a fleet of collective cars (electric at that), in what might be considered the model for Communauto.[2]

In 1969, he studied Hispanic civilization at the University of Granada in Spain. Silverman's resumé does not list any degree from these studies and possibly it involved only a semester of courses.

Reborn on a Bike
"A Reason to Live," a short poem

> Robert Silverman:
> Killed by a car, reborn by a bike:
> That's the story of my life.

It was also in 1969 that Silverman rediscovered bicycling.

"I went to Besançon, France, to study French at the university there. They had a program for non francophones and I stayed the summer. Encouraged by my Danish wife, I rediscovered bicycling while studying in France in 1969."

The terrain in Besançon is fairly flat, despite the town being close to the Alps. This makes local roads conducive for bike riding. Unlike in North America, bicycling never really fell out of favour in France. The most prestigious bike race in the world, the Tour de France, is staged in that country every year, drawing up to twelve million roadside spectators. But the sport is not only for elite athletes; everyone can ride a bike in France. Understandably, bicycling is a national sport for the French. France is also one of the countries that claims to have invented the bicycle.

"The idea of bicycling for adults was a new concept for me. After getting back to Montreal I picked up some good used bikes at La Porte à bicyclette (bike shop) on de Bullion Street."[3] Silverman at this time "did not have the means to buy a car." His bookstore bankruptcy meant that his "credit rating precluded any instalment option," so he soon became what he termed as "a bicycle freak."[4]

> "Encouraged by my Danish wife, I rediscovered bicycling while studying in France in 1969."

Credentials for a Real Job, 1970

In 1970, Silverman graduated with a TESL (Teaching English as a Second Language) diploma from Concordia University. This diploma today generally takes about three years of full-time study.

His TESL diploma was a continuation of the vocation that Silverman embarked on in Castro's Cuba, but now he had the academic qualification. He parlayed those credentials into securing work for the Catholic School Commission's COFI (*Centre d'orientation et de formation des immigrants*) program, teaching French to immigrants. His studies in Besançon, France, presumably helped with that.

Socialism Can Only Come by Bicycle

Silverman enjoyed cycling in Montreal and quickly noticed that, despite the growing popularity of cycling, there were essentially no facilities for cyclists. Furthermore, as a prodigious reader, he became familiar with the ideological underpinnings of the cycling movement. The authors whom he read also described what was wrong with automobiles and the automobile culture.

A 1973 article in *Scientific American* urged readers "not to take the bicycle too much for granted." While often overlooked among history's greatest inventions, the bicycle was described as a "humane and efficient machine (that) played a central role in the evolution of the ball bearing, the pneumatic tire, tubular construction and the automobile and the airplane." This same article pointed to the unparalleled efficiency of bicycles as expressed in calories consumed per gram per kilometre travelled.[5]

Foremost among the authors read by Silverman was Ivan Illich and his book *Energy and Equity* (1974). Inspired by that 1973 article in *Scientific American*, which described bicycles as "no. 1 among moving creatures and machines" in terms of efficiency, Illich starts his book with the quotation "*El socialismo puede llegar solo en bicicleta.*" ("Socialism can only come by bicycle.")

The significance of this quote cannot be overestimated. Silverman's own writings suggest that socialist countries that do not free themselves from extensive use of private cars are doomed to repeat the same errors of capitalist countries. Such extensive use of private cars serves to increase social inequities as Illich notes:

> People on their feet are more or less equal. People solely dependent on their feet move on the spur of the moment, at three to four miles per hour, in any direction and to any place from which they are not legally or physically barred. An improvement on this native degree of mobility by new transport technology should be expected to safeguard these values and to add some new ones, such as greater range, time economies, comfort, or more opportunities for the disabled. So far this is not what has happened. Instead, the growth of the transportation industry has everywhere had the reverse effect.[6]

As Silverman summed up Illich's thesis: "more energy means less equity." The bridges over the St. Lawrence River are but one example where improving access for motorists excluded cyclists and pedestrians, preventing them from crossing the river. Bridges built prior to the Second World War at least tended to have sidewalks, whereas the original Champlain Bridge, the Ile-aux-Tourtes Bridge and the Louis-Hippolyte-Lafontaine Tunnel—all dating from the early 1960s—were built with no provision for cyclists or pedestrians.

New highways, while improving mobility for motorists, are also significant barriers to cyclists or pedestrians who want to cross them. Setting vehicle speed limits at over 30 km/h on residential streets puts cyclists and pedestrians at greater danger of death or bodily harm, diminishing their mobility. The youngest and more elderly are typically the most vulnerable.

Illich also wrote that, in the context of industrial growth, "high quantities of energy degrade social relations just as inevitably as they destroy the physical milieu."

As opposed to automobiles, bicycles are among the most energy-efficient forms of transportation ever devised. A bicycle will use between ten to twenty-five times less energy per distance travelled than a personal car, depending on fuel source and size of the car. In addition, a bicycle typically requires one to two hundred times less energy to produce than a gasoline-powered automobile.

Illich did not really touch on electric cars, today considered almost a panacea for transportation woes. But Illich did write:

> Even if non-polluting power were feasible and abundant, the use of energy on a massive scale acts on society like a drug that is physically harmless but psychically enslaving. A community can choose between Methadone and 'cold turkey'—between maintaining its addiction to alien energy and kicking it in painful cramps—but no society can have a population that is at once autonomously active and hooked on progressively larger numbers of energy slaves.

Silverman also pointed to the large size of electric cars (relative to the driver), their speed, and their energy consumption as "reasons why they will lose."

Over their life span, electric cars require a lot of energy and metals to manufacture and maintain. As with conventional cars, they encourage urban sprawl with all the environmental problems that entails. It should be noted that electric cars—with only one person aboard—consume about three times as much energy per passenger as conventional trains do. Illich was a big advocate of cycling. He wrote,

> Man on his feet is thermodynamically more efficient than any motorized vehicle and most animals. Man on a bicycle can go three or four times faster than the pedestrian, but uses five times less energy in the process. He carries one gram of his weight over a kilometre of flat road at an expense of only 0.15 calories. The bicycle is the perfect transducer to match man's metabolic energy to the impedance of locomotion. Equipped with this tool, man outstrips the efficiency of not only all machines but all other animals as well.

Energy and Equity, together with Illich's *Tools for Conviviality* (1973), form the foundation for much of Silverman's ideological thinking about bikes and about cars.

It is important to note that Illich wrote about cycling at a time when most bicycles were heavy, simple, and robust. Any gears tended to be inside the rear hub and protected from harm. Until about 1970, typically only elite cyclists had ten-speed-type bikes with more delicate derailleur gears. Since then, high-end sales have been pushed by the industry, sometimes with price tags comparable to economy cars and often requiring proprietary parts or expertise to service. It is not uncommon to find bicycles today with about thirty gears or speeds. Thus, some of the things that Illich wrote about how bicycles are affordable and easy to repair might not always apply today.

Cyclo-Frustrations in Montreal

When Silverman was riding around the Plateau Mont Royal district in the early 1970s, he was not a typical cyclist. There was always something about him that stood out:

"You always knew when he was coming; nobody rode a bike like Bob. He embodied love of biking and was visible everywhere," recounts Diane Larson. She did not know Silverman well, but mutual friends often pointed him out riding his bike. At the time, Larson had just moved to Montreal's Plateau district, in 1972. Silverman might have been flamboyant, but his bicycles usually looked like something salvaged from a scrap yard.

Meanwhile, Silverman was "enjoying cycling in the city but I noticed there were no facilities for bikes—no parking, no paths, no bridge no metro access, nothing. I became 'cyclo-frustrated.'"

The Save Montreal Movement

IN 1973, the Van Horne Mansion, on Sherbrooke Street at the corner of Stanley, was a classic greystone house and dating from 1869, was demolished. More precisely, it was bulldozed in the middle of the night by a private developer, ultimately to be replaced with a concrete tower. The stately and classic Golden Square Mile mansion had been purchased in 1890 by Sir William Van Horne, builder of the Canadian Pacific Railway. That very lucrative railway was the first to span Canada. Van Horne was also a notable art collector.[1] The mayor claimed that, because the Victorian mansion was built and occupied by English-speaking Montrealers, it was not a typical piece of Quebec architecture.[2] Whatever the case, a five-dollar demolition permit was "gladly delivered" by the administration of Mayor Drapeau.[3]

After the Van Horne mansion demolition, Michael Fish helped found what eventually became Save Montreal. Fish nonetheless describes himself as "a background guy" in the group. Save Montreal brought together housing groups and environmental organizations, calling for an end to demolitions of historic buildings and the destruction of green spaces.

The core group of Save Montreal consisted of about 20 people. Among others, these included: architects Joe Baker, Michael Fish, Phyllis Lambert, Peter Lanken, Mark London, and Jean-Claude Marsan; Gazette reporters Donna Gabeline and Dane Lanken; McGill architecture professor Julia Gersovitz; longtime activists Dimitri Roussopoulos, alongside his wife, Lucia Kowaluk; and Silverman, of course. This group eventually morphed into Heritage Montreal with the aim of saving the city's architectural legacy. The group's victories include saving Dawson College, the Grey Nuns mother house in downtown Montreal; the Collège de Montréal (the oldest building of its kind on the continent); and la Prison des Patriotes. Fish speaks very highly of Silverman and recently spearheaded unsuccessful efforts to award the Order of Montreal to him. "Bob was fearless, and had imagination; when he said he'd do something, he would not let people down. So many activists let supporters down. He wasn't in it for himself, but was totally devoted to the cause of urban betterment."

"When I first met him, Bob was one of the top three or four actors protesting what ailed the city," explains Fish. "At the time, there were regular demonstrations against the Vietnam War. That kind of background noise crept into the Quebec nationalist movement and other issues in Montreal."

Fish maintains that opposition to the war spilled over into other popular issues; a better deal for Quebec, a better deal for blacks, etc. "There were 100 different issues to choose from." Historian Sean Mills, writing about the period from 1963 to 1972 in Montreal's political history, also notes how diverse protest movements often worked together. Fish participated in anti-war protests in front of the US Consulate, including one where Dimitri Roussopoulos was arrested. "But I stayed near the back of the crowd," says Fish, who did not want to be apprehended by police.

"The Save Montreal movement brought together the same people at weekly meetings. We became confreres; with perhaps twenty people listening to what each other did but working on different issues. When one of us did something, the others turned up. We were there at each other's press conferences. Bob was a leader," says Fish.

The above examples highlight how civil rights, environmental, anti-nuclear, church, student, feminist, trade union, and Quebec nationalist groups worked together to protest the Vietnam War. They also gained appreciation for each other's causes. Silverman credits the protest marches in Montreal with forcing the US consulate to relocate to a more secure location in the Complexe Desjardins towers downtown. The protest movement in general is arguably credited with eventually ending American involvement in the war. The US consulate has since moved a few times—always to high-security locations—and is now found on Sainte-Catherine Street West at the corner of Stanley, very close to where Silverman once had his bookstore. Ultimately, US President Nixon was forced to end an unpopular, expensive, and what many people saw as an unwinnable war. A peace treaty was signed with Communist forces under Ho Chi Minh in 1973, and US forces had mostly left by 1974. Within months, the anti-Communist South Vietnamese government, which the United States had been supporting, collapsed.

On April 28, 1975, Bing Crosby's "I'm Dreaming of a White Christmas" began playing over the US embassy loudspeakers in Saigon, Vietnam. This was the signal for helicopters to start frantically evacuating personnel from what is now called Ho Chi Minh City. Two days later, People's Army of Vietnam (PAVN) tanks crashed the South Vietnamese presidential palace gates. The Vietnam War was finally over and Silverman was already redirecting his energy toward MàB.

There were other factors involved, but anti-war protestors felt that they had succeeded in doing what initially seemed impossible: forcing the world's most powerful nation to withdraw its "invincible" military machine from Vietnam. This led to an effervescence and general feeling of optimism in the counterculture movement. What could they *not* do?

When Did Silverman's Bike Activism Really Begin?

Silverman insisted that his bicycle activism began at that May 1975 meeting in his apartment, but there is considerable evidence to suggest it began much earlier. According to Ross (2016), Silverman visited with the Provo movement in the Netherlands in 1967. The Provo had already established a collective bicycle fleet there and this may well have been the inspiration for Montreal's BIXI program.

Nick Peck, formerly with Association for Bicycle Commuting in Boston, distinctly remembers Silverman's name as being involved with cycling activism circa 1972. But most convincing is the 1974 election platform of the Montreal Citizens' Movement (MCM) was advocating for the establishment of reserved bus lanes and bike lanes as of 1974, a year before the founding of MàB.[4]

Given that Silverman was a member of the MCM, the likely explanation is that he probably constituted its "bicycle lobby" and was responsible for crafting the party's position on bikes. Who else would have believed in bicycles strongly enough to do that? Gail Tedstone, a former member of the MCM, recounts how she and Silverman were the only two party members who rode their bikes to party functions.

> Nick Peck, formerly with Association for Bicycle Commuting in Boston, distinctly remembers Silverman's name as being involved with cycling activism circa 1972.

Not One Inch of Pavement Dedicated to Bike Lanes

Cyclists had much to be "cyclo-frustrated" about when Silverman began riding the streets of Montreal in 1969, a situation that did not change much throughout the mid-1970s. Not only did the city offer nothing for cyclists, but it also ranked very poorly in comparisons with other cities. Carbon monoxide gas, a lethal pollutant of which ninety-eight percent came from car exhaust, reached unsafe levels (over thirteen parts per million) on some fifty-five days in 1974 in Montreal. Yet the city did nothing to discourage automobile use or encourage alternatives.[5]

In fact, Montreal saw massive "urban renewal" projects in the 1960s and 1970s that sometimes saw the demolition of whole neighbourhoods, often to make way for highways, wider roads, and parking lots. The Silverman family home on Iona Street—sacrificed for the Decarie Expressway—was but one casualty. Residences on both sides of René Lévesque Boulevard were knocked down to create an urban boulevard there. The Faubourg neighbourhood was razed where Maison Radio-Canada stood for many years (and where now a new residential neighbourhood is planned) and large parts of the Little Burgundy were demolished for various transportation projects. Half of Chinatown was demolished to make way for the Ville-Marie Expressway, Complexe Guy Favreau, and Palais des congrès (Montreal Convention Centre). Old Montreal narrowly escaped the wrecker's ball because of this highway project. Meanwhile, large parts of Hochelaga and Viauville were torn down for the eastern part of Ville-Marie Expressway, which was never built. The village of Longue-Pointe was levelled, along with the second-oldest Catholic church in North America, to build the Louis-Hippolyte-Lafontaine Tunnel. "Overall, about forty percent of the pre-war city was destroyed for highways and parking lots," said Silverman. Some considered this to be "progress!"

> Old Montreal narrowly escaped the wrecker's ball because of this highway project.

Some ninety-five percent of the city's transportation budget was consecrated to automobiles and not one inch of pavement was dedicated to bike lanes. Other cities were already developing bike lanes; Toronto had a network of some 373 km planned.

Montreal—which is on an island—had no dedicated bicycle bridge links. Meanwhile, both Calgary and Ottawa—while not on islands—boasted dedicated bike bridges.[6] In Montreal, bikes were barred from the metro and buses while New York City was already allowing bikes on its subway.

To add insult to injury, cycling was illegal in city parks such as Mount Royal Park and Saint Helen's Island with police occasionally setting up "traps" to catch errant cyclists. Absurdly, cyclists were also banned from going into the Botanical Gardens, while motorists were encouraged there. Today, a similar situation persists with some Montreal cemeteries.

The mayor of Toronto, John Sewell, could sometimes be seen on a bike, as could the mayor of New York, John Lindsay. But this could not be said for Montreal's mayor, Jean Drapeau. At this time, some 150,000 commuters in Amsterdam were riding bikes daily.

The Drapeau administration saw bicycles as a "thing for kids." Adult cyclists were perceived as being "marginal" types, with many of them being hippies or otherwise penniless people. But things were changing and the sport was undergoing a boom in popularity, attracting a wealthier clientele, due in some part, to new, lightweight, and affordable ten-speed bicycles becoming available.

The famous "Earthrise" photo of a green and blue Earth taken by Apollo astronauts orbiting the Moon in 1968 may have contributed to the burgeoning environmental movement, increasing bicycle sales. The anti-Vietnam War movement had also buoyed environmental causes.

The 1973 Oil Crisis—when oil-exporting nations cut off sales to countries that had supported Israel in the 1967 War—pushed up the prices of gasoline and diesel. So many people were buying bicycles that bike shops were having trouble keeping up with demand. In the United States, at fourteen million units sold annually; bicycles were outselling cars. By early 1974, some one hundred million Americans owned bikes and John Dowlin, a spokesman for the Philadelphia Bicycle Coalition, predicted that "this spring, we're going to see twice as many bikes as we've ever seen before."[7] In Canada, annual sales doubled from 1970 to 1972, reaching two million units. But there was no real safety in numbers; Quebec saw an average of sixty-eight cyclists dying annually on its roads. The situation was as dangerous elsewhere in North America.

In 1974, the UCI World Road Championships (Worlds) were held in Montreal. This was a very rare departure from Europe for this event, won by Belgian Eddy Merckx after a gruelling seven-hour ordeal. That race in Montreal crowned Merckx as the first ever victor in the same year of the planet's three most prestigious bike races: the Tour de France; the Giro (Tour of Italy); and the Worlds. There was undoubtedly some spill-over from such a high-level elite cycling event into increased enthusiasm for bicycling in general, including the non-competitive urban cycling preached by Silverman. Montreal continues to occupy an enviable spot in top-level road cycling. Since 2010, the Grands Prix cyclists de Québec et de Montréal (GPCQM) race annually in Quebec City and in Montreal. These UCI

> Adult cyclists were perceived as being "marginal" types, with many of them being hippies or otherwise penniless people.

ProTour bicycle races are the most prestigious in the Americas and they are free to watch for those nearby.

A Mayor Hostile to Bicycling

Jean Drapeau was mayor of Montreal in the 1970s, a position he was first elected to in 1954. He did not hold the office from 1957 to 1960, but when Drapeau finally stepped down in 1986, he had been the mayor for almost three decades. This time period stretched from Quebec's "Great Darkness" through the "Quiet Revolution" and beyond. Originally elected promising to eradicate corruption when Montreal was known for its brothels, gambling, and loose liquor laws, Drapeau's Civic Party is described as having a conservative, populist, and federalist ideology. But his partly modernist legacy is most remarkable for its ambitious achievements like Montreal's metro and an extensive highway system that Silverman despised.

> Drapeau's crowning achievement was to bring the 1967 World Fair—Expo 67—to Montreal and make a success of it.

Drapeau's crowning achievement was to bring the 1967 World Fair—Expo 67—to Montreal and make a success of it. His legacy also includes bringing the 1976 Olympics to Montreal as well as a Major League Baseball team, the Expos. While the metro did much to promote public transit usage, many new highway projects were built under Drapeau. These include the original Champlain Bridge, the Louis-Hippolyte-Lafontaine Tunnel, the Decarie Expressway, the Ville-Marie Expressway, and the Bonaventure and Côte-de-Liesse highways. Massive highway-building projects invariably encourage a massive increase in automobile use. Unsurprisingly, car culture dominated Montreal in Drapeau's time and for decades that followed.

Sometimes accused of extravagance, Drapeau is also described as a "modernist," bringing symbolic monuments like the Olympic Stadium, Place des Arts, and downtown skyscrapers to his city. He is credited with lifting Montreal into the modern world and onto the world map. Drapeau tried to stop French president Charles de Gaulle from taking a microphone in 1967 at city hall to declare "Vive le Québec Libre!"—a declaration that invigorated the independence movement in Quebec. Drapeau was also in office during the 1970 October Crisis when the FLQ kidnapped two prominent officials, killing one. Ottawa then declared martial law, arresting some 468 "subversive characters" and holding them without trial. The detainees were overwhelmingly francophone, but Silverman's former bookstore employee, Nick Auf der Maur, was among the few anglophones incarcerated during the October Crisis.[8]

Taking political advantage of the October Crisis, Drapeau's party accused the opposition FRAP party was of "being a front for the FLQ." His Civic Party succeeded in scoring 92.5 percent of the popular vote on October 25, 1970, and winning all fifty-two council seats. Drapeau's party almost repeated that performance in 1978, then winning fifty-two of fifty-four seats.

Of the two lonely opposition councillors elected in 1978, Nick Auf der Maur was elected with the Montreal Action Group. The other opposition councillor was Michael Fainstat, leader of the Montreal Citizens' Movement (MCM). Montreal was essentially a one-party state; the Civic Party faced only token opposition in City Hall during the 1970s. Initially, the Civic Party was elected largely on a law-and-order program, promising to get rid of corruption and the moral decay that was hitting the country's metropolis at the beginning of the '60s. Perhaps thirty thousand trees were cut down in Mount Royal Park by Drapeau's morality squad in the 1950s, causing long-term soil erosion and problems with invasive species. The intention was to reduce the "illicit and immoral" sex acts going under the cover of the trees, presumably an indirect attack on Montreal's gay community.[9]

The first biography written about Drapeau does not even include the words "environment" or "pollution," or the term, "bike path."[10]

"Most councillors under Drapeau were business types; it was not really a job. Everything was decided by the mayor or by Yvon Lamarre, chairman of the Executive Committee," relates Michel Prescott, an opposition MCM councillor first elected in 1982. In the late 1970s, while Montreal city councillors were being paid five thousand dollars a year; councillors in Ottawa and Toronto made four times as much. One wonders what the motive was for being elected as a councillor for Drapeau under such circumstances.

Among the councillors of Drapeau's party was Max Seigler, a business associate of Silverman's father. Seigler was first elected in 1930 while Camillien Houde was mayor; he later served as a councillor for the Civic Party. By 1958 he had become Montreal's longest-serving councillor. Silverman denied that this connection helped him in any way to communicate with the Drapeau administration.

"In the mid-1970s, Mayor Jean Drapeau's autocratic administration was hostile to bicycling. Communication with this administration was difficult; MàB's letters were rarely answered and there was no public question period [for members of the public] at city council meetings," wrote Silverman. He later corrected himself to say that Drapeau was simply "indifferent" to bicycling.

Silverman described the situation in 1975 as "cyclists have become frustrated and angry. They see that cars have all the road space and pedestrians have the sidewalks, and cyclists have nothing. They want to be able to ride to work, to school, to market, and to friends in perfect safety. They want to be able to park their bicycles without worrying that they will be stolen. They want to be able to cross over all tunnels and bridges. And they don't want hassles on buses and trains. In short, cyclists have cyclo-frustrations."[11] But all these "cyclo-frustrations" may also have been Silverman's secret weapon.

★★★

Silverman, an avowed anarchist and anti-authoritarian, could be seen as the natural enemy of the autocratic administration of Mayor Jean Drapeau. Indeed, Silverman was urged by his close friend Armand Vaillancourt to run for mayor of Montreal in the October 1962 election. Drapeau won that election with eighty-eight percent of the vote while Silverman ended up in Cuba.

"In Montreal we have a mayor who is particularly backward and anti-bicycle," proclaimed Silverman in 1978.[12]

"Drapeau built big concrete things like highways, stadiums, and a car-driven city; his vision was upside down to Bob's," says *Gazette* columnist Josh Freed. "Yes, Drapeau accomplished a lot of things, but many of these were failures. Bob's ideas were a success." The failures of Drapeau's legacy includes the 1976 Olympics, which were massively over-budget; the Olympic Stadium and its ongoing structural problems with the roof; the underutilized Olympic velodrome which ended up being converted into a zoo; and a Major League Baseball team, the Expos, which eventually left Montreal for Washington, DC.

Similarly, former MàBer Stéphane Desjardins believes that Silverman's legacy will eventually eclipse that of Drapeau's: "because Silverman's vision of a city is more grassroots. It touches day-to-day realities. The only real Drapeau achievement in this field is the metro." Louise Roy, a former administrator at Vélo Québec (VQ), described the Drapeau years as requiring big battles to obtain minor permits for bicycling events. According to fellow VQ administrator Michel Labrecque, Montreal cyclist advocates in the 1970s had to use every possible means to advance their cause.[13]

The head of Montreal's traffic department Jacques Barrière declared in May 1975 that promoting cycling was not a priority. He jokingly suggested that if the city encouraged bikes too much, "we will have to put the cars in our pockets." New bike paths typically lead to the elimination of hundreds of car parking spots.

Barrière once declared that automobiles were "the invention of the century," according to Silverman. Ironically, while Montreal had forgotten its urban cyclists, it was preparing for the 1976 Olympics. As part of the $1.6 billion Olympic installations built for the event was a $86.5 million velodrome, reserved for elite cyclists, which was denounced by Silverman. At its inauguration, this

Figure 6.1. Silverman on his bike, October 1976.
Source: Photograph by Tedd Church; reproduced with permission of Montreal *Gazette*, a division of Postmedia Network Inc.

state-of-the-art installation was the only covered velodrome in North America. Such irony only served to add insult to injury as far as MàB was concerned. Silverman wanted the millions to instead be spent on bicycle infrastructure accessible to and for the benefit of Montrealers. After the Olympics, the velodrome was under-utilized and ultimately converted into a zoo, the Biodome. There were other problems, too, with the Olympics. Drapeau made a statement that he would live to regret: "The Montreal Olympics can no more lose money than a man can have a baby." Soon after, the *Gazette* ran a political cartoon depicting a very-pregnant Drapeau trying to telephone an abortion clinic.

In fact, the 1976 Olympics ended up costing much more than projected and running up a billion-dollar debt. Auf der Maur and others had been predicting such horrific cost overruns. It took thirty years for the city to finish paying for an Olympics that Drapeau promised could not possibly incur a debt. Perhaps only a committed idealist would have been motivated to advocate for bicycling in such a bleak landscape. Some described Silverman as "quixotic," for which some synonyms are "idealistic, unconventional, unbusinesslike, romantic, extravagant, starry-eyed, visionary, or utopian." Every adjective here is appropriate. Silverman liked the comparison with Don Quixote; asking for bike paths in the 1970s probably seemed as pointless as charging windmills like the hero of *Man of la Mancha* did. But after a few decades, Silverman eventually succeeded in achieving most of his "utopian" and "unrealistic" goals.

During the May 1968 unrest in France, protesters used the slogan: *Soyez réalistes, demandez l'impossible* (Be realistic, ask for the impossible). This fully applies to Silverman with his insolence, his humour, and a political message. It seems that Silverman in the mid-1970s was all revved up, just looking for a worthy cause.

Le Monde à Bicyclette

THE VÉLORUTION
Cars, cars everywhere,
what a stink!
packed together
street by street
eliminating our feet
we had nothing to like
then,
we rediscovered
the bike.

THE GROUP, later known as le Monde à Bicyclette (MàB), first became famous in early 1975. Mention is made in the *Montreal Star* on April 10 of a group initially called the "Montreal Bicycle Movement" that wanted to promote the use of bikes. Those interested in joining the group were invited to attend a public meeting. Silverman's name does not appear in this listing, but that of another cycling advocate does: Vicki Schmolka.[1] This was followed by an article in the *Star* May 2, 1975, entitled "MUC Planners Start Assessing Bike Paths" and began with discussion about the lack of cycling infrastructure within the Montreal Urban Community (MUC), which included Montreal and all independent municipalities on the Island. Near the end of the article was mentioned a cycling advocacy group, now called "Citizens on Cycles (CoC)" and of a May 24 bike parade downtown. Schmolka, not Silverman, was again presented as the spokesperson. But there was an organizing meeting of CoC planned beforehand at Silverman's apartment.

"Bob called to invite me to the meeting," relates Jacques Desjardins, at the time a student employee of the Fédération de Cyclotourisme du Québec (now Vélo Québec). The invitation was because Desjardins had recently written an article in the federation newsletter, calling for more urban biking. "We spoke in French on the telephone."

The Founding Meeting
When MàB first started in early 1975, it was one of the earliest cyclists' rights groups anywhere on the planet.

> "About 20 people showed up on bicycles for that organizing meeting, to the great annoyance of our uptight landlord, George."

"About 20 people showed up on bicycles for that organizing meeting, to the great annoyance of our uptight landlord, George," wrote Silverman. He was then living with Ruth Schou at 4323 Esplanade Street on the corner of Marianne in Montreal's Plateau district. Silverman has jokingly described the MàB as "a union of Quebec nationalists and anglophone anarchists."

"It was in those years that MàB was born. I was there with the other founders. I tell you this and no one will believe me," related Armand Vaillancourt in 2022. Today a famous sculptor and painter; very few know him as a longtime cycling advocate.

Vicki Schmolka, a writer and lawyer, was among those at the founding meeting, besides being an early spokesperson for Citizens on Cycles. However, she soon left the group, leaving Montreal for a job in Ontario. Today, Schmolka continues to actively support cycling and environmental causes in the Kingston area.

Jacques Desjardins was a student employee at what is now VQ, in early 1975, when he first met Silverman. Jacques Desjardins is therefore part of the "first generation" of MàB, thanks to that telephone call from Silverman, inviting him to attend the founding meeting, "I liked Bob as of that first telephone call; he changed my life." Desjardins would become one of Silverman's closest friends and strongest supporters. He was impressed by Silverman's experiences in Cuba and Israel, but described their meeting as "Earthlings meeting Martians, but finding that we had the same goal. Bob was part of the dream of the 1960s." That time period is etched in Desjardins's mind because he married weeks later, leaving the church with his bride on a tandem bicycle. He told the *Montreal Star* then that this was a reflection of the lifestyle that he and his bride—both keen cyclists—planned to live.[2]

"At that first meeting, I spoke in bad English," jokes Desjardins. Other meetings followed on a weekly basis. "I proposed the French name *le Monde à Bicyclette* for the group." This name can mean either "the gang on bikes" or "the world on a bike."

"I liked this name instantly because it united subject and object and was universal," Silverman later wrote.

Searching through the archives of the *Gazette* and *Montreal Star* (on the Newspapers.com database in 2021) revealed 182 mentions of "Monde à Bicyclette" since 1975 but just 99 mentions of "Citizens on Cycles." So, even English-speaking journalists in Quebec preferred the French name by a margin of almost two-to-one. French-speaking journalists, meanwhile, rarely use "Citizens on Cycles." The "Citizens on Cycles" name does appear however in a *Canadian Press* article describing the Easter Monday 1981 event where Silverman, dressed as Moses, tried parting the St. Lawrence. This story was picked up by eleven English newspapers across Canada, including the *Edmonton Journal*, the *Regina Leader-Post*, the *Vancouver Sun*, Victoria's *Times Colonist*, and the *Windsor Star*. The peak coverage in this database was in 1976 and 1981 with twenty articles mentioning MàB each year. Outside of Quebec, newspapers in four other provinces also covered MàB some twenty-three times collectively. Editors as far afield as Vancouver Island—4,500 kilometres to the west—considered MàB to be newsworthy, typically referring to the group by its French name.³ Perhaps adding to the allure of MàB's name, US cyclist Greg Lemond began to make sporting news in the late 1970s. He eventually won a World Championship in 1983 and became the first American to win the Tour de France in 1986. His prominence in competitive cycling caused the North American press to start covering a sport that it had previously almost ignored. There may have been a spill-over effect on coverage of cycling advocacy for MàB.

★★★

"Bob was way ahead of his time," explains Desjardins today. "For that reason, nobody took him seriously."

In the 1970s, Silverman's vision was not apparent, even to other cycling enthusiasts. Not only did Silverman have vision, but he could also speak.

"Montreal would never have become the leading city in North America for bicycles without Bob. Gabriel Lupien of VQ said that bikes were just for countryside, recreational use and not for utilitarian city riding," says Desjardins.

> "I liked this name instantly because it united subject and object and was universal," Silverman later wrote.

Desjardins worked closely with MàB, on full-time basis for five years, and is still very involved with a successor group, Encore du Monde à bicyclette. Despite his admiration for Silverman, he admits that the man was sometimes hard to work with. Silverman had many international bicycling connections and turned Desjardins onto some of them: "I went to Amsterdam for MàB and was hosted by a guy there who spoke French. But he didn't understand my French so we had to talk in English. After that, I thought 'don't fight it,' and learned English."

Today Desjardins lives in the Portuguese neighbourhood of Montreal that used to be the Jewish one, having been invited to the neighbourhood by Silverman. Desjardins was among those who tried to get Silverman honoured by Montreal and by the Quebec government; eventually VQ did recognize "Bicycle Bob's" contribution.

★★★

Most of the activists stayed with the group for brief periods and some refer to "five or six generations" of activists associated with MàB over some two decades. Schmolka and Desjardins were with the first generation.

It was remarkable, especially at this time that Quebec nationalists and anglophone anarchists could work together at all. That they enjoyed each other's company and became successful is extraordinary. Over time, the group became majority francophone. This was partly because some of the early anglophone members left Montreal, often in search of better job prospects elsewhere. The language shift was also led by Silverman who invariably wrote and spoke in French despite his strong accent. "It must be recognized that a movement which promotes a choice of what type of society we want in Quebec can hardly be solely anglophone," reasoned Silverman.

"Bob had a thick anglophone accent and we sometimes made jokes about it," says Stéphane Desjardins who joined MàB circa 1979. "But it was impressive that he did this. It was still the era of 'Two Solitudes' and we certainly noticed it."

★★★

Schmolka's impressions of Silverman were that "He was a brilliant guy, smart, interesting, and committed. He was also able to execute plans such as the race pitting a pedestrian against a bike against a car. He was well read; understanding the political underpinning of the bicycle movement."

Apart from Illich, other authors that Silverman was reading included American-Canadian activist Jane Jacobs and Danish urban planner Jan Gehl, both of whom advocated taking back public spaces in cities from cars. Such ideas, despite obvious merit, remain heresy today for some politicians, voters, and bureaucrats. Gehl did much work to prioritize pedestrians and cyclists in urban settings. He is credited with developing the term "Copenhagenize," meaning to develop a city around safe bicycle and pedestrian transport, rather than around transportation by private cars. The Danish capital, Copenhagen, became the world leader for this kind of model.

"I was a good organizer," said Silverman of his time with MàB. "I learned how to do it by demonstrating against the Vietnam War. This work seemed natural for me. What I did with MàB was a continuation of work I did against the Vietnam War."

"We were very naive at the start," said Silverman. "We thought that it would be enough to show authorities that the rights of cyclists were not being respected, and that they would of course meet our requests [...] At first we weren't transport specialists, but apostles of the bicycle. We believed ingeniously that car owners would take our advice and alter their lifestyles."[4]

> Apart from Illich, other authors that Silverman was reading included American-Canadian activist Jane Jacobs and Danish urban planner Jan Gehl, both of whom advocated taking back public spaces in cities from cars.

MàB and Its Manifesto

Encouraged by the initial public reaction to MàB, in 1975, Silverman wrote the Cyclists' Manifesto. A manifesto is defined as "a written statement declaring publicly the intentions, motives, or views of its issuer" by the Merriam-Webster online dictionary. Silverman's text was originally an eleven-page (2,250 word) typewritten document composed in French (readers may find an English translation in the Annex). This text is very brief compared to the *Communist Manifesto* (at 65,000 words) written by Karl Marx and Friedrich Engels in 1848, probably the world's most famous manifesto. Writing a manifesto can be a good thing to do for detailing an elaborate plan for making a better world. But Silverman, instead of wanting to trigger revolutions, hoped to trigger a "Vélorution."

There were also two other "made in Quebec" manifestos of note at this time; the *Refus global* (which helped precipitate the Quiet Revolution) and the FLQ manifesto. This violent nationalist group (which would be described today as "terrorist") demanded that its manifesto be broadcast on Radio Canada by *Téléjournal* host Gaetan Montreuil during the October 1970 crisis, which the authorities agreed to in the hope of resolving the crisis. This manifesto struck a chord with francophones, because the text reflected many of their economic and social concerns. The manifesto even sparked a wave of sympathy toward the FLQ, but this evaporated when it was announced that the FLQ had assassinated Minister Pierre Laporte. Obviously, the MàB manifesto is of a completely different order than that of the FLQ, even if it speaks of liberation. Spelling out what MàB stands for is also a good way of ensuring that the organization stays on track with its stated mission over many years and despite important changes in personnel. An abbreviated version of the 2,250-word manifesto was published in *Le Jour* newspaper.[5] The document is surprisingly bold in calling for cars "to be replaced by bicycles in the long-term." Silverman later softened his position on this to limit the replacement by bikes only to urban areas. The first three of the original eleven pages were devoted to denouncing cars before an alternative—the bicycle—is mentioned.

John Dowlin—a Philadelphia-based custodian of cycling information and unofficial liaison officer for putting 1970s bike movements in touch with each other—was an important inspiration for Silverman. Contacted in late 2020, Dowlin was unable to recall another cycling group worldwide that so boldly called for bicycles to replace cars. Silverman's document is quite avant-garde in its call for an extensive system of bike paths and bike lanes when there were none in Montreal. In fact, Silverman felt compelled to define both bike paths and bike lanes for a public then so unfamiliar with these concepts. The text is also prophetic, especially in regard to the logistics of its call for communal bicycles more than three decades before Montreal launched its BIXI communal bike program in 2009.

By 2024, BIXI counted more than 11,000 bikes (including 2,600 electric ones) and over 900 docking stations, exceeding the 10,000 bikes that Silverman called for almost fifty years earlier. Silverman's text goes beyond promoting bicycles, and demanding bike lanes; the MàB also promoted public transit and called for express bus lanes.

Silverman wryly concludes by borrowing from the 1848 *Communist Manifesto*; "Workers of the world unite, you have nothing to lose but your chains" and adapting it for cyclists who have a different kind of chain.

To give a better idea of Silverman's overall vision, in a magazine interview he expressed his wish for a city where people only work four hours a day; transport is focused on bicycles, public transit, and cross-country skiing; solar panels are on all houses and factories; money is replaced by work exchanges; there are no hierarchies; volleyball is played in former parking lots; there are flowers and trees on all streets; men, women, young, and old are all equal; we can swim in the St. Lawrence River; we eat good food; and we pedal to our heart's content.[6]

The First Demonstration

LE MONDE À BICYCLETTE held its first big bike parade, blocking car traffic, on Ste Catherine Street West on May 31, 1975. Despite rainy weather, some three thousand cyclists arrived at the finish line in Parc Lafontaine. A sideshow event featured a race, pitting a cyclist against a motorist and against a transit passenger in rush-hour traffic. Silverman, who organized that race, said it was inspired by a similar contest in San Francisco:

"The cyclist won by four minutes; about twenty percent faster than the motorist (over 4.3 km) from Place Ville Marie downtown to the corner of St Denis and St Joseph streets," recalled Silverman. "The transit user finished third. All were supposed to stop at red lights, but the cyclist might have cheated."

A few days earlier there was also a bicycle—intended for official use—presented as a gift to Mayor Drapeau. Silverman's friend from the bookstore days, sculptor Armand Vaillancourt, was tapped to present the bicycle as part of an Athletic Committee of Montreal event. City councillor Jean Laroche accepted the bicycle on behalf of the mayor but was unable to commit whether Drapeau would make it to the bicycle parade.[1] The mayor's office never acknowledged this gift. Silverman suggested that it was an alderman's son who ultimately inherited the bike. Nonetheless, the media liked the idea and took an interest in MàB.

"After our first demonstration, someone just gave us five thousand dollars," recounted Silverman in 2013. The group now had a media presence and a war chest.

Deeming the 1975 events to be a success, the cyclists vowed to repeat the experience annually. MàB collaborated with VQ to schedule these events, trying to revive what used to be known as Canada Bicycling Week, originally initiated in 1916 for early June. The intent was to restore bicycles to their former glory.

"[...] from 1977 to 1983, the two organizations held a demonstration on this day. It was not unusual to see a procession of over a thousand cyclists set out on city streets at 10 km/h to bike the few kilometres separating Parc Lafontaine and Dominion (now Dorchester) Square. It was one way of showing the City and motorists that cyclists also had their rightful place in Montreal," states VQ on its website.[2]

"We were frustrated by our bicyclists' reality and still held weekly meetings at our apartment. Those who did not visualize bicycling as transport dropped out... [But] we received a lot of media attention," according to Silverman.

Applying for Job Creation Grants

Before she left Montreal, Schmolka applied for a federal job-creation grant. "The Local Initiatives Program (LIP) funding came through and Silverman was among those hired to work on this project," as she puts it.

"I had no job title," explained Silverman, before wondering out loud, "or maybe I was the manager?" Such job-creation grants routinely demand specific job titles for each employee, but hierarchies were anathema to Silverman and there is little enforcement for such job descriptions to be adhered to. The funding for nine months included a modest provision to rent office space. MàB leased a small room at the International YMCA on Park Avenue.

Whatever his job title was, the next few months were a busy time for Silverman. Plans were made for storming the metro, for parades, and for die-ins.

"The Milton Park Citizens' Committee gave us some money they didn't need and Le Château clothing store chain bought a large quantity of our T-shirts *Perds Pas les Pédales* [...] We were on our way," wrote Silverman about this period.[3]

"Le MàB grew rapidly as there were more and more bicyclists and then no facilities to accommodate them. Bicycle advocacy became my life work and the only job I ever really liked," Silverman also wrote. Over the next year, MàB activities included producing the newsletter and leaflets and organizing public debates, press releases, and press conferences. The group developed relations with other activist groups, such as trade unions, including some in Europe and the United States. And there was planning for the next Bicycling Week, including a die-in.

"We fought for cycling to be considered a means of transport and not simply a sport or leisure activity," wrote Michel Camus, one of MàB's employees, "This clearly distinguished us from other pro-cycling movements in Quebec. We were iconoclasts, breaking preconceived ideas anchored in the concrete of the automobile civilization. It was one of the most beautiful experiences of my life."

Finding an Equal in Claire Morissette
Excerpt from the poem:

ROBERT SILVERMAN
Spécialiste de l'impossible,
Génie sans diplôme,
Jeanne d'Arc à bicyclette,
Claire Morissette, je t'aime.
(Specialist of the impossible,

Genius without a diploma,
Joan of Arc on a bicycle,
Claire Morissette, I love you.)

Excerpt from the poem "D'où viens-tu Claire Morissette?" ("Where Do you Come from, Claire Morissette?"), which Silverman wrote for Morissette. Perhaps nobody else influenced Silverman's life as much as the eco-feminist Claire Morissette. She was absent from the first MàB meetings in mid-1975 and it was not until Silverman met her at an environmental rally that December, when he explained what MàB was about, that she promptly joined the group. Morissette might even have been more "anti-car" than Silverman; she apparently never drove one. Morissette poetically described her first meeting with Silverman, saying he was "an epic bikeshevik." She added that "he was a little breathless, but full of love and common sense."

Some sources erroneously list Morissette as a "co-founder" of MàB, but she did later share the title of co-president with Silverman. The title underlines how she was not so much a follower of Silverman's, but his equal.

"I realized that global threats were also local issues. I had met Bob Silverman and came to realize that the number one environmental menace was, and still is, the automobile. I could no longer stay with flowers and bugs (at the Botanical Gardens); I had to connect with the sociological issues of the time," explained Morissette years later.[4]

"The arrival in 1976 of Claire Morissette gave us a giant boost forward," wrote Silverman, who did not seem to feel threatened by her. "She quickly felt at home in our movement and for many years she assured the coordination of our group. Her loyalty, her competence, her high sense of responsibility, her accounting and organizational skills greatly contributed to our being an effective and visible lobby. And Claire's constantly growing literary skills were manifest in every issue of our quarterly newspaper."[5]

The two complemented and greatly encouraged each other and were sometimes referred to as "Bonnie and Clyde." This dynamic shifted over time, with Morissette assuming more control. Despite sharing a vision with Silverman, she may have perceived him as being disorganized.

"My first order of business was to bring order to the MàB office, which was chaotic," commented Morissette. "Then we worked on producing a newsletter for our members. The first versions were put out on a Gestetner machine."[6]

A 1977 trip to the Netherlands confirmed her vision of a new society. The notion of "cyclists' rights" was already established there. Prior to joining MàB, Morissette had worked as an illustrator for Montreal's Botanical Gardens, apparently collaborating on a book about boreal flora. These experiences, combined with natural talents for reading and writing, helped her proficiently produce the quarterly MàB newsletter. Pragmatically, she solicited advertisements to help pay for the newsletter, which was free for readers. From 1977 through 1998, 280 different advertisers found their way into the MàB newsletter, some opting for full-page ads while others chose simple business-card-size ads. Such ads were competitively priced at five dollars a column inch. The newsletter had an estimated circulation of twenty-five thousand readers. Over two decades, the bulletin went by various titles, including A vélo vers une ville nouvelle, Pour une ville nouvelle, or simply Le Monde à bicyclette. In general, about 80 percent of the content was written in French, the rest in English, often by Silverman. In 1980, Quebec held its first referendum on independence, which sharply divided the population along linguistic lines: half of French-speakers were in favour of independence, while English-speakers were almost unanimously opposed (on May 20, 1980, the "sovereignty-association" project proposed by the Lévesque government was defeated by 59.56 percent of the votes cast). The MàB newsletter stands out as a rare model of linguistic harmony in a divided society. The content of the newsletter was generally well researched and it exuded an optimistic tone. One issue in the late 1980s featured an article calling for a bike path on de Maisonneuve Boulevard West. It was accompanied by images of MàB volunteers dressed as surveyors, professionally measuring the street. The images alone conveyed a strong message of the inevitability that a bike path would one day be built there. In 2007, this became reality, and in 2008, the city named the bike path after Morissette. Some archived MàB newsletter issues (keywords are "Monde à bicyclette") are available online through the Bibliothèque Nationale's archives at https://numerique.banq.qc.ca/. There were rumours that MàB's "Bonnie and Clyde" were romantically involved, but Silverman denied this. Perhaps he had feelings for her, but were they reciprocated? When they first met, Morissette was just twenty-five while Silverman was forty-two. Most other members of MàB were closer to Morissette's age.

Silverman was the initiator while Morissette was the implementor. "Bob was the granddaddy of the bike move-ment in Canada. He was the first to advocate for cyclists'

> Silverman was the initiator while Morissette was the implementor. "Bob was the granddaddy of the bike movement in Canada. He was the first to advocate for cyclists' rights. Bob provided the vision while Claire provided the organization.

rights. Bob provided the vision while Claire provided the organization. MàB became successful between Bob and Claire as she efficiently organized his visionary ideas. In her own right, Claire was a real talent, the organizational brains behind MàB," as Angela Bischoff, puts it.

"The duet with Claire was very strong: Claire was organized, she took care of the numbers, was an example of a person who has ideas, convictions, structured in an organized action. She took care of funding, grants, and contributions [...] She allowed several of Bob's ideas to be structured over time," comments Michel Labrecque, a biking advocate who is credited with launching VQ's Route verte. Later, he became CEO of the STM transit authority and of Montreal's Olympic facilities.

Silverman mentioned that Morissette had been a top student and her parents had wanted her to become a doctor, but she dropped out of university. As per the poem above, Silverman described her as a "genius without a diploma." Morissette worked with various food co-operatives in the early 1970s; some of which, like the Co-op St-Louis and the Co-op aux petits oiseaux (now Amaryllis), were pioneers in the distribution and retailing of organic produce in Quebec. Her work there notably involved bookkeeping. Morissette thus developed a good sense of pragmatism about the methods needed to advance her causes. She compensated beautifully for Silverman's organizational weaknesses while helping him develop his ideas.

Morissette was also quick to understand the situation of reporters, realizing that weekends were often quiet times for news. So, putting together colourful and witty theatrical demonstrations by MàB on Sundays almost guaranteed front-page coverage in the Monday morning newspapers. This was especially true in the summer, when other news stories were scarce.

"I wouldn't be lying to say that MàB was in the news every week. We launched big and small biking campaigns. We adopted a theatrical approach and journalists liked it a lot," said Morissette.[7] Like other members of MàB, Morissette also often wrote letters to the editor of major newspapers. The flavour of such letters is typified by one published in La Presse entitled "Automobile, je te hais" (Car, I hate you) on March 9, 1977.

After joining MàB, Morissette continued her involvement with food co-operatives where she served on the board of La Balance Co-op. According to one anecdote, she stood up to the rest of the board, championing the rights of employees there who were being exploited. According to another, she urged the board to be open to opportunities outside the co-op movement, such as distributing to private stores.

In his poem (above) Silverman describes Morissette as "Joan of Arc on a bicycle," noting how she would sometimes forget herself while advancing her various causes. Like Silverman, she spent years advocating for cycling while living a precarious existence financially. However, living precariously did not prevent her from sometimes being very generous: "As a thirteen-year-old I received an incredible birthday gift from Aunt Claire; a Fiore Roma bicycle that was (circa 1989), worth about $500. For her it was a great sacrifice. And it was a gift much appreciated. Now, I'm a city cyclist," recalls Morissette's nephew Christian. Morissette was also very committed to the MàB cause and quite willing to be arrested or go to jail to make a point. She would have argued that cars, apart from being environmentally destructive, gobbling up land, and killing or injuring many people, also drive a wedge between the sexes. It must have offended Morissette that—because men tend to be higher income earners—women are often dependent on men for access to cars. Images of women are also often used to market cars.

"The car degrades our values, our tastes, our ideals. Not only does it steal precious material resources from us, but it steals our integrity as human beings," reads an excerpt from an editorial in a MàB newsletter, presumably written by Morissette.[8] In presenting a book by Maurice Brinton (see *Authoritarian Conditioning, Sexual Repression and the Irrational in Politics* in the supplementary bibliography) to Morissette, Silverman wrote this inscription (our translation): "I give this original book to my friend Claire, ecologist, botanist, anarchist, androgynous, Vélorutionary and revolutionary, gifted, convivial and unforgettable, so that she can sharpen her critical awareness and deepen her knowledge of human beings. Bob."[9]

"I was with MàB from 1984 to 1990, but it was not the golden age of the organization," recalls Yvon Dinel. "I saw that Claire was taking up a lot of space, she was steering the MàB. As a joke, we called our group 'Le Monde à Morissette.' During this time, there were few member assemblies, it was like a sort of private club revolving around Bob and Claire; the newsletter was very important. Some issues took a lot of our time: the Missing Link, between Montreal and the South Shore, a bike path on de Maisonneuve Blvd. And there had been a crisis before I arrived at MàB: some volunteers had left for VQ." During this time, Silverman was also becoming very concerned with trips to Vietnam, vision problems, and cyberspace, which he saw as a new and interesting universe. The internet was still taking form, but Silverman saw it as full of promise for opening up possibilities to communicate and to mobilize.

"By 1987, Claire was running operations at MàB while Bob had become a sort of elder statesman for the cause," says Stéphane Desjardins who was with MàB in 1979, returning to the group in 1987. "The dynamic between them was very different in 1979 versus 1987. To be clear, Claire was in charge in 1987."

"I was responsible for graphics and layout for a few editions," continues Desjardins. "Norman Nawrocki had been doing it before and I assured some continuity. I also wrote a few articles for each edition. Claire was the editor-in-chief."

"Claire was also in charge of soliciting ads; between these and some subsidies we received, the newsletter was never in a deficit situation. I think it may have even made some money for MàB. Claire regularly held planning meetings to discuss possible content for upcoming editions."

"There was an extensive distribution system for the newsletter. Apart from using bike shops as distribution points, we also used food co-operatives," says Desjardins.

In the 1980s, progressive people often distrusted technology; they considered it a means of alienating people, as described in Orwell's *Nineteen Eighty-Four* and Huxley's *Brave New World*. But Morissette was very fond of technology and especially of the Macintosh computer: it was easy to use in political combat. For her, technology was something that could liberate people from the damaging aspects of capitalism, such as cars.

"The MàB had a very holistic perspective on everything, not just bicycles. The bicycle was simply a revolutionary mechanism for the MàB," explains Zvi Leve, a cycling advocate who met Silverman years after Morissette's death in 2007. And for Morissette, the bike was a vehicle to advance feminism, especially in the Global South.

In May 1993, Morissette stepped down from MàB to concentrate on writing her book *Deux roues, un avenir, le Vélo en ville* (Écosociété, 1994). This book summarises much of her ecological and cycling thinking. "I believe that women have especially benefited from the current 'Vélorution.' They have experienced a huge sentiment of freedom," she explained.[10] In approximately two hundred and fifty pages, Morissette wrote about the issues and ideology of urban bicycling. The book was reprinted after her death. The preface, written by Silverman, describes how "the reader discovers the key role played at that time in furthering the social liberation of women: gains such as personal mobility for women, the right to wear pants and to be athletic." After writing her book, Morissette looked at solutions to problems caused by automobiles. Her research pointed to car-sharing co-operatives operating in Germany and Switzerland. Benoît Robert was in the process of setting up Communauto, a similar car-sharing system in Quebec City in 1994, and Morissette became his business partner. As such, Robert developed the Communauto branch in Québec City while Morissette concentrated on Montreal.[11]

Communauto, in 2023, counted fifty-thousand members (14 percent of Montreal households) and two thousand cars between Canada (Quebec) and France. The service expanded into Ontario and ordered 1,300 new vehicles in 2022 and another 750 in 2023. The reader will appreciate how a typical private car sits unused perhaps ninety-five percent of the time, as demonstrated by Donald Shoup of UCLA, in his ground-breaking research in the mid-1980s. Members of Communauto are able to occasionally rent a car at low cost, freed of the obligation to buy a car and thus reducing the number of cars on the road. Apparently, the original business model for Communauto was that of a co-operative, where most of Morissette's business experience came from. Communauto is now a private company, with Peugeot-Citroën as a minority shareholder. Morissette ultimately had a falling out with Benoît Robert. She next worked on setting up Cyclo Nord-Sud (CNS) in 1999, a charity modelled after the Boston-based *Bikes not Bombs* that collects and sends used bicycles from North America to the Third World. CNS notably ships to Cuba, Ecuador, Haiti, and Togo. This effort can bring about tremendous improvements in living conditions for impoverished rural residents there, especially for women. To Morissette, her efforts with CNS must have seemed like a continuation of the eco-feminism work she did with MàB; she even transferred MàB's telephone number to CNS.

In developing countries, women are typically tasked with procuring water and firewood from kilometres away; a bike lets them do that in a fraction of the time of walking. As of mid-2020, CNS claimed to have shipped 63,711 bicycles over twenty years. Apparently an unfortunate and unexpected news article about corruption within CNS associates in Haiti had a devastating psychological effect on Morissette. A previous traumatic event occurred in 1993, when she was hit by a car while riding her bicycle near Jarry Street, resulting in a broken pelvis. Colleagues have suggested that the emotional impact of that news article, combined with the side-effects of the medications she took for the pelvis injury may have somehow contributed to the breast cancer that killed Morissette when she was only fifty-seven. Morissette's character was quite particular: "She was the most honest person I've met in my whole life: integrity towards herself and her philosophies was paramount," says Stéphane Desjardins who worked closely with Morissette in the late 1980s. "Bob told me the same thing. Claire lived in poverty all her life, but was happy because she lived politically according to her beliefs."

Silverman wrote an obituary for his long-time friend, an excerpt of which appears below:

"A strong feminist, Morissette believed that bicycles helped to empower poor women who did not have easy access to cars [...] She worked tirelessly for the people of Montreal and for our planet, yet lived in poverty all her adult life. For these exceptional ecological contributions, Claire Morissette will long be remembered."[12]

***

At Morissette's wake—held at the Cyclo Nord-Sud offices—it was suggested that the various organizations she founded, co-founded, or otherwise advanced should be thought of as her children.

In June 2008, Montreal City Council voted unanimously to name a 3.4 km section of downtown's de Maisonneuve Boulevard bike path in honour of Claire Morissette. The MàB had long advocated for a major east–west bike path along this boulevard. Appropriately, this has become one of the most popular bike paths in Montreal—and Canada—recording 1.3 million trips in 2015.[13] By 2019, this bike path saw up to one thousand cyclists per hour.

Gomberg graduated with an arts degree focusing on environmental studies in 1980, then founded one of Canada's first curbside recycling programs according to Greenspiration. At the same time, he became active with the anti-nuclear and bicycle advocacy movements, also hosting his own environmental show on CKUT, the student-run radio station at McGill University. In the late 1980s, Gomberg took a job in Alberta where he became very involved with the Edmonton Bicycle Commuters

> In June 2008, Montreal City Council voted unanimously to name a 3.4 km section of downtown's de Maisonneuve Boulevard bike path in honour of Claire Morissette.

Figure 8.1. Richard "Tooker" Gomberg.
Source: MàB Archive.

(EBC) group. With his influence, this group became a bike advocacy–oriented movement. Emulating tactics used by MàB in gaining access to the metro, the EBC called for bike access to the Edmonton Light Rail Transit (ELRT) system. EBC copied the MàB stunt of carrying all kinds of large and awkward items—including an ironing board, ladder, and bike parts—onto the ELRT without trouble, but were stopped trying to bring a bicycle aboard. Gomberg later moved to Toronto where he worked with Greenpeace as a climate activist. In 2000, he ran to become mayor of Toronto and was notably endorsed by Jane Jacobs, an author influential to Silverman's ideology. Gomberg finished second–albeit distantly–behind winner Mel Lastman. Gomberg's 8.5 percent of the vote was feeble compared to Lastman's 80 percent, but was well ahead of 25 other candidates.

Gomberg once wrote a humorous blog, "Sofa, so good," about getting arrested for sitting on a discarded loveseat—not his—that was left in the street for the garbage truck. This incident highlights the distorted amount of space our society accords to car drivers at the expense of everybody else.[14]

Gomberg was charged with "obstructing traffic" even though the sofa was in the parked car lane, not the one for moving traffic. And police saw no problem when the same sofa was moved back onto a crowded sidewalk where it clearly obstructed pedestrian traffic. In subsequent adventures, Gomberg took part in various environmental, anti-nuclear, and anti-corporate protests in Holland, Quebec City, and Edmonton. During this time, he was arrested and sometimes tear-gassed. At one point, he locked himself into a vault in the office of Alberta

Figure 8.2. Procession of cyclists on a downtown street.
Source: MàB Archive.

premier Ralph Klein, trying to confront Klein about the Kyoto Protocol and climate change. This led to a "brutal arrest."

After so many years of being so active, Gomberg developed depression. In 2004, he left a suicide note before apparently jumping off a bridge in Halifax, Nova Scotia. Since Gomberg's death, the "TaketheTooker" initiative has been launched in Toronto, intended as a living legacy to the bike and climate activist. The idea is to promote cycle priority beside the Bloor/Danforth subway, creating a bicycle expressway from Mississauga to Scarborough through the city core.

Eight Thousand Cyclists Take Over the Streets

The second edition of the MàB's cycle week in 1976 saw eight thousand participants riding along Sainte-Catherine Street West in downtown Montreal on June 5. Thanks to communication facilitated by John Dowlin in Philadelphia, cycling advocacy groups worldwide coordinated efforts to hold such events on the same day. As such, cycling groups imitated a tactic from the anti–Vietnam War movement.

Some credit Silverman with dreaming up the idea of International Bicycle Day, which was officially recognized by the United Nations in 2018 and is celebrated on June 3 every year.[15] However, the United Nations' online notice on this subject does not mention Silverman. This is perhaps not surprising, Stéphane Desjardins

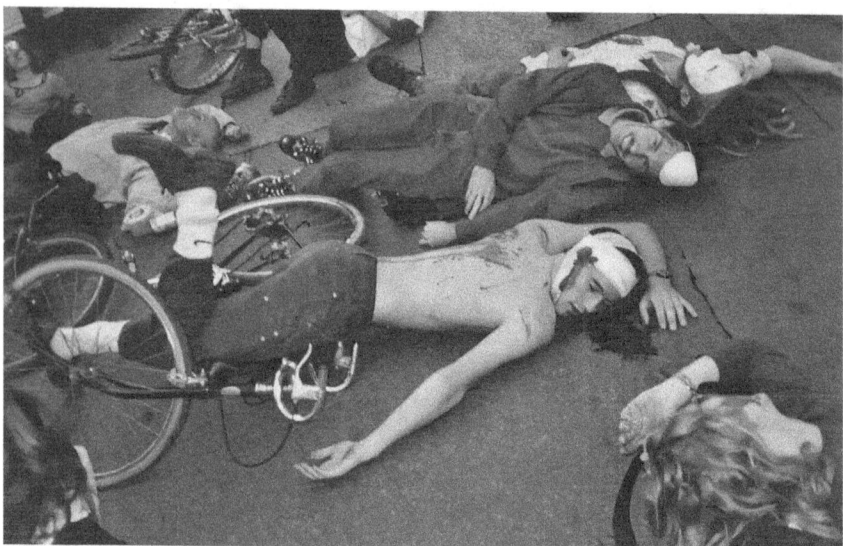

Figure 8.3. The "die in" protest by MàB.
Source: MàB Archive.

recounts how descriptions of later work that Silverman and Morissette did on the "missing link" tend to ignore the role of these two bike advocates and instead credit the politicians who voted to fund the project. Sometimes, these same politicians get the credit after initially opposing the idea.

The First "Die-In"

Also in 1976, the MàB also held its first official "die-in" on October 12, during which some 200 cyclists lay down in the street, pretending to be dead and covered in ketchup to make it appear as if they were bloodied. The event was initiated at 5:30 pm on Ste Catherine Street W at the corner of University Street.

"We ensured the blocking of cross streets by one or two cyclists at each street in constant rotation," recalls Michel Camus, who was in charge of security by the MàB. "Drivers honked their horns, shouted at us or tried to sneak past. But we remained calm and jovial, trying to make them wait or convince them [...] Once, one of them knocked me down with his sports car and we had to calm the crowd down so as not to hit him in turn."

The incident with the impatient sports car driver seemed to be a recurring theme with future die-ins; security for participants was paramount. Silverman mentioned attempting a die-in on Park Avenue before realizing that the street configuration there was too dangerous; the one-way streets downtown were much safer. During the event, a more realistic creation of a "crime scene" is accomplished by using sidewalk chalk to trace the silhouettes of prostrate participants. This also has a more lasting impact on those passing by hours or even days afterward. Police could have arrested die-in protestors for impeding traffic, but instead they read the MàB leaflets and scratched their heads. Perhaps they had seen too many dead pedestrians for real.

Reversing Normality

In his preface for Claire Morissette's 1994 book *Deux roues, un avenir*, Silverman wrote:

> For the last 19 years, Claire Morissette and myself, as part of our long term mission to convert Montreal into a bicycle-friendly city, have co-organized dozens of theatrical demonstrations to illustrate the present unjust and absurd reality for bicyclists and proclaim our demands. [...] But of all the numerous cyclodramas le Monde à Bicyclette has done, there is one that I will always cherish the most. On a bleak early October afternoon, at 5:00 p.m., the day after Thanksgiving Monday in 1976 [...] about a hundred people, cyclists and pedestrians lay prostrate on the street at the corner of Sainte-Catherine and University (now Robert-Bourassa). Mangled bicycles, blood illustrated as ketchup, gas masks, canes, a coffin and a 4-year-old child carried on a stretcher mingled among the hundred people 'lying dead' in the intersection. It was the Great Montreal Die-in to dramatize the car's most irrevocable consequence: death. I was lying on my back prone on the pavement amongst the auto victims dead in the square. Claire, a bullhorn in her hand, was passionately proclaiming the 10 deadly sins of the automobile. Other sympathizers handed out explanatory leaflets to baffled motorists and pedestrians. The police gave us ten minutes while one policeman, intensely reading our leaflet, shook his head back and forth continuously. After a few minutes, the drivers stopped honking, and an unusual and solemn silence fell. Prostrate, I became joyous. For I saw, we all saw, how insane the daily reality was. We were exposing this collective insanity. We had reversed normality.

Storming the Metro

AMONG THE MANY "cyclo-frustrations" in 1975 in Montreal, there were no bike paths, no bicycle access to public transit, and no way to legally traverse the St. Lawrence River with a bike. After discussions, members of the MàB chose bicycle access to the metro (subway) system as their first objective.

"The lack of access to the metro was a frustration for all Montrealers," said Silverman. "It was due to pigheadedness on the part of the *Commission de Transport de la Communauté urbaine de Montréal* (CTCUM), the transit authority's management." This same transit authority is now known as the *Société de transport de Montréal* (STM).

The Montreal metro system, built in 1966, now includes four lines with sixty-eight stations stretching over sixty-nine kilometres. It forms the backbone of Montreal's public transit system and is the fourth busiest subway system in North America. Presiding over the CTCUM from 1974 to 1985 was Lawrence Hanigan. Mayor Drapeau appointed Hanigan to the position after he served five terms as a municipal councillor for Drapeau's party.[1] Described as being "authoritarian and remote," the most indelible image of Hanigan is of him riding to work in his chauffeured limousine during some twenty transit strikes that took place under his tenure.[2] Meanwhile, transit users were trying to get to work or school by walking, cycling, or hitchhiking.

Hanigan seemed to have little empathy for regular transit users and even less for cyclists wishing to ride the metro. Today, many cyclists have transit passes; they combine biking and public transit on a daily basis. "Transportation cocktails," is the current terminology for combining different types of transport. Cyclists who are occasional transit users may experience a flat tire or other mechanical problems, bad weather, darkness, fatigue, and so on. Bicycle access on the metro's yellow line to Longueuil would also provide bicycle access across the St. Lawrence River. "Yet the transit management was adamant in their refusal," as Silverman put it. Hanigan cited alleged "safety concerns" as well as the belief that bicycle grease would get on the clothes of other passengers.

Silverman compared Hanigan to his own father, "taking indefensible positions." It is not clear why Hanigan was so hostile to bicycles, but his ideology was conservative. After leaving the CTCUM Hanigan was an unsuccessful candidate for the federal Conservatives under Brian Mulroney in the 1984 elections. In 1978, Hanigan claimed that he would reconsider the ban on bikes in the metro if it could be proven that it was safe. He also promised to check what other transit systems were doing about the issue. But Silverman got there first.

"We checked to see what the situation was in other cities; it was only transit authorities in fascist countries that didn't allow bikes on their subways. Even Toronto said 'yes' to bikes," Silverman told the Gazette in 1978.[3]

The comment about fascism dredged up some old animosities: Camillien Houde, who preceded Jean Drapeau as mayor of Montreal, openly admired fascist leader Benito Mussolini and opposed mandatory conscription prior to the Second World War. Consequently, he was interned by the Canadian government for four years at Camp Petawawa. At that time, Drapeau, serving as his lawyer, argued for Houde's release.

MàB first tried storming the metro on June 1, 1977, with many cyclists attempting to enter the metro at Berri station, but being prevented from doing so by metro constables. Five other cyclists attempted the same from St. Laurent station, successfully reaching Longueuil station on the South Shore without incident.

"Our first action was at Laurier metro station, but we made the mistake of letting ourselves be arrested outside of the station and thus legally on the street; we lost (in court) as a result," Morissette told Vélo Mag. "The next time, we lifted our bikes over the turnstiles and made it to Berri metro station where we were arrested and put in holding cells."[4]

Figure 9.1. Members of MàB with Bob and Claire in the centre.
Source: MàB Archive.

An Unwritten Prohibition against Bikes

"There are specific prohibitions against other things: smoking, bringing an animal with you, carrying a firearm, etc., but nothing about bikes," Silverman told the *Gazette* in 1978. Further to Hanigan's "safety concerns" about bikes on the metro, Silverman cited correspondence from the New York City and San Francisco transit authorities stating that there had been no insurance claims against them regarding bicycles since these had been allowed on the subway or trains there.[5] Silverman and the MàB came across in the press as knowing more about the topic than did Hanigan. Drawing attention to how other transit authorities allowed bicycles, Silverman once tried to get on the Montreal metro with a bike pass issued in New Jersey. To look the part, he wore a tie and tweeds. CTCUM employees were confused, unsure what to do when confronted with the fake bike pass.

Thus began a four-year struggle for the MàB to obtain access to the metro for bikes. The MàB used public demonstrations, civil disobedience, comparisons with other transit authorities worldwide, research on metro ridership, media influence, and ultimately the courts. But probably MàB's most effective weapon was humour, making made short movies of transit users taking all kinds of large, cumbersome, and awkward objects onto the metro and being permitted aboard.

A Life-Sized Papier-Mâché Hippopotamus Takes the Metro

The list of objects allowed on the metro included skis, a toboggan, a twelve-foot ladder, and a television set. But when MàB members tried to take a bike onto a train, they were arrested. A very large papier-mâché hippopotamus—borrowed from a zoo—almost made it onto the metro, but observant guards noticed that bicycle wheels were incorporated into the beast. There are also reports of an "elephant" trying to board the metro; it is unclear if this elephant also concealed a bike.

Despite media support and the feeling that public opinion was with MàB, Silverman received an anonymous death threat around this time; as a precaution he slept at a friend's house.

MàB members continued their efforts as Silverman described:

"In the spring of 1978, cyclists began to step up pressure on the local subway system to gain access for cyclists. On May 10, two hundred riders, dividing their forces, entered the subway from eight different stations. Then they headed for the chief transfer point on the subway [now Berri-UQAM], and there sang and danced to the amusement of subway passengers."

Not everything went peacefully, however, and two MàB members, Claire Morissette and Françoise Guay were arrested after some sort of incident.[6]

Convicted of disturbing the peace, Morissette and Guay refused to pay their fines of seventy-five dollars, including costs, and were sentenced to three days in jail. The pair were released, however, after serving only one day. In a joint MàB and Vélo Québec venture, about fifty cyclists carried their bikes over the turnstiles at Ile Ste Helene station in June 1979.[7]

Sheindl Rothman was a MàB member in August 1979 when she and five others, including Silverman and Tooker Gomberg, were arrested for deliberately trying to take bikes onto the metro.

"We had a planning meeting beforehand, but no rehearsal. One of us managed to get an ironing board and another got a stepladder past the wicket before some of us were stopped with bikes. This was to demonstrate the absurdity of the rules. We were arrested, but ultimately did not do jail time or community service."

Figure 9.2. Police Arresting an Elephant.
Source: MàB Archive.

Rothman, who has never provoked any other run-ins with the law, admits that this episode was quite out of character for her. But she justifies her renegade action by saying "I wasn't alone. There were many of us who felt very strongly about cyclists' rights and how bicycles should be allowed on the metro. Also, I didn't think that I would go on death row for committing such an action."

"Let Cyclists onto Métro," read the *Gazette* editorial page headline on August 24, 1979. Some sixteen letters to the editor were published there and were "heavily in favour of allowing [cyclists outside of rush hour]," as the *Gazette* noted. A letter by Silverman speaks of other cities where bikes were allowed on metros "and where no incidents have been reported." Silverman also pointed out that there was then no safe way for cyclists to cross between Montreal and Longueuil.[8] Media coverage in other newspapers, like *La Presse*, was also favourable to MàB. "The media got friendlier all the time," said Silverman.

The Court Battle (1978–1981): A Young Lawyer Takes the "Test Case"

A young lawyer named Dida Berku represented Tooker Gomberg and Claire Morissette, in what was to be the "test case" challenging the CTCUM rules that prohibited bikes.

"I was working with *Services Juridiques St-Louis* on St-Hubert Street," says Berku. "We were public defenders, acting as legal aid before there was officially legal aid. We also represented the LGBQ community (*droit des gais*) and the Milton Park Coop, etc."

"I knew about MàB; they were causing a ruckus and were funny. If we were paid for this case, it wasn't for much money."

"Claire and Tooker were better witnesses than Bob; you had to have some sort of decorum. Bob could be seen as wacky."

"From my perspective it was fun to challenge rules in front of a court; this was not just about getting arrested," continues Berku. The two defendants admitted they tried to take bicycles onto the metro and were arrested. With their guilt established, the question became whether the rule prohibiting bikes was legal.

According to internal documents, the CTCUM cited two main justifications for its refusal to allow bicycles on the metro: (1) the risk of sullying people's clothing (presumably by a skirt or pant leg coming into contact with an oily bike chain) and (2) the fact that it is difficult and dangerous for bicycles in the metro space, notably for getting through the turnstiles.[9]

Yet, there was nothing specific in the CTCUM guidelines banning bikes from the metro or from buses. Instead, the CTCUM relied on Article 5 of its Regulation 18, stipulating, "Everybody on board a CTCUM vehicle or in the [metro] stations or other nearby public places must conform to the posted directives of the CTCUM or [directives] given by its personnel."[10]

The CTCUM also argued that payment of a ticket gave the user the right to travel in the metro with objects that they could easily transport without danger or causing a nuisance for other passengers. It is curious why ladders, skis, an ironing board, a cardboard elephant and even a large papier-mâché hippopotamus were permitted on the metro, but not bikes. The earlier objection about difficulties getting a bike past a turnstile would presumably have also applied for wheelchairs, wheeled luggage, and baby strollers.

MàB Loses in Municipal Court, 1978
The first reference to a court case regarding bicycle access is on December 7, 1978, with a Montreal municipal court judgment in the case of Montreal (on behalf of the CTCUM) v. Claire Morissette, dossier 9525. She was found guilty and ordered to pay a twenty-five dollar fine or spend three days in jail; she chose the jail sentence.

As her nephew Christian understands these events, it was to make a point that Morissette chose imprisonment but not because she was unable to find the twenty-five dollars:

> It was a colourful demonstration involving all kinds of large objects, including an imitation pink elephant that people took on the metro, then she tried to get on the metro with her bike. This was segregation: you could get on the metro with all kinds of large objects, but she was arrested trying to bring her bike with her. This was calculated for political and media effect [...] She did not pay her fine. She was ready to go to jail to advance her cause.

There are also references to another person being accused—presumably Gomberg—and tried on another date. City prosecutors were getting convictions, but the CTCUM's case had holes in it:

> The (legal) problem that arises is that of the imprecision of Article 5 in the name of which the prohibition of cycling in the métro is carried out. Since it is the only presence of the cyclist that is involved, and no longer the delimitation of a public order in which he must be registered, the only regulatory possibility to exclude these individuals from the station is to appeal with the obligation to follow the directives of the staff of the métro. But this shift presupposes at the same time that it is no longer really a conception of a general order which anchors these directives but rather what one could qualify as a construction of what a traveller should be (therefore of course a traveller without a bike) directly linked to," wrote Garnier in 2006 (our translation).[11]

Complicating things for the CTCUM, MàB defendants produced a subpoena demanding that Hanigan, the CTCUM president and CEO, justify the legitimacy of banning bicycles from the metro as per Article 5 of the CTCUM regulations. Silverman recalled a law student named Louis Poisson handling the subpoena. Berku insists that she did not handle that aspect of the case.

This subpoena—referred to by the CTCUM legal team as *farfelu* (wacky)—provoked detailed correspondence within the CTCUM about how to add the words: "bicycle, tricycle, and unicycle" to the transit authority's regulations; all this to reduce the number of people trying to board the metro with bicycles. For reasons unknown, CTCUM management never spelled this out clearly in its regulations.

On another occasion, three groups of cyclists entered the metro at the same time from different stations, all heading for Berri station. Expected confrontations with security failed to materialize. One of the cyclists, Stéphane Desjardins, recalls an annoyed Morissette and Silverman asking: "Why are they not arresting us? That's what we want, that's our strategy."

"Please Arrest Us!"
The cyclists' ultimate destination at Berri-UQAM station was a famous black circular bench nicknamed "the hockey puck," a central location within the most strategic station in the whole system. It is also a stone's throw away from the metro constabulary office where a handful of officers stood.

"I went over to the police and asked if they were going to do something about the cyclists," says Desjardins. "A constable responded that people elsewhere were getting attacked, raped, and robbed. 'You are wasting our time,' he said. I replied that it was not time wasted and that bikes were illegal in the metro."

"Perhaps ten minutes later, two cops came over and told us that we must leave. When we refused, they told us we were under arrest and should follow them. They led us to their station and into two holding cells," continues Desjardins.

"I was in the cell with Claire who remained very calm; her attitude helped calm me. The group in the other cell was loudly making jokes. 'Tabernac, I forgot my hash!' yelled someone. There were other similar jokes, which remained respectful of the constables. The cops were trying to remain serious but couldn't help laughing."

"After filling out paperwork, the cops let us go, but they kept our bikes."

"A month later, we went down to the old Craig [now Viger] Street streetcar terminus to recover our bikes. This magnificent neoclassical building was demolished soon after to make way for the hideous Palais des congrès (Montreal Convention Centre)."

★★★

On November 20, 1979, nine protestors were arrested trying to board the metro with bicycles. But, because the CTCUM was unable to clearly show that these protestors were warned that bicycles were not allowed on the metro, they were all acquitted.

On April 11, 1980, another thirteen protestors were arrested. Prosecutors were putting pressure on the CTCUM to clearly spell out that bikes were not allowed, but the CTCUM did not do this, clinging instead to its flawed Article 5. The verbal instruction not to board the metro held little weight; protestors with bicycles told to leave one metro station by CTCUM police could simply go to another nearby station. This way, they could pretend they were not warned that bikes were banned.

A MàB study, as published in the organization's newsletter, conducted in early 1981, counted the number of passengers on 259 trains outside of rush hour and found an average of 1.19 passengers in the last car, built to accommodate thirty-nine. This study was referred to in the CTCUM internal documents, suggesting embarrassment, even if there was no official reaction.

MàB Wins on Appeal

On August 24, 1981, a hearing took place that saw an appeal in Quebec Superior Court of Morissette's December 1978 municipal court conviction.

The case for the appeal rested on four grounds: (1) that nowhere in the CTCUM regulations is a ban on bicycles specifically mentioned; (2) the vagueness and ambiguity of Article 5 (which supposedly banned bicycles without mentioning them); (3) the "illegal" sub-delegation of power (presumably to metro constables to interpret the regulations); and (4) that the 1978 judge did not accord Morissette a presumption of innocence.

The Honourable Claire Barrette-Joncas rendered her judgment on August 25. While not ruling on three of the grounds of the appeal, Barrette-Joncas concluded: "The CTCUM cannot delegate its powers to its constables." This means in practice that a breach of a commission staff directive does not constitute an offense and is therefore not punishable by law. If bicycles are banned from the metro, this must be clearly indicated in CTCUM regulations rather than an interpretation by constables.

After the ruling, Hanigan is quoted as saying that the bicycle ban would continue, disputing how much such things need to be spelled out. Another source with the CTCUM suggests perhaps rewording their regulations or appealing the decision to a higher court. Silverman then threatened to meet with Montreal area MNAs to discuss the Quebec government withholding subsidies to the CTCUM.[12] The Parti Québécois government had been elected promising to allow bikes on the metro. The CTCUM had ten days to register an appeal, but apparently never did so.[13]

Silverman recalls that "the CTCUM originally claimed that the judgment meant only Claire Morissette could have access with her bike to the metro." An August 27 *Gazette* article also indicated that cyclists boarding the metro would still be fined despite the ruling.[14] "But I had a call from the president of the metro constabulary union. He said that his members were obeying the court, not Hanigan." The CTCUM had seen bitter strikes under Hanigan, and the unions were not endeared to management.

"Silverman's adversaries completely underestimated him. Hanigan never saw it coming," chuckles Stéphane Desjardins, a former MàB protestor who provoked these famous arrests in the metro.

The CTCUM Allows Bikes in the Metro

Gracious in victory, Silverman noted publicly how bicycles were permitted in the subways of New York, Manchester, Liverpool, Amsterdam, Rotterdam, Oslo, Sydney, and San Francisco, but particularly praised Washington, DC. He also noted how "we want access in a civil, regulated, and secure manner as is the case in other cities."[15] MàB submitted its proposed new regulations to the CTCUM, which then began studying these and how bicycles were accommodated on metro systems of other large cities, especially Washington, DC. Hanigan had already promised to do exactly that some three years earlier.

"Silverman's adversaries completely underestimated him. Hanigan never saw it coming," chuckles Stéphane Desjardins, a former MàB protestor who provoked these famous arrests in the metro.

In April 1982, the CTCUM finally established its initial rules under which bicyclists could have weekend access to the metro as part of a pilot project. Speaking to the media, a jubilant Silverman urged cyclists to obey the new rules "to the letter" and avoid further confrontations with the CTCUM.[16] MàB members went out postering that night, indicating what the rules were for taking bikes on the metro and urging cyclists to be very respectful of other passengers. Over the years, some stipulations have been relaxed and the hours of use have been expanded as detailed in the following paragraphs.

"Regarding metro access, in June 1982, the CTCUM—now the STM—issued a $5 photo ID bike permit providing access to the last metro car on weekends. As of July 1986, this permit was no longer necessary."[17]

By 2020, bicycles were permitted in the metro for 92 of the 132 hours that the system operates in a normal week. In 2023, the hours that bicycles are permitted were extended to 107 hours per week. In 2020, Silverman remarked that there has never been an incident of bicycles interfering with metro operations and none that he knows of with getting other passengers dirty. He did regret, however, that the STM has no bike racks on its buses, as is common with other transit authorities across North America. For example, the RTL transit authority in Longueuil has had bike racks on its buses—during the warmer months—since 1983. Similarly, just north of Montreal, the STL authority in Laval has had bike racks on its buses since 2013.[18]

Getting aboard Commuter Trains

After the victory for Montreal's metro system, MàB turned its attention to getting bicycles accepted on the Vaudreuil and Deux-Montagnes commuter train lines. These train lines run from between Montreal and off-island towns in the far suburbs such as Candiac, Hudson, and Deux-Montagnes. Previously, the trains were operated by the CTCUM, which also oversaw Montreal's buses and metro.

Video clips from this campaign indicate MàB using very different tactics than it did with getting bicycle access to the metro or over local bridges. Well-dressed and soft-spoken MàB members stand outside downtown train stations with large-scale diagrams of train cars showing how they can be converted to have folding seats, permitting bicycles when the seats are folded up. There is also an image of MàB members symbolically driving a "last spike" into the track by Windsor Station, presumably to celebrate their eventual victory. This campaign apparently involved little wacky street theatre, no die-ins, and no civil disobedience. The passengers on these commuter trains tend to be a more educated, more affluent, and more subdued crowd than that found on Montreal's metro system so the new tactics probably went over well.

Hanigan remained president and CEO of the CTCUM until 1985. He was succeeded as director by Robert Perreault, somebody much more sympathetic to the cause of "cyclists' rights," from 1986 to 1994.

Bikes Allowed on Three Commuter Train Lines

In the early 1990s, train cars on the Hudson and Deux-Montagnes lines were converted to accept bikes in the entrance area of each car. MàB's demands had become reality. As with the metro, there was no extra charge for bringing a bike aboard.

In 1996, management of the commuter trains was transferred to the *Agence métropolitaine de transport* (AMT); these same trains are now operated by Exo. Within about ten years, this service was extended so that bicycles were accepted on all six commuter train lines then operating around Montreal. Bikes are also conditionally allowed on the *Réseau express métropolitain* (REM) trains that began running in 2023. The REM, a train, is a new component of the Montreal transit system.

A Bike Activist Takes Control of the CTCUM

After Robert Perreault, Michel Labrecque took over as head of the transit authority now known as the STM in 2009. For Silverman, this was like icing on the cake. Labrecque, a well-known cyclist, previously led Vélo Québec from 1985 to 2000. Like Silverman, he used to participate in demonstrations calling for bicycle access to the metro.

"Wow, Michel, this is incredible!" Silverman said in thickly accented colloquial French to Labrecque. "You there, a bicycle activist at the head of the CTCUM! Amazing!"

The same year that Labrecque took over, Hanigan died. Obituaries for him in 2009 noted that Hanigan presided over acrimonious strikes at the CTCUM, served eighteen years as a municipal councillor for Mayor Jean Drapeau's Civic Party and was also a friend of former Conservative prime minister Brian Mulroney. The obituaries mention nothing about bikes on the metro.[19]

The Battle for Bike Lanes

> Under a government which imprisons any unjustly,
> the true place for a just man is also a prison.
> Henry David Thoreau

IT ALL STARTED MYSTERIOUSLY on a summer evening in 1980. Claire Morissette began telephoning members of MàB, asking if they were doing anything around 11:00 p.m. Without specifying the activity, she simply gave a location. The activity was creating the first urban bike lanes in Montreal. Because the city was not prepared to do that, MàB took it upon itself to create such infrastructure. Without permission from authorities, this activity had to be a clandestine operation and MàB could only do something symbolic, lacking the resources to create bike lanes across the city.

In early 1980, the Montreal Bicycle Path Committee, comprising senior civil servants and city councillors, including executive committee member Fernand Desjardins, and had proposed creating a bicycle corridor of about ten kilometres from Old Montreal north to Henri-Bourassa Boulevard. The Quebec government even offered to pay $300,000 for this corridor, but the Drapeau administration vetoed the proposal without explanation.[1]

Illegally Painting Bike Lanes on City Streets

"Our first action painting a bike lane was on St. Urbain Street, near the corner of Marianne," recalled Silverman, referring to the action that took place on July 23, 1978. Perhaps no small coincidence, Silverman's apartment on Esplanade Street was only a few steps away.

"A bunch of us went out the first night to paint *voie cyclable* (bike lane) on the asphalt and were not caught. We gave fake parking tickets to motorists parked in the unofficial bike lane. We went out again two weeks later on Marianne Street when a police car pulled up. The cops asked what we were doing and we explained that we were painting a bike lane," recounts Scott Weinstein. The police had to ask: "what's a bike lane?" The police officers' bewilderment was understandable; there were almost no bike lanes in the metropolitan area at that time. Nor was there much public discussion about bike lanes or bike paths.

Figure 10.1. We want bike lanes now!
Source: MàB Archive.

"While some of our non-status friends disappeared when the arrests were made, I volunteered to get arrested," says Weinstein. The charge was "creating mischief."

Silverman was arrested with paint still on his hands. "I went to court with Bob and Claire and we were convicted," says Weinstein. Silverman said that their plea was "guilty with justification." While some other judges accepted this plea without handing down a sentence, Judge Louis-Jacques Léger was a former councillor with Mayor Drapeau's party. He termed their offense "a grave crime" and sentenced them to pay a fine of twenty-five dollars plus costs of sixteen dollars or go to prison for eight days.

"Even in 1981, twenty-five dollars was not a big fine," Weinstein notes. They refused to pay on principle and as a protest against how Montreal was refusing to create a north–south bicycle corridor; this despite the Quebec government offering to pay for the endeavour.

Between late 1979 and September 1980, some twenty-five members of MàB were arrested for painting unofficial bike lanes in Montreal. Their actions and the resultant publicity may have forced the city administration to consider not "if" but "where" it would create bike lanes. Montreal Executive Chairman Yvon Lamarre was quoted that year saying that the city did not want to put bike lanes on a street "where there will also be automobile traffic."[2]

Figure 10.2. MàB members clandestinely painting unofficial bike lanes.
Source: Photo by Guy Kosak; MàB Archive.

The Three Criminals Surrender to Police

At first, there seemed to be no follow-up from the court system. After six months, Morissette, Silverman, and Weinstein staged a press conference in front of the Court House on Gosford Street, announcing to the media that they were going to jail for painting bike lanes. The three "criminals" then walked into the local police station to surrender to the authorities.

In those days, there was still no widespread use of computers, and police were unable to find the files for them. "Rules are rules," the constables said and then told them to get lost. Finally, some six months later, the three notorious criminals finally received their summons to report to jail. After their press conference, Weinstein was particularly moved when a colleague whom he didn't particularly know well came up to him at work and said: "I saw you on TV with the bike lane thing and am proud of you. If there were bike lanes, I would feel safe riding my bike." This incident made Weinstein fully realize the significance of the event in which he had participated.

Figure 10.3. Enthusiastic MàB supporters at inauguration of unofficial bike lane. *Source*: MàB Archive.

Off to Bordeaux Prison

Despite previous arrests for taking his bicycle on the metro, Silverman had never served time in jail. Now it was different:

"Jail conditions are never described in the travel sections of the weekend papers like the other trips one can take," wrote Silverman, explaining that he did not know what to expect for his time behind bars.

"At first we were placed in a large room with about ten other men at Post 1 on Bonsecours Street. We stayed there for two hours. Finally at about six, we were transferred with two other [convicts] to Bordeaux Prison in a panel truck with escape-proof grilled windows."

"The other two passengers had not paid a few hundred dollars of parking tickets. I later discovered that over one hundred of the men were in for auto-related crimes; parking tickets and speeding." While many inmates were there for car-related crimes, Silverman was there because of promoting bicycles.

Bordeaux Prison is the largest provincial prison in Quebec, housing up to 1,189 male inmates serving sentences of two years or less. Silverman and Weinstein were put in different cells. Morissette, meanwhile, was sent to Tanguay, a women's prison.

Other inmates were encouraging; even one of the guards said to Silverman "*ne lâche pas*" (don't give up), suggesting that Judge Louis-Jacques Léger may have been out of step with public opinion. To help pass the time, Silverman lifted barbells and skipped rope in the cell block exercise room. He also remarked that "the two solitudes existed in prison. There were two TV sets in cell block A; one for French inmates; the other for English ones." Both TVs were on too loudly.

Silverman, a vegetarian, was not pleased with the meat-and-potatoes cuisine served in prison. He wrote: "I don't consume milk nor dairy products. Unlike [in] airplanes, there are no provisions here for vegetarian meals. So, I had to eat a little meat [...] and other food I wouldn't ordinarily go near. I got diarrhea and [felt] groggy."

But Silverman took his nourishment from looking out the window of his prison cell. In the year since his arrest there had been some progress on the bike lane dossier. Ironically, one of the very first "official" bike lanes built by the City of Montreal was along Gouin Boulevard—within sight of Bordeaux Prison.[3] Probably few cyclists were riding there in October, but he imagined what it would look like in June. Adding to his pleasure, there was also a volleyball court visible from Silverman's window in cell AD3/23. Because of prison overcrowding, the three were released early. Silverman only served three days of his eight-day sentence.

> Other inmates were encouraging; even one of the guards said to Silverman *"ne lâche pas"* (don't give up), suggesting that Judge Louis-Jacques Léger may have been out of step with public opinion.

Convincing Drapeau to Do the Right Thing

DURING THE FIRST HALF OF THE 1980S, Montreal's first "urban" bike paths were installed along Gouin Boulevard and Notre-Dame Street East, as well as along the north–south corridor bordering Christophe-Colomb Avenue, Boyer, Brébeufm and Berri streets.[1] Not only was Montreal now building bike paths, but these were also avant-garde designs as the first protected bike paths in North America.[2]

Mayor Jean Drapeau remained in power until 1986; his administration was described by Silverman earlier in this text as "hostile" to bicycling. Silverman in retrospect amended his description of the Drapeau administration's attitude towards bicycling as "indifferent." So, the big mystery is what finally convinced Jean Drapeau to start building bike paths? Assisting at the inauguration of the new bike paths was Guy Tardif, the Quebec transport minister at the time. Silverman recalled Tardif as a big supporter of bicycling. News reports from the period also mention generous provincial subsidies for municipalities that built bicycle infrastructure. This included bike paths going from one municipality to another and for bicycle parking.[3] Subsidies were also provided to Vélo Québec for the organization of regional conferences providing information about bicycling facilities, presumably to inform municipal officials on the right way to build such things.

This could probably be referred to as "push-pull" pressure on Drapeau. The MàB's consistent public protests and frequent news stories about the need for bicycle infrastructure pushed Drapeau while the provincial subsidies pulled him in that same direction. Drapeau might still have been hostile to bicycling, but he was pragmatic. Once convinced of something, he could be quite effective in getting it accomplished.

René Lévesque's Parti Québécois government sometimes also needed a little prompting to deliver its promised funding for bike paths. Silverman once provided such prompting by standing in front where the party's annual convention was being held, dressed completely in red like a cardinal, holding a large cross, and attempting to "exorcise" the building of evil spirits.[4] This led to a front section photograph of Silverman in costume with curious cabinet ministers peering at him from a distance. Embarrassed by this publicity, the Lévesque government soon fulfilled its promises leading to the inauguration of bike paths in Montreal as described above.

Montreal Builds Its first Modern Bike Paths and Lanes

In the 1980s, some of the first municipal bike paths and lanes in Montreal were once considered of avant-garde design for protecting cyclists from automobile traffic, but much has changed since then.

"Montreal's bike network was built in the 1980s and is no longer adapted to our reality. New infrastructure needs to be built to meet the needs of today's cyclists. I travel by bike every day and I see how many problems there are and how great the need is," states Valérie Plante, mayor of Montreal, on the Copenhagenize website.[5] These days it is common to see bicycle traffic jams on some of these paths, especially along rue de Brébeuf, boul de Maisonneuve, or Rachel Street. Silverman saw this as a positive thing, a sort of "teething problem," as testimony to the growing popularity of cycling.

Bike paths and lanes alone are not enough to create a cyclist-friendly city, but they are essential and easily measurable infrastructure. While Montreal's first bike path, along the Lachine Canal, was built in the late 1970s, the situation has changed a lot since then. By 2024, Montreal's cycling network will span 1,065 kilometres, 729 of which will be open year-round. In 2022, the Plante administration promised an additional 200 km of bike paths by 2027, including 10 new sections of the Réseau express vélo (REV) spanning 60 km, notably on Jean-Talon, Henri-Bourassa, Lacordaire, Berri/Maisonneuve, Côte-de-Liesse, Édouard-Montpetit, Bellechasse, Viger, Saint-Antoine and Saint-Jacques. In 2022, there were also 3,450 km of cycle paths in Greater Montreal, including municipalities in the suburbs.

In the 2019 "Copenhagenize Index," Montreal already ranked first in North America and eighteenth worldwide in terms of "bicycle friendliness." Cities in northwestern Europe tend to rank highest on this index. The Danish capital, Copenhagen, invariably leads the annual rankings. A sophisticated methodology is used to derive these scores.

The Copenhagenize Index

The Copenhagenize Index gives cities points for their efforts towards re-establishing the bicycle as a feasible, accepted, and practical form of transport. Countless cities around the world are taking up the challenge of modernizing their public realm, to chip away at the decades of auto-oriented street design—implementing bicycle infrastructure, better policy, bike-share systems, restricted car use, and more. These actions are catalogued and coded in order to paint a holistic picture of bicycle-friendliness around the globe. That is the Copenhagenize Index.[6]

Over six hundred cities with over six hundred thousand inhabitants (as well as national capitals) from all corners of the world are logged into the database. Cities with a bicycle-modal share above two percent (with reliable data) are put through to the next round. Modal share is the number of trips or the percentage of travellers using a particular type of transport.

The remaining one hundred and fifteen cities are given between zero and four points across thirteen different parameters, as well as in a fourteenth bonus-point category, awarded for particularly impressive efforts or results.

The fourteen scores taken together are effective at determining the bicycle friendliness of any given city, showing what's been happening on the ground in the two years leading up to the ranking. The bonus points allow us to highlight extra efforts that are difficult to see in the parameters. For example, a city may score down the middle on politics because the mayor and other politicians are promising infrastructure. Bonus points can assist in determining the level of the political will and the scope and timeline of the proposed work. Once the infrastructure starts being built, the city will score higher in the infrastructure parameter on the following ranking.

The modal share of cycling on the entire island of Montreal was estimated at 3.3 percent in 2018 (latest figures available at the time of writing this book), according to Vélo Québec, and 5.5 percent for central neighbourhoods, according to the daily newspaper *La Presse* in 2023. Cycling is much more popular in certain central neighbourhoods than on the outskirts: the Plateau Mont-Royal recorded 13.1 percent, the Sud-Est 8.7 percent and Villeray 7.0 percent in 2018.[7]

It might seem incredulous that a hilly city famous for its long, cold, and snowy winters could figure so well in international ratings. One of MàB's longstanding demands is for bike paths to be cleared of snow in winter; Montreal now claims that 729 km are accessible year-round. Those who have never tried might be surprised how easy it can be to ride a bike in the winter, provided you have the right clothing and equipment (lights, fenders, good tires, etc.) and adapt your riding habits for winter conditions. As for the cold, "Let [Montrealers] do as in Beijing. It is as cold as here and every day a million Beijing residents go to work by bicycle," said Silverman in 1982, suggesting an alternative transport option during one of many transit strikes.[8] Another example is Oulu, Finland. Despite

Figure 11.1. Silverman participating in a "die-in" holding a volleyball.
Source: MàB Archive.

a cold, snowy winter comparable to Montreal's, this city boasts a 20 percent modal share for bicycling, year-round. Through the winter, adults pedal to work, young children go to school on their bikes, and grandmothers pedal to go shopping.[9]

The MàB Campaign for Bus Lanes

The MàB's demands extended beyond making bike lanes to include calls for expanded bus service, express bus lanes, and even free public transit. There are photos of MàB members putting down removable mats on the pavement, with one side saying *piste cyclable* and the other saying *bus lane*. Just as there used to be no bike lanes, there were no bus lanes either in Montreal in 1975.

"Then we had a movable bike path," as Morissette put it. "We wrote 'bike path' on a 100-foot roll of roofing paper and unrolled it on top of parked cars on the sides of streets. The effect was satisfying."[10]

Silverman talked about how bikes "marry well" with public transit. The current terminology speaks of the transportation cocktail as an intelligent mix of different means of transport including active and collective modes of transport, taxis, rental or car sharing, carpooling, etc., instead of solely relying on private automobiles.[11] For instance, bikes can be fast and convenient from the home to a train or subway station from where passengers continue on their trip with buses, subways, and trains. The term "active transport" as used in this text includes cycling, but also incorporates walking, jogging, rollerblading, etc.

Reasons for promoting a transportation cocktail extend beyond reducing greenhouse gas emissions (GHGs), increasing the level of physical fitness in the

Figure 11.2. 1,200 cars per hour is too many!
Source: MàB Archive.

general population, improving safety on the street, and making cities more liveable. Private automobiles also take an exorbitant amount of space.

"We are simply going to lack enough space for cars, even in the suburbs," prophesied Morissette in 1995. "Private cars will lose their dominant position and be replaced by real transportation solutions: collectively owned cars, taxis, and a truly efficient system of public transit." Strangely, she did not mention bicycles in this quote, but surely intended to.[12] This is another example of MàB's holistic view of the world; the group was concerned with much more than simply making the world a better place for cyclists.

A Brief History of Montreal Bike Paths

BICYCLES FIRST BECAME POPULAR in the 1870s but did not at that time resemble their current form, having an oversized front wheel, the most well-known type being the Penny Farthing. By 1885, however, the Rover Safety Bicycle appeared, which looked similar to modern bicycles.[1] Montreal opened its first official bike paths in 1874 and had an impressive bicycle path system in the 1890s, but these had all disappeared by the 1960s.[2] There were even petitions against the bikes, which were dubbed dangerous. Readers might be astonished at how extensive Montreal's network once was. It was the same story in other Western cities in the 1890s during the first "bicycle boom."

Paved Roads Were Originally Made for Bicycles

Readers might also be astonished to learn that the first paved roads in many cities were built for bicyclists, not for motorcars. This history is spelled out in Carlton Reid's 2015 book, *Roads Were Not Built for Cars*.

The invention of the automobile is generally attributed to Karl Benz in Germany in 1885 and it is evident that few cars were on the roads of North America until the early decades of the twentieth century. The first cars were seen on the roads of Montreal around 1899.[3]

An exhibit at Montreal's Château Ramezay Museum shows the French-made De Dion-Bouton automobile that was one of the first cars in Montreal, dating from 1902. Amusingly, it looks more like a go-kart than a modern car. Adding to the comedy, the first cars in Montreal were required to be equipped with bicycle licence plates as none were available specifically for cars. Bike shops at this time typically provided parts for car repairs. Karl Benz's 1886 car had to be fuelled with petroleum ether—then used to clean laundry stains—bought at a pharmacy.[4] The increasing popularity of motor cars in the first half of the twentieth century pushed cyclists off the roads originally created for them.[5] This dynamic became entrenched following the Second World War and by 1951, American suburbs had become more populated than the cities, thus changing the landscape: streets and roads became the logical way of developing communities. Suburbia, centered around cars, became the urban model of development in

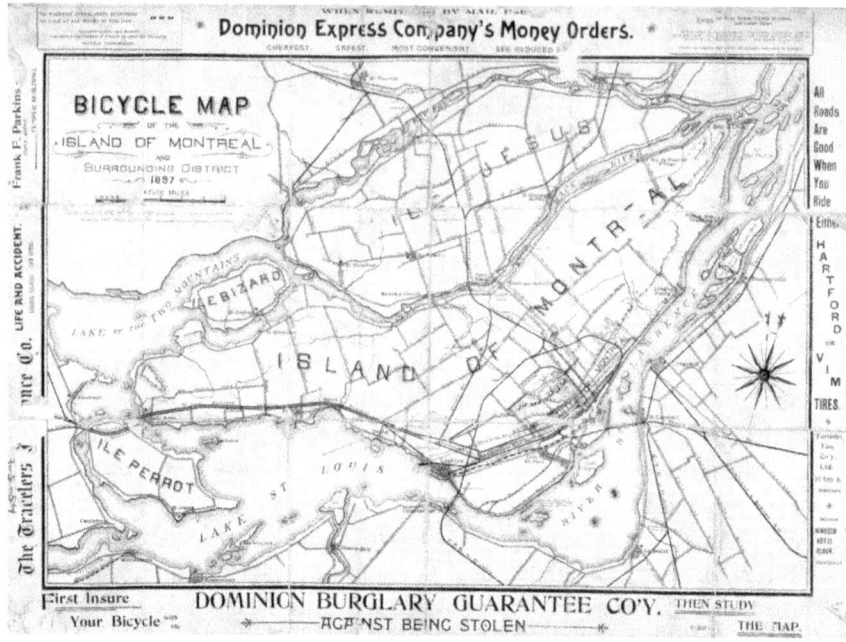

Figure 12.1. Map showing bike lanes in Montreal from 1897.

North America. Silverman and MàB were fighting to change this order of urban organization.

Many Montrealers are surprised to learn that bicycling—as a spectator sport—rivalled hockey in popularity until the 1940s when the city boasted three velodromes. John Symon interviewed hockey legend Henri Richard in 2006; Richard recounted how he and his brother, Maurice (also a hockey legend), used to watch track cycling races during their free time. The City of Westmount—an enclave within Montreal—apparently had a bike path in 1975, but Montreal itself had none. Traffic safety expert Gilles Roger Prevost had been urging Montreal to create bike paths or bike lanes since 1972.[6]

In 1975, Montreal finally announced plans to build eleven kilometres of bike lanes in the east-end Mercier district. Speaking to the press, Silverman decried Montreal's first timid attempts to build urban bike paths and lanes as "nothing less than tokenism," pointing out how insignificant the costs were.[7]

This historical background puts Silverman's comments into context about "the reconquest of the city, taking it back from the private car." By some estimates, up to sixty percent of the land area in the central core of typical North American cities is devoted to roads, parking lots, and other car infrastructure.[8] People are now realizing that free (i.e., subsidized) parking is a bad idea and asking if cities should be built for cars or for people? Donald Shoup is one author who examines this subject in his book, *The High Cost of Free Parking*.

Modern Bike Paths as an Afterthought

Today Montreal has many bike paths and bike lanes, but these were generally created as an afterthought in the urban landscape. As such, they rarely take the most direct route from point A to point B. This means that cyclists can spend a lot of extra time travelling extra distances compared to motorists. And this is in sharp contrast to the situation in the 1890s.

Apart from highways, very few roads are forbidden to bicycle traffic, but some are generally avoided because they are dangerous or impractical. Riding on the sidewalk is illegal in most places and cyclists risk being ticketed, even where the road is obviously dangerous and when no pedestrians are in sight. Following some highly mediatized cyclist fatalities under viaducts, some boroughs now allow cyclists to ride on the sidewalk in certain situations.[9] There are also large areas without bike paths. Meanwhile, crossing railroads, highways, and rivers can pose significant barriers to bicycle travel.

If Bikes Were the Size of Cars

One cyclodrama street theatre stunt that Silverman and the MàB did was to attach boards to their bicycles, giving them the dimensions of an average car. This stunt was bound to evoke anger among motorists who found their way blocked. But the average car takes up that much room and has only one person in it, the driver.

"MàB members demonstrated remarkable imaginative power," once noted Morissette. "For instance, we did a spatial demonstration, using wooden frames attached to our bikes to make them the same size as a car. The image was worth a thousand words. We wanted to demonstrate how much public space was lost to private automobiles." This same stunt has since been copied by other bike groups elsewhere.

Readers might be surprised to learn that car drivers pay for only a small portion of road construction and

Figure 12.2. Silverman prepares for the spatial protest.
Source: MàB Archive.

maintenance costs. Fuel taxes in North America pay for only a fraction of such costs, with the difference coming out of general government revenues. This means that Silverman—who had not driven a car since the 1970s—spent many decades subsidizing car drivers. Different studies in various jurisdictions produce different numbers but come to the same general conclusion: car drivers are heavily subsidized by governments. A 2017 study found that automobile travel in Quebec cost various levels of government $6.4 billion in 2015. That study states: "Contrary to popular belief, only a third of these costs are covered by user fees through fuel taxes, fees related to vehicle registration and driving license fees. The rest of the financing of the system is absorbed by all taxpayers through general infrastructure funds, such as the $2.9 billion dedicated by municipalities to their public roads."[10] Similarly, George Poulos, a Vancouver-based researcher, calculated that for every dollar motorists pay to drive their car, costs of $9.22 are incurred by taxpayers. By comparison, for every dollar that bus passengers pay, costs of only $1.50 are incurred to taxpayers. "Reconquering the city" also means dramatic changes in how public monies are spent.

One Million Cyclists Trapped on Montreal Island

THE ICONIC JACQUES CARTIER BRIDGE is almost as symbolic of Montreal as the Eiffel Tower is of Paris. In fact, there are four miniature replicas of the Eiffel Tower placed on the high points of this bridge. Named after the first French explorer to sail up the St. Lawrence River to the site of present-day Montreal in 1534, the Jacques Cartier Bridge links east-central Montreal to the South Shore city of Longueuil. The Jacques Cartier Bridge is the third busiest in Canada for motorized traffic, but probably the busiest for cyclists. In 2017, some 411,000 cyclists used its bike path, averaging some 1,750 cyclists daily between April 2 and December 20 when the bike path was open that year.[1] This gives some indication of how many cyclists might have wanted to use it in the 1970s. The bridge span is 2.7 km, but only 0.7 km of this is over water, including the St. Lawrence Seaway where large freighters pass. Saint Helen's Island—part of a municipal park—can also be accessed from the Jacques Cartier Bridge.

Bridge Authorities Deaf to Cyclists' Pleas

The bridge is among those overseen by the Jacques Cartier and Champlain Bridges Incorporated (JCCB), a federal agency. That agency, much like the Jean Drapeau administration at city hall and Lawrence Hanigan at the CTCUM, was deaf to pleas from cyclists in the 1970s.

This bridge was inaugurated in 1930 with two sidewalks, each 1.5 metres wide; three lanes for road traffic, as well as two lanes reserved for tramway cars but apparently never used for that purpose. Initially, a toll of fifteen cents was demanded of cyclists using the bridge while motorists had to pay twenty-five cents.[2] The tolls were abolished in 1962 though the former toll booth still stands in Longueuil.

Between the 1930s and 1960s, however, cars gained prominence and the tramway lanes were converted into extra road lanes. Meanwhile, sidewalks suffered from neglect though bicyclists and pedestrians could still use them at their peril. It was also illegal—but usually tolerated—to ride on the sidewalk and cyclists risked being ticketed by police if caught. The issue of cycle access to the South

Shore was personal for Claire Morissette; she used a bike as her main means of visiting her mother who lived in Longueuil.

"There were then a million bicycles in the Montreal region," wrote Silverman later. "In spite of this we still can't legally cross the St. Lawrence River. Bicycles are barred from all bridges and tunnels that cross the St. Lawrence River in the Montreal region. However, bicyclists are tolerated on the sidewalks of the Jacques Cartier Bridge. Unfortunately for we cyclists, these sidewalks disappear into the very dangerous Taschereau Boulevard on the South (Shore)."[3]

On Sunday, June 8, 1975, some four hundred cyclists defied the law, riding onto Jacques Cartier Bridge, demanding better bridge access for cyclists. They rode in the car lanes from Montreal to Saint Helen's Island and back despite threats from police to arrest them all.[4]

MàB Forces JCCB to Reopen Jacques Cartier Bridge Sidewalk

In March 1977, a portion of sidewalk from the Jacques Cartier Bridge collapsed and fell into a parking lot below. The JCCB promptly closed both sidewalks on the bridge, thus depriving cyclists of their only access across the St. Lawrence River.

The MàB and its allies first telephoned and wrote to the authorities but were told that a sidewalk repair was not a priority. Cyclists then decided that if no bikes could cross the bridge, no cars should be allowed across either. Preparations were made for a mid-bridge die-in, with plans to stop car traffic there. A leaflet was prepared and a press conference organized. This information was allowed to leak out.

"On April 9, the day before the scheduled die-in, the authorities caved in and reopened one of the sidewalks, covering up the hole and other weak points," wrote Silverman.[5]

"We scared them into fixing the sidewalk on a Saturday night," recounted Silverman in 2015.

"Instead of halting the action, the cyclists decided to go ahead. The next day, contingents of pedestrians and cyclists, walking their bicycles, departed from both ends of the bridge, blocking traffic as they went."[6]

Participants stopped traffic and even played some volleyball in the middle of the bridge. The JCCB promptly responded by doing more temporary repairs and promising additional work later.

Citizen Repairs to Jacques Cartier Bridge Sidewalk

By July 1977, impatient with the speed of promised additional repairs, some thirty volunteers from le Monde à bicyclette as well as Serge Mongeau's South Shore cycling group, la Rive sud à bécane, pulled a small cement mixer onto the bridge and poured a cubic yard of concrete onto the sidewalk "that had fallen into ruin." Cyclists also put down carpets—bought at Canadian Tire—on the bridge's metal grilles so that bicycle tires would not get caught and stuck.

"It is thanks to our efforts, and particularly to the article published yesterday in Le Devoir, that the JCCB has finally announced it will immediately undertake the needed repairs to the Jacques Cartier Bridge sidewalk," Mongeau told Le Devoir.[7]

"The sidewalks of the Jacques Cartier Bridge will be repaired, and bicycles will be able to cross without risk of falling into the river through the holes," wrote La Presse columnist Pierre Foglia on July 8, 1977. "But do not send your thanks to mayor Jean Drapeau. [Instead thank] Bob Silverman of le Monde à Bicyclette, it is he who took care of the [sidewalk repair] with his own cement!"[8] Simultaneously, MàB was soliciting messages and resolutions of support from local city councils, mayors, provincial MNAs, and federal MPs. Many letters of support were received from local politicians, all asking for proper bicycle links across the St. Lawrence River. The only other alternative was by metro to Longueuil, but the CTCUM prohibited bikes.

MàB Seeks Divine Help with Bridge Access

Apart from the aforementioned temporary sidewalk repairs and offer of an escort, the JCCB was deaf to the cyclists' demands. To make fun of both the CTCUM and the bridge authority, the MàB staged a cyclodrama on Easter Monday, April 20, 1981.

Inspired by the story of the Biblical Israelites fleeing Egypt with the Pharaoh's army in hot pursuit, MàB intended to re-enact Moses calling upon the Almighty for help crossing the Red Sea. The Bible story has an army of chariots trying to chase down and crush the escaping Israelites, making this metaphor even more appropriate. These details, however, were kept as a surprise for the media who had simply been told that the group finally had a solution for how to get bikes across the river. MàB members rented costumes and props from a local theatre company, then turned up on the waterfront. A natural for the role, the bearded Silverman was cast as Moses, carrying a staff and replica stone tablets. Speaking in French, he cried out (our translation):

"There are a million [cyclists] of us stranded on Montreal Island and God, only You can help us."

Silverman then issued the "Ten Commandments of Bicycling," beginning with "Thou shall not pollute…" For dramatic effect, "Moses" walked into the river and shouted louder:

"We people of cyclists, we have been subjected to automobile civilization for many years. Endured pollution, noise, risk of being crushed. Today we are on this island of our masters who occupy the doors of our prisons […] O you the Great Almighty […] separate the troubled waters of this river and allow cyclists to leave this island." The old adage is "if you do not get satisfaction, go up the chain of command." Obviously, MàB was getting no satisfaction from the JCCB, so appealing instead to a higher authority was the only choice. When the expected miracle again failed to happen, some twenty volunteers instead tried draining the river with buckets. This was about as effective as readers can imagine. While God did not answer Silverman, watching journalists took full note of the performance and loved it. This was a colourful and unusual story with tremendous photos; it was also very funny. Some photos of the event show another MàB member, Philippe Coutu, playing Moses. Despite Silverman being a ham and enjoying centre stage, he shared the lead role with Coutu.

This spectacle netted MàB a full page in the first section of Tuesday's *Journal de Montréal*, together with three striking photos. Other daily newspapers reporting on this event the next day were *Le Nouvelliste*, *La Presse*, *Le Soleil*, and *La Tribune*. The *Gazette* was present, too, but reported on the event later.

Outside of Quebec, a dozen English newspapers also published a *Canadian Press* report of the Easter Monday event; these included the *Edmonton Journal*, the *Regina Leader-Post*, the *Vancouver Sun*, the (Victoria) *Times Colonist*, and the *Windsor Star*.

After Moses, Icarus Comes to MàB's Aid

On July 20, 1981, MàB held their "fly-in" cyclodrama at the flower gardens of what is now Parc Jean Drapeau, on an island in the river. This time an Icarus character (not played by Silverman) was the star instead of Moses, attempting to fly across the river. Icarus had a bicycle equipped with big white duck wings, rented from the same place that provided the Moses costume. While Icarus did not achieve liftoff, he did make the news. The incident mentioned in the Foreword, in which Silverman and his "wingmen" chased down Mayor Drapeau in his car in 1980, showering him with pamphlets, was presumably a practice run for the Icarus cyclodrama.

Another rally was organized by le MàB, held on the Jacques Cartier Bridge on August 8, 1982, with some sixty cyclists protesting how difficult it was to ride bikes on the bridges linking Montreal to the South Shore. They also showed support for Daniel Lacoste, a cyclist due for a court appearance the next day for once riding across the nearby Champlain Bridge at 1:00 a.m. Canoe paddlers and scuba divers (frogmen) were also enlisted in attempts to take bicycles across the St. Lawrence River. At some spots, the St. Lawrence River is two kilometres wide.

In 2002, the Jacques Cartier Bridge deck was rebuilt, including a widening of the western sidewalk to 2.5 metres and its transformation into a veritable bike path. The eastern sidewalk was reserved for pedestrians but cyclists can walk their bikes there.

Year-Round Bridge Access

The next battle was for bridge access twelve months a year. Much of each winter, there is little snow or ice on the Jacques Cartier bike path, but authorities insisted that it was "unsafe," deciding to lock access gates. The dates of the beginning and end of the winter closings varied widely from year to year. In 2017–2018, the bike path was closed for 131 days but only 82 days in 2012–2013. Some cyclists hopped over the gates regardless.

Since 2023, over 500,000 cyclists have been using this bridge annually. While cycling is much more popular in the warmer months, there are still many cyclists who ride in winter. In July 2022, almost 3,000 cyclists and pedestrians crossed the Jacques Cartier Bridge daily. During the winter of 2021–2022, some 37,190 cyclists and pedestrians crossed the bridge, presumably just more than 400 daily.[9] On average, cyclists represent 85 percent of this traffic or about 340 daily crossings. Arguing that ice on the bike path was hazardous for cyclists, the JCCB resisted this initiative for years. Cyclists countered that the JCCB had a huge budget for de-icing the rest of the bridge; why not spend a tiny part of that budget on the bike path? The JCCB also cited difficulties in evacuating traffic accident victims by ambulance should cyclists be injured on the bridge. Cycling advocates responded with the suggestion of adapting bicycle trailers to carry a stretcher as some bike trailer manufacturers mention in their product literature.

It became a yearly event for bike advocates to hold a *pelle-t-in* (mass snow-shovelling event) to symbolically clear snow from the bridge access. By 2019, the JCCB experimented with a pilot project to keep the bike path open that winter.

In 2020, the JCCB officially opened both the bike path and sidewalk to wintertime use from 6:00 a.m. to 11:00 p.m. daily with the night-time closures intended for maintenance and snow clearing. The bike path was open 24/7 as of spring, 2022.

Other Bridges to Montreal Island
While bicycle access in the 1970s was problematic on the Jacques Cartier Bridge, it was non-existent on most other bridges: The Victoria Bridge (Highway 112), the first bridge across the St. Lawrence River, was inaugurated by Prince Albert, Queen Victoria's consort, in 1860. At the time, it was the longest bridge in the world. It also predated the invention of the car by about two decades. Primarily a train bridge, it was originally built with two lanes for pedestrians, horses, and eventually also cyclists. Over time, these were converted into road traffic lanes. By the 1970s, only motorized vehicles and trains could use the bridge; the same is true today.

In August 1979, MàB, in conjunction with Vélo Québec, stormed the renovated Victoria Bridge. Two baton-wielding bridge police officers failed to stop forty cyclists from crossing the bridge as Silverman later wrote. After crossing the bridge, the cyclists headed for the "streetcar museum [Exporail in St-Constant] to mark the twentieth anniversary of the elimination of Montreal's streetcars."[10] After their illegal ride, the cyclists were offered an escort across the bridge if they telephoned in advance.

The original Champlain Bridge, inaugurated in 1962 at the height of the automobile period, was never equipped with a sidewalk or bike path. This bridge crossed the St. Lawrence from Nun's Island (Montreal) to Brossard. The new Samuel de Champlain Bridge, which opened in 2019, also crosses the St. Lawrence from Nun's Island to Brossard. It incorporates a 3.4 km multi-use path for cyclists and pedestrians, sometimes referred to as "the Mercedes of bike paths." Accessible from René Lévesque Boulevard on Nun's Island, the multi-use path links to the Riveraine bike path along Brossard's riverfront. Panoramic views are offered from four lookout posts and cyclists are requested to respect the twenty kilometres per hour speed limit. There are nine "assistance buttons" in the event of an emergency. The multi-use path is advertised as "being open 24/7," except for special occasions such as major snowstorms that will be announced on the Signature on the Saint Lawrence website. Signature is the private consortium that manages the bridge.

Transport Quebec Recognizes Cyclists

In 2006, Transport Quebec adopted a policy recognizing cycling as a means of transportation. This policy, which stipulates that any new bridge or major work on a bridge must include a bike path, was inspired by the Silverman and Morissette protests of the 1980s and 1990s. Although the Samuel de Champlain Bridge is under federal jurisdiction, the integration of a bike path was part of the design of the new bridge from the outset, as was the separate deck of the REM, a commuter train inaugurated in 2023. This bridge, which was also designed by an architect, is considered the best-designed link to the South Shore.

In May 1976, MàB also addressed Papineau-Leblanc Bridge (or simply Papineau Bridge), crossing from Montreal north to Laval Island across the Rivière des Prairies (Back River). Silverman was quoted as saying it was "shameful" that people need to own a car just to cross that bridge. He threatened to block the bridge to automobiles unless provisions were made for cyclists and pedestrians to cross. It is unclear what happened to Silverman's threat. Today, the Papineau Bridge, which is a highway, is still not cyclable. Considering that work on the bridge deck and cable stays resulted in one lane being closed in each direction for nearly two years (in 2023 and 2024) without causing major traffic jams, there seems to be room for a bike lane.

A Bike-Friendly Mayor Is Elected

THE MONTREAL CITIZENS' MOVEMENT (MCM) administration of Mayor Jean Doré was elected in 1986, ending almost thirty years of rule by Jean Drapeau. Promising to do much for cyclists, the MCM's ideology is described as "Communitarianism, Social Democracy, Progressivism, and the Third Way." This party also had affiliations with the NDP while Jean Doré himself previously worked as an attaché for PQ premier René Lévesque. Silverman was a card-carrying member of the MCM as were some other MàB members. The party was advocating for cyclists even before the founding of MàB; the MCM program from 1974 called for the establishment of reserved bus lanes and bike lanes. The party program from 1982 called for bike access to the metro, especially for the Yellow Line crossing under the St. Lawrence River, as well as bike parking around stations.[1] By 1990, when the party was in power, its program called for bicycle access to commuter trains.

"The MCM literally opened the door to City Hall," recalls former MCM councillor Michel Prescott. While Drapeau had initiated a question period—reserved only for elected officials—circa 1974,[2] it was Jean Doré who expanded the question period, allowing members of the public to also ask questions. Prescott remembers often seeing Silverman and Morissette there, asking questions and pushing the agenda for cyclists.

Silverman Becomes Disillusioned with Mayor Doré

While improvements were being made, these were not done fast enough or extensively enough for Silverman. In 2020, Silverman favourably compared Drapeau's accomplishments on bicycling to the subsequent Doré administration that was supposedly "pro-bicycle." Is there a lesson here that even administrations hostile or indifferent to bicycling can be coaxed to do the right thing? And even administrations supposedly "pro-bicycling" need to be reminded, coaxed, cajoled, and pushed to do the right thing?

Lavallée Defends Mayor Doré's Record
In 2021, André Lavallée, a high-ranking member of the former Doré administration, took strong issue with Silverman's suggestion that Doré's MCM party "did

Figure 14.1. André Lavallée (*left*) and Jean Doré.
Source: André Lavallée.

little" for bicycling from 1986 to 1994. Lavallée first met Silverman in 1975 when the two were activists doing a "squat" on a St-Norbert Street block. Some forty apartments were destined for demolition to make way for a parking lot. Lavallée later embarked on a long career in politics, then in the civil service. The whole time Silverman remained an activist.

Lavallée pointed to the inauguration of new bicycle paths—including the 5.3 km east–west "Rachel Street Corridor" and extending the "Christophe-Colomb Avenue to Downtown Corridor" to 10 km—during Doré's tenure. There was also the implementation of "a real bike path network" (as opposed to unconnected sections) and ferries for bikes to cross the St Lawrence from the Old Port to Longueuil and Bellerive Park to Charron Island and the Boucherville National Park[3]). Further, there were zoning law changes that required car parking lots to provide some bicycle parking while downtown office towers were required to provide showers, a nice perk for sweaty cyclists arriving at work.

Lavallée attributed the conceptualization of many of these projects to Silverman and the MàB, but it was the politicians and bureaucrats who transformed such ideas into reality. It is not just Lavallée who sang Doré's praises as an environmentalist. The Federation of Canadian Municipalities selected Doré—out of all the mayors in Canada—to speak for them at the 1992 United Nations Conference on Environment and Development (UNCED), or "Earth Summit" held in Rio de Janeiro, Brazil.

Furthermore, under the MCM, Montreal began rolling out its curbside recycling pickup program, starting in NDG in 1991. This program was eventually extended to the entire city. Prior to 1991, there was a modest recycling program operating in Outremont—then an independent municipality. Tooker Gomberg may have been implicated with the initiation of the Outremont recycling program. Lavallée also emphasized that part of the Doré administration's time in office coincided with a global economic recession,[4] high interest rates, and high unemployment rates, all resulting in reduced municipal revenues. Lower revenues necessarily slowed—or cancelled—many planned municipal initiatives. The Quebec government reduced its funding for Montreal's public transport during this time and the Doré administration responded with a new tax. That public transport tax was unpopular and probably contributed to the MCM's electoral defeat in 1994.

And while the artistic community was the vanguard of social changes during the Quiet Revolution, this does not seem to have been the case while the MCM was trying to make Montreal more bicycle-friendly: "When we implemented the St-André Street bike path beside parc Lafontaine, many people were opposed, including singer and songwriter, Plume Latraverse," noted Lavallée. Latraverse even composed a song, *La piste cyclable*, in which he pours insults on bike paths.[5]

Dispelling Silverman's notion that the MCM did not do enough, Lavallée asked: "Did Mayor Jean Doré try to do too much? There was just so much to do."

Lavallée also suggested that the MCM could have used the services of someone like Silverman to better communicate its accomplishments to the electorate. Unlike his predecessor, Mayor Doré could sometimes be seen riding a bicycle. But the MCM's commitment to bicycling is also questioned by Gail Tedstone, a former candidate for the MCM in district 47. She remembers party leader Michael Fainstat scolding her for riding her bicycle arriving to do door-to-door election campaigning, as if the MCM only gave lip service to bicycling. "I also rode my bicycle to MCM meetings," she recalls. "But the only two bikes tied up outside were mine and Bob's."

On June 7, 1990, a cyclist was struck and killed while avoiding a car parked on the Rachel Street bike path. The path was not yet finished but was already being used by many cyclists. Despite public pressure to complete the bike path and make it safer, five weeks passed with the MCM administration doing nothing. MàB volunteers eventually painted "no parking" zones around where the cyclist was killed.[6] Some opposition politicians have echoed Silverman's anti-car rhetoric, but then failed to follow through once in power. John Gardiner, a councillor with the MCM, was an example, calling for a "car-free" city while in opposition.[7] Gardiner had joined Silverman and André Lavallée for the squat on St-Norbert Street in 1975 to save it from demolition. But things changed after Doré's 1986 election victory when Gardiner was named to Montreal's executive committee.

"Despite his radical roots, he quickly built rapprochement with the business community," wrote Marion Scott of the *Gazette* in Gardiner's 2015 obituary.[8] The same article notes that Gardiner, once in power, alienated many of his former supporters. Silverman lamented that "once Gardiner was in charge; he did very little. We worked with Doré and he let us down." Michel Prescott recalls walking on Duluth Street with Michael Fainstat, probably in early 1990. "We saw Bob and Michael asked if he would be a candidate in the next election for the MCM. I interjected, telling Bob that if he wanted to run, he would first have to win against me for the local nomination."

In November 1990, Silverman was frustrated enough with the MCM to quit the party and present himself as a candidate for the rival Montreal Ecology Party with Dimitri Roussopoulos, but that party failed to elect any councillors. Perhaps in reflection, Silverman saw the wisdom in Lavallée's defense of the MCM. In 2020, Silverman suggested that the current Projet Montréal administration of Valérie Plante could be seen as a continuation of Jean Doré's MCM administration. Projet Montréal is commonly perceived as "pro-bike." Echoing Silverman's suggestion, Projet Montréal councillor Alex Norris (Jeanne-Mance district) says that "All [Silverman's] direct action stunts allowed us to achieve a different image of what kind of a city we want. This allowed a political party like Projet Montréal to take root."

Reconquering the City

Silverman's first law of bicycling states that the likelihood of cyclists getting suitable infrastructure built somewhere is inversely proportional to the number of car drivers likely to be inconvenienced by this. The automobile lobby is quite powerful almost everywhere in the world, to the point where the safety of pedestrians and cyclists is of secondary importance to the priority of getting motorists to their destination a few seconds sooner.

In recent years, anti-bicycle city administrations such as that of former mayor Rob Ford in Toronto were actually removing bike lanes. This was done under the pretext that they posed a hindrance to motorists. Ford was openly antagonistic to cyclists; it was no coincidence much of his electoral support came from voters who commuted long distances by car rather than inner-city types who commuted by bike. There is also a great misconception that traffic congestion is best alleviated by building more roads. In fact, this invariably just creates induced demand for more cars, which in turn generally makes the congestion worse. At the time of writing, the Doug Ford administration in Ontario was about to order Toronto to dismantle some of its bike lanes. Doug Ford is the brother of the late Rob Ford. Other city administrations are not antagonistic to cycling, but neither are they willing to tackle car-driving voters. Instead, they tend to work to create extensive "recreational paths" in areas that will not inconvenience motorists too much.

Montreal, under various administrations, has recently been much bolder. In the late 1980s, the Rachel Street bike path was built through le Plateau on a major artery, against the will of many city bureaucrats. Executive committee president, Lea Cousineau, who pushed the project under Jean Doré's MCM administration, fought for a straight-line path with no detours, one of the conditions for success of an urban bike lane. The implementation of the path created monstrous traffic jams at the corner of Papineau and Rachel streets. Montreal backed off for decades, making a detour on a south side street, but cyclists did not take the detour and the intersection was deemed one of the most dangerous in the city.

Finally, in 2020, the Valérie Plante administration re-established the bike path in a straight line. Borough mayor Luc Ferrandez eliminated hundreds of parking spots along the path, which were a safety hazard for cyclists, pedestrians, and motorists. The new configuration also adds much flora.

The 3.4 km Claire Morissette bike path along de Maisonneuve Avenue in downtown Montreal, opened in 2008 at a cost of $3.5 million,[9] displacing some 350 car parking spots by our estimation. The six hundred BIXI docking stations also displaced over one thousand car parking spots. Ottawa, meanwhile, actually closes some of its main thoroughfares to motorized traffic on Sunday mornings, to the delight of cyclists.

"We're not just talking about a change. We're talking about the reconquest of the city, taking it back from the private car and making it a quieter, cleaner, healthier and friendlier place for people," Silverman told the *Gazette* in October, 1976.[10] The issue is not only where to build the bike paths, but also what purpose to make them for. To some, bicycles are a recreational toy, primarily for use on weekends. This way of thinking also suggests that it is unimportant whether the bike paths connect with each other, lead anywhere important, or are safe in weekday traffic. A competing vision, espoused by MàB, is that bike paths should be built so as to provide corridors for cyclists to efficiently, safely, and quickly commute to work, go to school, and access important services.

As mentioned, the cities of Longueuil and Westmount had been building bike paths or lanes in the mid-1970s.

The first real plan for urban integration of bike paths came with the construction of the Collectivité nouvelle, part of Longueuil, in the 1980s.[11] The design was inspired by European urban planning practices; bike paths were separated from motorized traffic, with underpasses or overpasses across main arteries. Unfortunately, this design was rarely reproduced in Quebec.

The federal government also built what were among Canada's first bike paths in modern times, starting with a 14 km path along the St. Lawrence Seaway dyke from St. Lambert to Sainte-Catherine circa 1976, followed by a 13.5 km path along the Lachine Canal from Lake St. Louis to Montreal's Old Port, in 1978. Another bike path was built along the river from Lake St. Louis through LaSalle and Verdun, but all were designed for recreational use and not very practical for everyday use. Nonetheless, the Lachine Canal bike path can be a practical commuting route for some cyclists who work near Old Montreal and reside in western parts of the Island.

"For a long time [municipal authorities] made cycle lanes for [use on] Sunday mornings. But we [at MàB] wanted lanes to be used from Monday morning to Friday evening, which changes your way of life," says MàB co-founder Jacques Desjardins.[12]

The St. Lawrence Seaway and Lachine Canal bike paths caused no inconvenience for car drivers, thus making these easy, early victories. The bike network that has been built since then has required fortitude on the part of authorities. Today, it is very difficult to imagine Montreal without bike paths. By extension, it is very difficult to imagine Montreal as if MàB, or Silverman, had never existed.

The Missing Link

The smaller Concorde Bridge from Montreal to Notre Dame Island—now the site of the Montreal Casino—is open to cyclists.[13] Unfortunately, it was impossible to continue onto the St. Lawrence Seaway bike path and the South Shore until 1989 when a small footbridge was built close to Victoria Bridge. "The solution [for 'the missing link'] was to build a simple land link between Île Notre Dame and the St. Lawrence Seaway cycle path, which was already connected to the South Shore," Silverman later wrote.[14] This mainly involved building half a kilometre of bike path, a small bridge for cyclists, putting the bike path underneath Victoria Bridge, and some fencing. All this was estimated to have cost some $300,000. Complicating MàB's request was that such a link involved four different jurisdictions: the City of Montreal, the Quebec government, the St. Lawrence Seaway Authority (federal para-governmental agency), and the Société de gestion de l'île Notre Dame (a municipal para-governmental agency). It was essential for all to coordinate the building of this structure. The bureaucratic slowness was frustrating with this project; the main stumbling block was finding the necessary funds.[15] At least the local city council in St. Lambert was enthusiastic, adopting a motion in August 1988, urging that this link be built.¹⁶ Soon, others would follow.

"Patiently, le Monde à bicyclette requested and obtained letters of support from eighteen MNAs in the region. At our request, resolutions supporting this solution were passed by municipal councils of the South Shore. Repeated questions, both written and verbal, were presented to the Executive Committee of the City of Montreal," Silverman continued.¹⁷

Blackmailing a Government Minister

Morissette had heard about how one of Premier Robert Bourassa's cabinet ministers had spent about $300,000 of public funds to construct a small bridge to a remote fishing lodge (*pourvoirie*) used by only four people. As Silverman recounted in 2015, Morissette then contacted the office of Yvon Picotte, minister of recreation, hunting and fishing. She mentioned the need for a 500 m link and small footbridge connecting Île Notre-Dame to the Maritime Seaway, which would be used by an estimated 150,000 cyclists annually.

She then threatened to hold a press conference to highlight this issue and embarrass the minister. Within days, the minister's office called back and promised $250,000 for the "missing link" footbridge. Soon after, the City of Montreal announced that it was building this link at a cost of $550,000, with $250,000 to be provided by the Quebec government. This link was inaugurated in May 1990. Morissette joked beforehand that Moses, Icarus, and a frogman would be at the inauguration, sharing "a toast of champagne."¹⁸ Silverman considered the building of this footbridge to be one of the MàB's greatest victories.

The Estacade and the Rabbit Trail

An ice-breaker bridge, often called by its French name, the *Estacade*, is slightly upstream from the Samuel de Champlain Bridge. Dating from the 1960s, it was built to protect the Samuel de Champlain Bridge and Expo islands from ice flows and flooding.

"After our success with the Jacques Cartier Bridge, we planned a die-in on the Champlain Bridge," recounted

Silverman in 2015. "Then authorities opened the ice breaker bridge." Accessible to non-motorized traffic since about 1990, this two-kilometre span allows bicyclists and pedestrians to cross from Nun's Island to a bike path on the St. Lawrence Seaway dyke. The bridge is closed seasonally to the public, typically from December through May. For the rest of the year, some refer to it as "the longest bike bridge in the world."

To reach the South Shore from this bridge, a detour is required via the St. Lambert locks. Initially, the one-kilometre link between Nun's Island and Verdun (now part of Montreal) was even more problematic. To reach Nun's Island, cyclists had to cross a smaller bridge from Verdun and follow footpaths.

"The portion between Nun's Island and Verdun was dangerous and unpleasant," later wrote Silverman.[19] His group described the access to Nun's Island as "a rabbit trail" without pavement or proper signage. "We dressed up as rabbits on two occasions to illustrate the inconvenience of having to go from one short end of the trail to another." The costumes were part of a cyclodrama for the benefit of photojournalists. "At the same time, having learned from our previous experiences, we requested and obtained letters of support from eighteen federal MPs and we obtained resolutions from six municipalities on the South Shore [calling] for a cycling link on [Pont de l'Île-des-Sœurs], which gives access to Nun's Island. Finally, in the summer of 1994, the JCCB decided to build a protective fence that had been requested and the City of Verdun completed the work by building the bicycle access at the entrance to the Champlain Bridge. Another cyclo-frustration was thus eliminated. Well done!" wrote Silverman on his blog.

The Bikepath that Stops Halfway across the St. Lawrence River

The Honoré-Mercier Bridge, or simply Mercier Bridge (Highway 138), from LaSalle to Kahnawake and Chateauguay until the early 2000s had a narrow sidewalk on the upstream side that bicyclists could use at their peril. You could see the river below through holes in the sidewalk while nothing separated cyclists from fast moving traffic.

Now there is a multi-use (bicycle and pedestrian) path, but over only one-half of its length, stopping dramatically at the half-way point before Montreal! That southern part of the bridge is administered federally. The northern section—administered by Quebec's Transport Ministry—was closed "temporarily" in 2009 and remains so today with not even a framework for an eventual bike path. Cyclists and pedestrians trying to cross the river there are now faced with a 30 km detour.

On the north side of this bridge is the Montreal borough of LaSalle with a population of some 77,000 and many retail stores. To the southwest of this bridge is Kahnawake, a Mohawk First Nations community of 8,000 people. Silverman in 2016 cynically suggested that the Mercier bike path closure is supposed "to keep Mohawks out of LaSalle."[20] Officials at the Quebec Ministry of Transport were upset to hear this comment relayed to them.[21]

Protesting the Auto Show

THE MÀB went beyond promoting cycling, notably in protesting against cars and what Silverman termed the "auto-cracy." This differentiates the group from many other bicycle lobby groups. Silverman insisted that "cars are the problem" whereas other groups, such as Vélo Québec, try to promote peaceful coexistence between motorists and cyclists.

In January 1976, just prior to the annual Montreal Auto Show (*Salon de l'Auto*), MàB issued a press release describing cars as "public enemy no. 1." The same press release claimed that "since 1900, [cars] have killed 25 million people, more than all the wars of this century."[1] The MàB also referred to the January 9 auto show as the "Salon de la Mort" (the Death Show). While the group had previously held a few demonstrations, MàB's protests against the 1976 auto show were apparently the group's first cyclodramas or street theatre events.

The 1977 Auto Show

One year later, prior to the 1977 Montreal Auto Show, MàB distributed leaflets that stated: "[The Auto Show] is a million-dollar pornographic circus of chrome, or carpets, of dancing girls which sells the illusion that we cannot live without this machine, that a person without a car is not quite complete.[2]" Silverman duly promised to "drive" the auto show out of town.

MàB member Tom Berry—now an accomplished film producer—made a short film about their group's interruption of the 1977 auto show.[3] The event was supposed to be a dignified affair, presided over by Jacques Duval, a journalist who authored the *Guide de l'auto* and wrote about cars for various publications. There were elegant female models standing beside luxury cars at Place Bonaventure. Then, shortly after the national anthem is played, a loud noise erupted from the back of the hall. An unruly gang of MàB members arrives from the metro, waving placards and some wearing gas masks. Accompanying them are members of Save Montreal and the Society to Overcome Pollution (STOP).[4] They also carry a ketchup-smeared supporter on a stretcher. Silverman is very prominent in the group holding a placard reading "*un tour d'étau au tour du monde.*" In English, this placard could read "a vice grip around the world" or "a car trip around the world."

Other placards featured skulls and crossbones, accompanied by the words "your turn is next," or icons depicting cars with a line crossing them out. Their chants reached a crescendo when Silverman—still wearing a gas mask and holding his placard—was hoisted high on the shoulders of other MàB members. Duval and company looked horrified at the disturbance. Duval, later speaking on CKAC Radio, called Silverman "*un monstre*" (a freak).

Twenty-Seven Million People Killed by Cars

MàB mainly protested the carnage (or is that "car-nage"?) caused by cars. Silverman subsequently wrote in 1980 of twenty-seven million people killed worldwide by cars since 1900, as well as fifty-five thousand Americans killed yearly, without citing a source.[5] Silverman's numbers are similar, however, to those of the World Health Organization (WHO).[6] There are more than 1.35 million traffic fatalities a year worldwide or one death somewhere every twenty-four seconds according to WHO. MàB group also objected to the pollution and huge waste of resources caused by cars, the indebtedness incurred by car ownership, and the sexism used to market cars.

"The ten largest companies in the world are all producers of either cars or oil. General Motors and Exxon have [annual] sales in excess of Canada's [federal] budget. And the car/oil multinationals have molded the world to suit their interests. Urban geography reflects the stamp of auto-necessity. And their billions have corrupted everyone's heads and value systems," wrote Silverman in a 1980 *Open Road* article.[7] Silverman often wore a T-shirt featuring the message "cars killed more people than all the wars of the 20th century." Another T-shirt featured the message "I support Zero Automobile Growth," echoing the words of consumer advocate Ralph Nader. Suffice to say that Silverman was very strong in his belief that cars are bad. Silverman was not expressing original ideas on this. Authors such as Jane Jacobs and Jan Gehl pioneered this view, noting how cars have taken away so much of the public space while Ivan Illich describes how cars detract from conviviality (friendly interactions). Cyclists and pedestrians can easily recognize someone in passing and stop for a chat; motorists can rarely do the same. More recently, concerns about climate change heighten sentiments that the private automobile has brought much suffering to the world.

The Evolving Father and Son Relationship

"Bicycle Bob" was certainly in the news a lot; it would have been difficult for family members not to notice. To his very conventional and materialistic father, Silverman probably appeared as a kook. There was a certain "Peter Pan" quality to Silverman; his lifestyle long remained that of a teenager while he embarked on quests of romanticism with little regard for materialistic reward.

According to Terrence Regan, a longtime close friend, Silverman's wealthy father tried to get his son into a profitable career. "With his bookstore, the problem was that Bob would give books away for free. His father became frustrated with that."

There was the dichotomy of his father's constant criticisms versus the praise from Che Guevara and from Ivan Illich. If only his father could see what Guevara and Illich saw. Or what his fans at MàB saw ... Did this make Silverman want to always prove himself? Was he always hoping for his father's approval? Communications between father and son must have been strained. But Bert Silverman seems to have nonetheless assisted at least once at one of "Bicycle Bob's" rebirthings, perhaps in the 1980s. Silverman's father was apparently "quite moved" by the experience.[8]

While "scraping and scrounging" to get by for much of his life, and living frugally, Silverman nonetheless travelled widely. His destinations included Europe, Cuba, Vietnam, Israel, Australia, and South America, as well as frequent trips in Canada and the United States. Friends wondered how he managed and whether his father helped. While his father never seems to have appreciated Silverman for who he was, perhaps the opposite was also true. Silverman publicly repudiated his father's values, yet still expected the father to accept him and leave him much of the family wealth.

Paradoxically, Silverman said that "my father had no expectations of me." Yet, almost in the same breath, explained that his father "did not leave me a penny because he expected me to give it all to charity." Expecting someone to give generously to charity is certainly an expectation, if not a great virtue within Montreal's Jewish community.[9]

"Silverman also had a habit of denouncing his mother and father publicly; doing so dogmatically. His father was upset with the insults and they had a falling out. When they opened his father's will, Bob got nothing," said Regan. His father's 1993 obituary, while mentioning "Bob," also lists his sister, four grandchildren and four great-grandchildren,[10] the apparent heirs of the family fortune, all on his sister's side. His mother, Florence, passed away in 1987.[11]

Contributing to the father–son animosity was the fact one was an unabashed capitalist while the other was an unapologetic communist in an era of deep ideological divides. Quebec independence was anathema to most anglophones—especially to the business class—while Silverman was unperturbed by the idea and many of his friends were sovereigntists. The father was presumably also a strong supporter of Israel while his son criticized the Jewish state, eventually meeting with Palestinian leader Yasser Arafat.

There was a certain *rapprochement* between Silverman and his sister, Rona, in the years before Silverman's death. The two often talked and she visited, for instance celebrating Silverman's eightieth birthday with him in Val-David. Three generations of the sister's family participated in the April 2022 commemorative ride for Silverman. Many assume that Rona also provided financial assistance in Silverman's latter days.

Silverman, the Communist, Cashes in on the Stock Market

Around 1991, John Symon was playing volleyball in Jeanne-Mance Park and saw Silverman. They chatted about Symon's work for a health charity that dealt with Parkinson's disease. Silverman smiled and said that he had inherited some money after his mother died in 1987. He then made a stock market investment in a company marketing a new drug for Parkinson's, Toronto-based

Deprenyl Research. Symon must have whistled upon hearing this; the company's stock had recently surged on the markets! Silverman probably paid between three and nine dollars[12] for shares soon worth about twenty-three dollars.[13] He then confided that his reasons for making the investment were because he thought "that the company was doing good things for humanity," and nothing to do with its financial potential. The company founder, Dr Morty Shulman, was also an eccentric fellow sharing some characteristics with Silverman. They both had a good laugh at Silverman's incredible beginner's luck with the stock market.

The Communist Aristocrat

Despite being an impoverished Trotskyite and a Vélorutionary, Silverman could still sometimes project the image of an aristocrat, as someone from his family background could be expected to do. He was not alone in this apparent contradiction; much the same could be said of Cuba's Fidel Castro or Chile's Salvador Allende.

The Philadelphia Bicycle Coalition and International Connections

IN THE 1970S, Silverman got in touch with John Dowlin, founder of the Philadelphia Bicycle Coalition (PBC), now known as the Bicycle Coalition of Greater Philadelphia. This group's material gave him further inspiration and the conviction that there was a "new and global bicycling consciousness" in the West in 1975. Like Silverman, Dowlin was opposed to the Vietnam War, seeing support for Southeast Asian oil production as the real reason for US involvement there. Documentation that Dowlin possessed includes a 1973 map of the extensive oil leases in the South China Sea. Superimposed is a poster of a bicycle with the inscription "No American soldiers were killed to fuel this vehicle," showing one way that Dowlin tied the war to bike advocacy.[1]

PBC notably agitated for bicycle facilities in Philadelphia, much like MàB did in Montreal. Dowlin was also involved with the Bicycle Network (equally known as the Réseau cycliste and the Red de Ciclistas), which ran a clipping service, sharing bicycle information worldwide with some forty bike advocacy groups in its Network News,[2] published on a quarterly basis from 1980 to 1999.[3] Silverman often contributed to the Bicycle Network;[4] he and Dowlin started a long history of complicity. In 1995, Dowlin joined Silverman for a group bike trip in Cuba.

Some of the bike groups linked by this publication included

Figure 16.1. John Dowlin, in Philadelphia, on his cargo bike in 2019.
Source: Bicycle Coalition of Greater Philadelphia.

Eco Kyoto (Japan), the Leningrad Bicycle Club (now Russia), Power Tasmania (Australia), La Fédération Française des Usagers de la Bicyclette (France), and Todos en bicicleta (Mexico). But MàB was probably the most militant bike movement anywhere, with its aim to turn Montreal into a "no-car city."[5] While still advocating for no cars in Montreal, Silverman did later make an exception for cars in rural areas, where he conceded that they have a practical benefit. The equivalent of the Jacques Cartier Bridge for Philadelphians like Dowlin would be the Ben Franklin Bridge across the Delaware River from Philadelphia to New Jersey. In 2019, a ramp was finally installed on this bridge, replacing many stairs, which had been a bicycle obstacle. Dowlin had meanwhile suffered a stroke. He made the inaugural ride on the ramp as a passenger on a cargo bike. This inauguration followed more than ten years of advocacy efforts by PBC.

The Many Campaigns of le Monde à Bicyclette

The Monde à bicyclette supporters were constantly confronting authority figures, mostly older men in business suits, who tried not to listen. On MàB's side was mostly a younger crowd with shaggy hair, marginalized by mainstream culture, but making noise, being creative, and doing street theatre.

With approximate dates, these campaigns included calling for:

- access to the metro, starting in 1976
- an end to the Montreal Car Show, circa 1976
- the building of bike lanes and paths, circa 1978
- better access over the St. Lawrence bridges, starting in 1975
- retaking public space from cars, circa 1981
- completion of the "missing link" from Île Notre Dame to the Maritime Seaway, in the late 1980s
- better signage along the Rachel Street bike path, in 1990
- the "Estacade" or "ice-breaker bridge" to be opened to cyclists circa 1990
- access to AMT commuter trains, in 1991
- better bicycle parking at public buildings, circa 1992
- improvement to the "rabbit trail" / better access to Nun's Island, in 1993
- more public bike parking facilities in the downtown sector, in 1998[6]

MàB sometimes expanded its theatre of operations from the streets of Montreal to areas of national concern. The group wrote to the Canadian Radio-Television and Telecommunications Commission (CRTC) in 1976, requesting a ban on automobile ads on all Canadian TV and radio stations.[7] By 1988, the CRTC had banned advertising for tobacco products because of the public health danger that smoking represents. MàB presumably used similar justification in asking for the car ad ban. André Lavallée contends that one of MàB's aims was to promote Montreal's central core as a "livable city." This was in contrast with the Drapeau administration's unofficial view that nobody really wanted to live downtown.

MàB against Nukes

MàB was not a single-issue group and its members took a holistic view of world problems. After the March 1979 Three Mile Island nuclear disaster in Pennsylvania, MàB was among a dozen diverse groups co-signing a Canadian Coalition for Nuclear Responsibility (CCNR) full-page ad in the *Gazette*, denouncing nuclear power.[8]

Gordon Edwards of CCNR spoke about how "the MàB would send a contingent to our demonstrations. They enjoyed ethically based demonstrations and wholeheartedly supported such things while advertising bicycles. There was a common cause; it was not a matter of choosing one thing over another."[9] He maintains that there was significant overlap between protecting the environment, civil rights, promoting good urban planning, and maintaining healthy lifestyles. There is no real distinction between military and "peaceful" uses of nuclear power according to the CCNR.[10]

In October 1977, members of MàB—including Silverman—and the CCNR travelled to the Gentilly nuclear station (now out of service and to be dismantled) in Bécancour, Quebec. There, they held a joint protest against nuclear power, holding signs that energy conservation was a better alternative.[11] Stuart Anthony Stilitz, a member of both groups, speaks of how CCNR members sometimes emulated the die-ins of MàB. Over the years, MàB worked together with other bicycling and environmental groups. Apart from Vélo Québec and *Bécane Rive Sud*, it worked with the environmental groups Greenpeace; the *Société pour Vaincre la Pollution* (SVP); Save Tomorrow, Oppose Pollution (STOP); and Transport 2000, as well as the CCNR. One of MàB's last major actions was to protest Canada's timid stand at the UN Rio Summit in 1992. Prime Minister Mulroney promised to reduce Canada's carbon dioxide emissions, but MàB considered this to be a sham: no emission targets were set and no timelines established.

MàB also opened a library, known as the "resource centre," sponsored bike mechanics' workshops, and hosted mass bicycle rides. There was also a recreational component to MàB's activities with free guided bicycle excursions being offered to various destinations outside of Montreal.[12] Mostly, these were one-day excursions, but some were over two days.

Perhaps as a continuation of these MàB excursions, Silverman also began leading bike tour trips to more distant destinations, such as the Maine coast, sometimes travelling by train before starting to ride. Some accounts have him leading bike trips in Cuba in the late 1970s and in Vietnam by the 1980s. MàB probably came to its zenith around 1980 until 1982, after which some initial victories diminished the cyclo-frustrations that powered the organization.

Leading by Example

Silverman also understood the importance of being a role model, both as a committed cyclist and as an anglophone choosing to speak French. While some other cycling advocates still used cars as their main means of locomotion, MàB showed the courage of their conviction, riding their bikes for everyday trips. "We all used our bikes to get to work even if those around us found it daredevilish or downright iconoclastic. [At the office where I worked, co-workers] were offended that I put my bike in my workroom," related former MàB-er Michel Camus on Facebook after Silverman's passing. Former MàB members are invariably proud of their participation in the Vélorution, but only Silverman and Morissette stayed with it for two decades. Being an unpaid activist can be emotionally and financially draining. Napoleon was famous for inaugurating the "pep talk" to his troops before battles to motivate them and explain what the tactical or strategic purpose of the battle was. Similarly, Silverman seemed to have instilled a great sense of purpose and camaraderie amongst his followers. Even "part-timers" within MàB have little trouble today articulating why they participated in various actions, such as declaring it was "to promote cyclists' rights."

Figure 16.2. MàB Logo.
Source: MàB Archive.

The MàB logo featured a bicycle set against five circles, with one representing each of the five continents. This logo was selected by a contest and symbolized how MàB was very much in communication with other bike advocacy groups worldwide. Evelin David Nogue was the designer.

MàB Slogans

In the context of this absurdly pro-car society, what choice is there but to be anti-car? MàB chants often had a distinctive anti-car flavour, such as "La voiture pue, la voiture tue" ("Cars stink, cars kill"). But there were less confrontational slogans:

"Les cyclistes existent, Où sont les pistes?," "L'essence de mon vélo, c'est moi," "Mon vélo est payé, pas ton auto," and "Vive la Vélorution."

("Cyclists exist, where are their paths?," "The gas for my bike, it's me," "My bike is paid for, not your car," and "Long live the Vélorution.")

The MàB personalized some of their slogans for former mayor Jean Drapeau "Drapeau, à vélo; à bas l'auto" ("Drapeau, get on a bike; down with cars").

The slogans, songs, and chants of the anti-Vietnam War movement helped alter public perception of that war. Silverman, the poet and wordsmith, guided MàB in using similar methodology to help change public perceptions toward bicycles.

MàB: A Victim of Its Own Success

"Every gain made the movement weaker," said Silverman to explain the demise of the group he co-founded. As the number of "cyclo-frustrations" diminished, so too did the MàB's *raison d'être*. The group was a victim of its own success. "I predicted it," stated Silverman.

He drew an analogy to the pro-choice (i.e., the freedom to choose an abortion) campaign in the United States that lost much of its momentum after the Supreme Court's 1973 Roe v. Wade decision essentially legalized abortion in all fifty states. However, in 2022, the American Supreme Court overturned Roe v. Wade. Consequently, 14 states have passed anti-abortion laws, which relaunched the fight for the freedom of choice.

The MàB as a Legal Entity

Le Monde à bicyclette was registered as a legal name, together with its English version, Citizens on Cycles, with the Quebec Registry of Enterprises in August 1975. Registering an organization is necessary to apply for government funding, but requires the holding of an annual general meeting, the writing of bylaws, and annual filings with the registry.

Four Factions Clash at Founding Convention

At MàB's founding convention in March 1977, about sixty people attending had to choose between four "tendencies," as Silverman later wrote. These four choices for which path MàB could follow were led by (1) the bike mechanics; (2) reformers who did not want to raise a ruckus, who said go easy, cooperate with the government, it's going to happen anyway; (3) the Trotskyites, who expressed the view that the car industry was so powerful, nothing could be done while capitalism continued to exist and suggested an alliance with the working class to overcome capitalism; and (4) there were Silverman and Morissette, the advocates for "poetic cyclists" and "Vélorutionaries," meaning revolution by the bicycle. The struggle for cyclists' rights is a new historical movement with a new consciousness and it requires a "poetic-Vélorutionary" approach.

Silverman recalled, "At the congress [convention] the Trotskyites called for a thirty-hour work week, the independence of Quebec, rights for homosexuals and women, but there was not a word about bicycles in their two-hundred-page program."

"I said, 'hey, if you prevail, the workers will work for thirty hours and then have traffic jams and nothing will change for the city bicyclists, us.' Then I recited some poetry."

"In the end, the poetico-Vélorutionary tendency, which I supported, received the most votes and the members of the technical, reformist, and revolutionary tendencies left."

Readers will appreciate the irony that Silverman, a Trotskyite himself, successfully resisted efforts by that movement to take over MàB. Anecdotally, there are accounts of Trotskyites taking over other groups during this time, such as CEGEP (college) student councils. As per Ivan Illich's quote: "Socialism can only come by bicycle," Silverman believed that transportation methods are more important than ideology in changing the world.

The Putsch

Later years also saw drama at MàB annual general meetings.

"In 1995 or 1996, there was a putsch at MàB. A new group got themselves elected onto the board of directors. They threw out the employees, hiring their friends instead. This led to complaints to the human rights commission. Good books were stolen from the MàB resource centre. Donors were wondering what happened. I tried to repair things. Bob was not on the board of directors then," said France Lebeau. The silver lining with this incident is that Morissette's eyes were opened to how a non-profit group can be "hijacked" and she put into the constitution of Cyclo Nord-Sud measures to prevent the same from happening there. Notably, members must sign up at least a month before the annual general meeting to be able to vote and only one-half of the board is up for election each year.

Many interviewed for this book claim that MàB closed down in the 1990s. But according to the Quebec Registry of Enterprises, the group was still in existence in the mid-2000s. In its later days, the organization had repeated difficulty filing its annual report with the registry by the required deadline. Because of this failure to file an annual report, since 2004, MàB was finally radiated (removed) from the list of legal entities in 2009. In MàB's final filing (for 2003), neither Silverman nor Morissette are among the names of directors.

MàB and Vélo Québec: Allies or Rivals?

THE MÀB was not the only bicycling advocacy group in 1975. Also active then was a cyclo-tourism federation, the ancestor of today's Vélo Québec (VQ). Despite some similarities between the two non-profit groups, they had very different visions and used quite different techniques to achieve their aims. The two groups were sometimes allies, but also sometimes rivals.

Gabriel Lupien's Vision versus Silverman's

The *Fédération cyclotouriste provinciale* was founded in 1967 by Gabriel Lupien, a physical education teacher and former Catholic priest.[1] Some called him "the good God on a bike." From 1973 to 1979, his organization became known as the Fédération québécoise de cyclotourisme before finally changing its name to Vélo Québec.[2]

"Our local *Fédération* (Vélo Québec) was not really interested in becoming concerned with public transportation," wrote Silverman, describing the mid-1970s.[3] Indeed, Lupien privately espoused that bicycles were recreational vehicles for use in the countryside and not for riding in the city.[4] Some of MàB's initial popularity might have been because urban cyclists saw VQ as irrelevant. Ironically, during the 1970s, Lupien was an advisor about bike paths and bicycle safety for the Quebec and municipal governments.[5] Did Lupien's apparent lack of enthusiasm for urban bike paths contribute in some manner to why so few were built during that period?

A New Gang Takes Over VQ

VQ's lack of enthusiasm toward urban cycling changed dramatically around 1976 after Guy Rouleau became director of the cycling federation. Rouleau is an unsung hero of the Vélorution; while playing a lesser role than Silverman or Morissette, his support was critical to many cycling victories. The two groups worked closely together on gaining access to the métro. A 1979 *Montreal Star* article by C. Bain even incorrectly cited Morissette as "the president of Vélo Québec,"[6] indicating how journalists could confuse the two organizations. Rouleau was assisted by Michel Labrecque and Louise Roy, each of whom eventually succeeded him as executive director of VQ. While Silverman never met Lupien, he did often meet—and frequently argued with—Rouleau. Former VQ director Suzanne Lareau remembers these, however, as "fertile arguments." That is to say, the two organizations successfully collaborated on certain projects.

"Our goals were the same, but our approaches were different. There were many arguments between VQ and MàB, but our approaches were complementary," said Lareau. Besides Silverman arguing with Rouleau, she also remembers him arguing with Morissette. Rouleau has been described as "an intellectual, man of action, and promoter of sustainable development" who "allowed the unrepentant band of idealists that we were to transform society's perception of cycling."[7]

Silverman often led informal rides, combining militancy and recreation; Rouleau sometimes joined them. One such ride led to a graveyard after midnight where participants sipped beer beside the tomb of the Molsons, owners of a large brewery and among Montreal's wealthiest families.

Activism versus Reformism

For a while, there was much collaboration and people from VQ went to MàB activities. But quietly over time, the two groups evolved to have distinctive tendencies: the activism of MàB versus the reformism of VQ.

"Bob was more radical than we were; he was too radical from our point of view," Lareau said when asked about MàB's stated objective to replace cars with bicycles. While MàB was revolutionary, wanting to change everything, VQ was reformist and willing to work within the system.

"Yes, we would like to replace some cars with bicycles. [That was the] division between our two organizations: Bob was an extremist. Authorities don't want to talk to you if you are an extremist. We are for the development of more bicycle infrastructure and promotion of the use of bikes." She sees VQ's mandate as covering all non-competitive bicycling in the province.[8] Silverman countered that VQ is "not overly against cars." He also criticized the group for timidity with its demonstrations and its reluctance to commit civil disobedience. "They didn't even chant anti-government slogans," bemoaned Silverman. In contrast, MàB's demonstrations were done with panache, involving colourful cyclodramas, designed to ridicule its adversaries.

Jail Time versus Paying the Fines
Despite VQ wanting to differentiate itself from Silverman's "extremist" approach to promote bicycling, VQ administrators Guy Rouleau and Louise Roy were among those arrested for attempting to paint unofficial bike lanes in the late 1970s and early 1980s. Lareau speaks of participating at such an event, but not volunteering to be among those arrested by police.

Louise Roy also recalled sometimes being held overnight at the local police station, but always paying her fines.[9] Similarly, Guy Rouleau was sometimes held by police for an hour or so, then released.[10] In contrast, MàB members preferred jail in order to make a principled stand.

A critical conjuncture involved a VQ organizing meeting circa 1981 to prepare for sending delegates to France to study how bicycling was encouraged there. All the delegates selected were from within VQ; none of the longtime militants from MàB were included. This caused many angry words being exchanged; as a result, Guy Rouleau resigned from VQ.[11]

★★★

In 1977, VQ officials learned of a Quebec government publication entitled *La bicyclette, un moyen de transport*, and obtained a copy. Soon after, the group presented itself as having expertise on how to make bicycles a means of transport. In 1979, VQ organized its first symposium on the construction of bike paths. By 1992, VQ had established itself as an authority on the subject, attracting some six hundred participants to Montreal from thirty countries for its *Conférence vélo mondiale*.[12]

Working within the system, as Lareau describes, involved months of collaboration with government officials on revising Quebec's highway code in 1979. The most dramatic moment was in August of that year when VQ administrators won reluctant permission from security guards at the National Assembly to bring a bicycle into the Salon Rouge, adorned in red like the British House of Lords. This symbolic action, before a parliamentary commission, recalled the long and difficult struggles to get bicycles allowed on Montreal's metro. More concretely, some fifty proposals for changes to the highway code, were advanced by VQ. For instance, the law previously stipulated that cyclists must always be sitting on their seat, even when climbing a steep hill. It was proposed that cyclists have the option instead of standing on their pedals. These proposed changes received positive comments from Transport Minister Lucien Lessard. This reception "astonished and enchanted" VQ officials, as they later recalled. Silverman was on the committee that proposed these changes.[13]

Inaugurating the Route Verte, then Fighting for Its Survival

In 2007, VQ proudly inaugurated its *Route verte*, a network of over five thousand kilometres of interconnected and mainly rural bike paths—North America's longest network of bicycle trails. This project probably epitomizes Lupien's vision for cycling. In 2014, austerity measures by the Quebec government involved the elimination of maintenance funding for the *Route verte*. VQ quietly organized opposition to this decision. An open letter was written to the government, signed by many prominent Quebecers, notably including those from the business world. There were no noisy street demonstrations, yet funding was eventually restored.

Changing the Law versus Changing Public Opinion

VQ did manage to work with various Quebec governments, but it was the MàB which made the news, helping to change public opinion.[14] And it was the MàB which really changed the situation for cyclists in Montreal according to British author, Carlton Reid, who writes about urban bicycling internationally.[15]

"I first heard of Robert when researching my *Bike Boom* book. I already knew Montreal had been a hotbed of cycle advocacy in the 1970s and 1980s so I poked around online from the UK and quickly discovered about Robert, Claire and the rest of the vélorutionaries," as Reid wrote in personal correspondence with us.

Jeff Mapes, an American writer who covers similar subjects, wrote in *Momentum Magazine* that Silverman: "sparked a revolution of bike advocacy in Canada."[16] MàB took a confrontational position that cars are bad, protesting at the Montreal Auto Show (Salon de l'Auto). This position was inspired by figures such as Jane Jacobs, among others, who underlined that municipalities need to take back public space from car use. While MàB sometimes received government job creation funding, these funds tended to be of short duration. Meanwhile, Silverman sometimes described VQ as "the Quebec government-financed cycle touring association." He also said: "Why do you think I was so amazing? Toronto never had a 'Bicycle Bob.' Their bike lobby was financed by the city, like Vélo Québec, but worse."

Regarding VQ's less confrontational approach with governments, Silverman grumbled that "it is unwise to bite the hand that feeds." But did his anger hide jealousy? VQ's website acknowledges work of "the activists of the 1970s, notably Bob Silverman, Guy Rouleau, Claire Morissette, and Michel Labrecque,[17] who fought valiantly to ensure that the bicycle received the respect and recognition it deserved."[18]

"Le Monde à bicyclette and Vélo Québec, each with a different strategy, but sharing the same goal, decided to show their solidarity on International Bicycle

Day, celebrated around the world on the first weekend in June," continues VQ. "As a result, from 1977 to 1983, the two organizations held a demonstration on this day. It was not unusual to see a procession of over a thousand cyclists set out on city streets at 10 km/h to bike the [three] kilometres separating La Fontaine Park and Dominion Square. It was one way of showing the city and motorists that cyclists also had their rightful place in Montreal."[19]

In the late 1970s, the MàB organized a mass tour of Montreal Island as part of its bike week activities, but participants were not obligated to complete the entire ride. The event was a free and fun activity. Although the shoreline of Montreal Island measures some 266 km around, most cyclists took much shorter rides of perhaps 50 km in this non-competitive event.

"Hijacking" the Tour de l'Île

In 1985, VQ organized its first official "Tour de l'Île de Montréal," attracting thirty thousand participants as well as corporate sponsors, such as Canadian Tire. Although VQ did not invent the tour, with such corporate funding, and good organization, VQ's tour soon won international recognition. But VQ's gain was MàB's loss: "After the hijacking of the Tour de l'Île by Vélo Québec—and making it a paying event—that killed us. In 1976, we had thousands of cyclists. But we couldn't do [the event] anymore," deplored Silverman. The VQ version is that "Guy Tardif, transport minister at the time, asked Vélo Québec to organize the very first Tour de l'Île de Montréal in October 1985. Just three years later, this event was officially recognized by the Guinness Book of World Records as the largest gathering of cyclists on the planet, a fitting tribute to the architects of the *Vélorution!*"[20]

The Largest Gathering of Cyclists on the Planet

At its peak, the Tour de l'Île was attracting some 45,000 cyclists. Silverman's discontent was softened somewhat once he saw so many people on bikes. Some even suggest that VQ, in certain years, deliberately underestimated the numbers in an attempt not to alarm Montreal's emergency services.

The number of participants in Montreal have since declined while events in other cities, such as New York's TD Five Boro Bike Tour, can today attract more riders than the Tour de l'Île. VQ has consequently added other peripheral events to its menu during the week-long cycling festival. Peripheral events include the "Tour la Nuit" nocturnal ride, the competitive "Métropolitain Challenge," and a bike-to-work program. These events typically take place in early June to incorporate International Bicycle Day, a global event allegedly "dreamed up by Bicycle Bob."[21] Apart from attracting up to thirty thousand cyclists to its annual Go Vélo Montréal Festival, which notably includes the Tour de l'Île, VQ also secured corporate sponsors over the years, such as Canadian Tire, the Dairy Farmers of Canada, and Desjardins credit union. Meanwhile, logistical support is provided by the City of Montreal such as providing police officers free of charge, installing barriers, and closing roads to car traffic. Montreal provides similar free support to other festivals, no doubt contributing to their success.

Currently, the local transit authority (now called the STM) encourages cyclists to arrive at the Tour de l'Île and leave using the metro. In recent years, only six bikes were allowed onto each train. But for the day of the event, the STM temporarily lifted this limit. In the 1970s and 1980s, MàB and VQ activists were arrested for taking bicycles onto the metro; this is now just a distant memory. One avid cyclist who participated in die-ins with the MàB and now regularly rides VQ's Tour de l'Île says the time with Silverman "was more fun."

When Silverman went to Vancouver for the 1976 UN Habitat Conference, VQ paid his bills. In 1984, he was writing an international column for the VQ publication *Vélo Mag*. Silverman also claimed that he was appointed to VQ's board of directors for about two years in the 1980s. However, former VQ director Michel Labrecque contradicts this claim, saying that Silverman instead was simply part of VQ committees focusing on helmet use, traffic law review, and election strategies. In any case, Silverman described that volunteer experience as "boring, often involving non-pertinent discussions."

Despite winning the "Vélorution," Silverman had no head for the art of administration. VQ deserves kudos for growing the Tour de l'Île to such a size and ensuring that the event runs so smoothly. But this level of organization typically involves a lot of boring meetings and attention to minute details, something that might not seem pertinent to a fervent visionary and Vélorutionary. It is also possible that the more moderate VQ have used the radical MàB to play "good cop, bad cop" with authorities in order to get more concessions. Comments by former *Vélo Mag* editor Pierre Hamel, that "MàB was the strong arm of VQ," reinforce this notion.

VQ Wins in Longevity

Over more than two decades, the MàB proved to be very effective as an independent lobby group. It loudly criticized the municipal and Quebec governments, precisely because it was not financially dependent on them. Almost three decades after MàB disbanded, the momentum that this group created is still going; today Montreal continues to lead the Americas with bicycle infrastructure. Montreal now has an extensive network of connecting bike paths and lanes. Additionally, since 2014, many city boroughs have lowered the speed limit on most residential streets. At thirty km/hour, collisions between cars and either pedestrians or cyclists are unlikely to be fatal; driving at lower speed also improves the driver's field of vision and reduces braking time. Higher speed limits of forty km/hour are still found on most arterial roads.

VQ certainly wins over MàB in terms of longevity, as the former group approaches six decades of operations with its less-confrontational approach to bicycle advocacy. Such an approach might mean more influence on society over time. And VQ pays its staff, foregoing them from having to make personal sacrifices in order to advance the cause.

Today, VQ still lobbies for cyclists, encourages cycling among businesses and institutions, manages the annual Go Vélo Montreal festival, publishes the magazines *Vélo Mag*, *Québec* and *Québec Science*, oversees the Route verte, organizes Le Grand tour (mass cycling tours in rural Quebec) and elsewhere, and runs a travel agency, a documentation centre and a bookstore, as well as a café. With all its subsidiaries, VQ probably employs some seventy-five people full-time. Since 1994, the VQ headquarters have been housed in Montreal's *Maison des Cyclistes*, at the intersection of two popular bike paths on the corner of Rachel and Brébeuf streets. Silverman visited often and in 2019, VQ gave him the title of honorary member. Today, VQ has become something different from Lupien's original vision; it now incorporates important aspects of what Silverman long advocated.

MàB Struggling in a Period of Austerity

In 1984, the Progressive Conservatives under Brian Mulroney swept to power in Canada, ending twenty-one years of almost uninterrupted Liberal rule. Despite their success nationwide, two Conservative candidates in the Montreal area failed to win seats. They included Silverman's nemesis, Lawrence Hanigan, who ran in Laval-des-Rapides and Nick Auf der Maur, Silverman's former employee, in Notre-Dame-de-Grâce. After his 1984 election defeat, Hanigan was named president of VIA Rail by Prime Minister Mulroney.[22] Silverman was also a candidate, but for the Green Party and was not elected. Changes brought in under the Mulroney government included austerity policies to reduce the federal deficit. This had ominous effects for bicycle advocacy; federal job-creation programs, such as Opportunities for Youth (OFY) and LIP, that MàB had depended on, began drying up. At the same time, it became more difficult to receive employment insurance (EI), the social security benefit on which Silverman lived for much of each year while working as a volunteer for MàB.[23]

In this more difficult environment, MàB started to decline. Past successes—such as obtaining access to the metro and bridges—also deprived it of much of its *raison d'être*. Meanwhile, Silverman was investing his energies into other things.

Participatory Volleyball, Good Volleyball Is like Good Sex

OUR VOLLEYBALL IDEOLOGY
I'd rather play with those I love
than those who come to win,
I'd rather play with those who Like to pass
than those who want to smash,
for our jobs our tough
and the nights are short
so, let's be kind,
on the volleyball court.

Silverman's Proudest Accomplishment?
One of Silverman's closest colleagues suggests that his proudest achievement is not making Montreal more cycle-friendly but, rather, in developing the city's first outdoor volleyball courts. Indeed, Silverman made the news promoting volleyball before he did so promoting bikes.[1] He was working on both causes in the mid-1970s and was known as "Volleyball Bob" even before he became "Bicycle Bob."[2]

Volleyball certainly is one of Silverman's long-standing passions, but (naturally) his ideas on the game differ from convention. He promotes the game as a non-competitive, egalitarian, all-inclusive sport.

Keeping it Up as Long as Possible
For Silverman, the objective is not to win a point, but rather to keep the ball in play as long as possible.

"Good volleyball is like good sex," joked Silverman. "The objective is to keep it up as long as possible." Continuing with this metaphor, he heaped scorn on the young guys—and some girls—who try to win the point on one quick, hard serve, also called a "smash."

Changing the Rules to Increase Participation
"Participation, not winning, should be the goal," he said. "I started a movement to eliminate hard serve. After two winning serves, the serve would be from the

middle. A referee would toss it in, much like the puck drop with hockey." Readers will probably appreciate that many novices to the game find the serve difficult to master, especially a hard overhand smash serve. This probably constitutes an obstacle or barrier, preventing many people from joining the game.

According to soccer legend, an incident that happened in 1823, when a player "broke the rules," picked up the ball and ran, and those who thought this innovative move was legitimate developed the game we now know as rugby. Today rugby and soccer are two different sports with different rules; perhaps volleyball will someday see a similar evolution if Silverman's followers become more numerous.

Silverman worked for years as a volleyball facilitator in the Milton Park area of Montreal. He began playing with an indoor recreational league in the early 1970s, then advocated for outdoor (or "beach") volleyball.

"I called the Sports Department of the City of Montreal," wrote Silverman. "Fortunately, at the other end of the line was Raymond Verschelden, who was in favour (of outdoor volleyball) We made an appointment for the next day. Driving around in Verschelden's car, we discovered, on that March afternoon, an unused and flat spot in Jeanne-Mance Park, south of Duluth Street."

Everything was ready in late June 1974, just in time for the St. Jean Baptiste provincial holiday. These were the first outdoor volleyball courts in Montreal. Among the first to play volleyball in Jeanne-Mance Park was Silverman's friend, Leonard Cohen, though he was not very good at it.[3] In season, volleyball is still played at this same spot.

"Volleyball is now more popular than baseball; it is played in ten different parks," boasted Silverman in 2020. His claim must have been a huge understatement; dozens of city parks now have volleyball courts. It is also worth noting that, as a youth, Silverman hated the competitive sport of baseball.

No Volleyball without Terrence

Terrence Regan worked alongside Silverman as a volleyball host. "There would have been no volleyball without

Figure 18.1. Silverman (*centre*) with Regan (*right*) at the volleyball courts. *Source*: MàB Archive.

Terrence," as Silverman has put it. He held a similar status regarding volleyball that Claire Morissette held within the MàB.

Regan, originally from Milwaukee, was another American who fled to Canada because of the Vietnam War. He also served as executive director of the Milton Parc Recreation Association for many years. Regan passed away in 2021.[4]

Regan was similarly full of praise for Silverman, but also gave hilarious accounts of him insisting on playing without eyeglasses—ostensibly for his vision improvement—and routinely missing the ball.

"Bob was swinging and missing balls. It was exasperating! Other people were diving on the gravel, just trying to keep the ball in play. Then Bob would flub!"

"When Bob wore his glasses, he could do a very good underhand serve and became a maniac about serving well. He hated when people missed a serve. He could be so rough on them." This description may seem inconsistent with other aspects of Silverman's personality, but we can all be afforded a few inconsistencies.

Volleyball Fascists Must Die!

While Regan usually subscribed to Silverman's non-competitive vision of the game, the two nonetheless had many arguments. Typically, this followed Regan permitting some jocks to play two-on-two when there was a free court. Silverman saw this as the beginning of the end of co-operative volleyball, with competitive two-on-two now tending to dominate in Jeanne-Mance Park. Upset with how competitive volleyball was starting to take over the Jeanne-Mance courts, Silverman apparently once wrote a letter to the *Gazette* entitled "Volleyball Fascists Must Die!"

"Bob was a wealth of knowledge," recounted Regan before adding that his friend was also "impossibly dogmatic and argumentative."

"Jeanne-Mance Park saw the first organized outdoor volleyball in Montreal," continued Regan. "It was run by the community. Elsewhere, you would find your level of play, pay in advance, and join a league, but we developed a system based on pickup volleyball. Initially, we charged players just twenty-five cents a game."

"Bob invited many passersby to play, but they were not necessarily athletic. One of the beauties of volleyball is that a range of abilities can have a good time playing the sport," recounted Regan.

In a 1974 interview, Silverman told the Gazette that volleyball costs little, "occupies the least space, can be played by young and old, men and women, and demands cooperation."[5] In addition, Silverman added that there is little risk of injury; it is egalitarian and everybody rotates into each role; the game is dialectical and improves your mind; and the game is not complicated.

Press Gangs Used to Recruit Players

The Gazette columnist Nick Auf der Maur jokingly wrote about "press gangs" used to entice newcomers to play volleyball when there were not enough players.[6] Silverman would commonly call out to strangers walking past the courts, inviting them to join the game. Officially, Silverman was the "organizer" of the Jeanne-Mance volleyball. When Regan was away for extended periods, Silverman literally carried the ball, as well as the nets. He would stay until dark and then ensure that the balls and nets were safely stored in the nearby park chalet. On warm days, he provided water bottles in this part of the park that previously lacked water fountains.

Games in Jeanne-Mance Park often involved seven players per side, with one rotating in to increase participation over the regulation six players. "This was better for beginners," as Regan said. Three hits were stressed before passing the ball over the net. There was a wide variety of ages and ethnicities playing in this lovely park nestled beneath Mount Royal. Cost was not a barrier to joining in; Regan even allowed John Symon to pay for the games with Canadian Tire money. The main disadvantage of this scenic and central location was that the ball would sometimes fly over a high stone wall into the grounds of an adjacent nunnery belonging to the *Religieuses Hospitalières de Saint-Joseph*.[7] Invariably a brave volunteer would have to jump the wall and recover the ball without getting caught by vigilant nuns. Jumping over the wall one time, John Symon was surprised to find a hidden orchard in downtown Montreal. "I played volleyball many times with Bob," recounts one participant. "He got mad when people didn't pass the ball three times. Bob couldn't see properly nor hit the ball well. But he encouraged us to play cooperatively; we all got it! We supported this and respected Bob. It brought us all joy to be respecting the rules. We enjoyed it when we were on his team and had good times playing volleyball."[8]

A federal OFY grant was secured to pay some minimal salaries for volleyball organizers, but Silverman was too old to qualify for this program. He then simply worked as a volunteer.

Did Losing His Job Lead to Bicycling?

Regan recalled Silverman in 1974 being on strike from his job as second-language teacher that he had held for years with the Catholic School Commission (today the *Centre de services scolaire de Montréal*). A 1974 *Gazette* article describes how strikers were asking for wages and working conditions similar to what privately run schools were offering.[9]

This same article quotes Silverman as the union spokesperson. He spoke about teachers occupying their schools to set up "self-education programs," including languages, yoga, and macrame. Furthermore, they converted the cafeteria into a gymnasium to play volleyball there. "Volleyball is the sport of strikers," Silverman told the *Gazette*.

A settlement eventually ended the strike, but one of the conditions on which management insisted was that Silverman—alone among all the teachers—would not be rehired.

For management, Silverman was either the most dangerous or the most difficult teacher to deal with. But losing his teaching job provided him an opportunity to delve into the bicycle movement.

Scraping and Scrounging for Money

Regan also described Silverman as living precariously, "scraping and scrounging for money." At the time, Silverman typically worked for six months, and then collected EI for another six months, supplementing his income with speaking engagements. "He lived in low rent apartments." Silverman made himself business cards over this period, variously presenting himself as a "poet and essayist" and "natural vision improvement (specialty: presbyopia)."

Despite living precariously, Silverman spent much of his life as a volunteer board member with various non-profit organizations, including the Association récréative Milton-Parc that sponsored the volleyball games in Jeanne-Mance Park.

Summer Camp for Inner-City Residents 1980 to 2015

Silverman was also part of the board of what is now the *Centre de loisirs multiethnique Saint-Louis* (formerly University Settlements) at 3555 St-Urbain Street. This is where Silverman began playing indoor volleyball. While on this board, he learned that this same organization owned a family camp on a small lake near Chertsey, northeast of Montreal.

Silverman suggested to Regan that their volleyball group visit *Camp Familial St Urbain* in late June and early September, just before or after when the summer camp was open for families. And thus began a tradition where—for over three decades—buses of multi-ethnic, inner-city adults and children rode north for an hour into the forests and hills for a weekend of volleyball, swimming, barbecues, and relaxation. Many of these urban dwellers did not have easy access either to cars or to the countryside.

"We went to Camp Familial St Urbain every year from 1980 to 2015," said Regan. "Bob had his own private cabin there; it was his place of honour. Bob was involved with starting volleyball; he was well respected. He was a big part of what we did."

The Handbook of How to Run a Vélorution

IN TERMS OF HIS POLITICAL ACTIVISM, Silverman was very influenced by the writings of Saul Alinsky and his book *Rules for Radicals*. The American establishment has been under "relentless attack from a bespectacled, conservatively dressed community organizer who looks like an accountant and talks like a stevedore," wrote Eric Norden for *Playboy* magazine in an extensive 1972 interview with Alinsky.[1] A criminologist by training, Alinsky is described as "the founder of community organizing."[2] Alinsky notably worked "helping poor communities organize to press demands upon landlords, politicians and business leaders."[3] Attacked by the *Chicago Tribune* once, he responded that "unlike humorless radicals, I have a hell of a good time doing what I'm doing."[4] United Farmworkers Union founder Cesar Chavez was among Alinsky's disciples. Hillary Clinton wrote a thesis on Alinsky and his writings. Conservatives often try to demonize him, linking both Clinton and former US president Barack Obama to Alinsky, but they also try to appropriate his theories for their own causes. Michael Patrick Leahy, an early Tea Party leader, wrote *Rules for Conservative Radicals* in 2009, as a reference to Alinsky's work.[5]

Much of MàB's strategy seemed to have been taken from the pages of Alinsky's work, a summary of which might be:

1. Power is not only what you have but what the enemy thinks you have.
2. Never go outside the expertise of your people.
3. Whenever possible, go outside the expertise of the enemy.
4. Make the enemy live up to its own book of rules.
5. Ridicule is man's most potent weapon. There is no defence. It is almost impossible to counterattack ridicule. Also, it infuriates the opposition, who then react to your advantage.
6. A good tactic is one your people enjoy.
7. A tactic that drags on too long becomes a drag.
8. Keep the pressure on.
9. The threat is usually more terrifying than the thing itself.
10. The major premise for tactics is the development of operations that will maintain constant pressure upon the opposition.[6]

Silverman, of course, was not only a radical but also an anarchist. So perhaps for him these were ironically his "rules for anarchists." Anarchism as a political ideology is closely associated with the radical left. While some anarchists agitate for the violent overthrow of all governments, others favour a non-violent, evolutionary approach. Silverman fits into this second group. According to one definition, anarchy "is the state of a society being freely constituted without authorities or a governing body. It may also refer to a society or group of people that entirely rejects a set hierarchy."[7]

Again, Silverman fits into the second group. His actions, including the painting of "illegal" bike lanes and citizen repairs of the Jacques Cartier Bridge sidewalk, point to an impatience with or even contempt for government authorities to do the right thing. So, citizens must take the initiative.

Taking his cue from Alinsky, Silverman hurls a secret weapon at adversaries for which there is no retort. Morissette's poem describes it as "He gives the villains their pill, of paradox, of ridicule." MàB also notably followed Alinsky's advice on point eight, keeping the pressure on local authorities for some twenty years. Beyond Alinsky's advice, Silverman and the MàB cultivated very good relations with journalists. A large part of MàB's extraordinary success over two decades is due to its good media coverage, both in English and French. And politicians detest bad press. As journalists, we often wrote about Silverman and his colleagues. Afterwards, it was common to find long messages from him on our phones, thanking us profusely for what we had done. In these messages, Silverman did not skimp on superlatives, calling us "the best journalists ever." Of course, we suspected he said the same thing to others. To get journalists interested in your cause, it can help to be interested in them. John Symon once asked Silverman about a sixty-year-old article concerning his bookstore; he immediately recognized the journalist's name and gave some details about what he had recently written. Internal communications can be as important as external ones. For about two decades, MàB ran its own bilingual newsletter. Although largely a volunteer effort, it kept to fairly high journalistic standards. This undoubtedly helped the group promote its message. Today, social media functions as an alternative space for promoting causes.

Die-Ins

Silverman excelled in cyclodramas, but his specialty was in die-ins. As previously noted, the location of die-ins is critical, especially for the safety of participants. Some car drivers may attempt crazy and dangerous manoeuvres when their passage is blocked. And contrary to popular belief, tomato ketchup does not make the best fake blood. Try this MàB recipe instead:

Fake Blood Ingredients
- 3/4 cup corn syrup
- 1/4 cup water
- 1/2 teaspoon red food colouring
- 5 drops blue food colouring
- 2 drops green food colouring
- 1 tablespoon cornstarch

Preparation
In a small bowl, whisk together the corn syrup and water. Add the red, blue, and green food colourings and whisk until well combined. Whisk in the cornstarch and let the liquid sit for ten minutes to thicken. Makes one cup.[8]

Message from the UN Secretary-General for 2021
The following text, which echoes Silverman's Cyclists' Manifesto, is excerpted from a June 3, 2021, statement by Antonio Gueterres:

> Bikes are freedom; bikes are fun. They are good for one's health—physical and mental—and good for our one and only planet. Bikes are popular and practical, providing exercise and transporting us not only to school, stores and work but to a more sustainable future. World Bicycle Day celebrates this great power and highlights the importance of non-motorized transport in achieving the Sustainable Development Goals and combating climate change. Today there are an estimated 1 billion bicycles in the world—about as many as passenger cars. Their use spans the generations, from toddlers to older persons; once you learn, you never forget. Even before the COVID-19 pandemic, cycling was a critical mode of transport, and bike-sharing programmes were increasingly common, providing free or affordable access to bicycles for short trips. The crisis has changed transport needs and behaviour: with gyms closed many people turned to bicycling as a way to exercise while avoiding crowds. Many cities are rethinking their transport systems, with bicycles playing a vital role in offering an economical and non-polluting alternative [...] To all the world's cyclists on World Bicycle Day, whether out for sport, exercise or an errand, keep those wheels turning!"[9]

Many of his contemporaries describe Silverman as unconventional or eccentric. There were also suggestions that he may have been bipolar or neurodivergent.

It is also important to note the transformation that Silverman experienced once he found his calling with MàB. In his own words: "I used to be anonymous, sloppy, and shy. Then journalists started putting a microphone in my face. CBC called me to the morning radio show and *Le Jour* [newspaper] gave us two pages.

I gave classes at university for professors who agreed with our cause. I could handle all challenges. I learned to dress well for speeches."[10]

Le Jour was a daily newspaper founded by Yves Michaud, and by Jacques Parizeau—before he became premier—who both had very close ties to the Parti Québécois (PQ).[11] At the time, the editorial pages of established newspapers were not favourable to the PQ. Le Jour published from February 1974 to August 1976, promoting the idea of a Quebec as an independent country, but also covering news as any other daily. More of a popular success than a financial one, the newspaper closed after two years. (During the 1976 electoral debate, Liberal Premier Robert Bourassa taunted PQ leader René Lévesque for "not being able to manage a newspaper.") The idea that Le Jour published articles on Silverman, an anglophone bike advocate is perhaps comical, but also shows broad support for his cause.

"The bike changed me; I didn't think I could write a newspaper article. When others asked 'Who can write a bicycle manifesto?'[12] I volunteered."[13]

"I was invited to visit foreign countries." As a bicycle activist, Silverman travelled the world. In many cases, once at his destination, he travelled about by bike.

Others from dysfunctional backgrounds, or otherwise estranged from their families may have been drawn to Silverman, seeing him as something akin to a father figure. Key figures in MàB often congregated at Silverman's apartment at Christmas, doing a communal cleanup of his place. The motivation being that his poor eyesight made cleaning difficult for him.[14]

Silverman, the Writer, Public Speaker, and Ambassador

From a boy who failed both English and French final exams in high school, Silverman went on to become a poet, prolific writer, and a gifted orator in both of Canada's official languages. One former MàB-er, Alain Brunet (today a celebrity journalist with La Presse), says this about Silverman's speeches:

"Typical of a left-wing activist of the 60s converted to the socio-environmental cause, 'Bicycle Bob' was a colourful character, very passionate, sometimes perched on the fence separating serious speech from oratorical caricature."

"His Anglo accent was delicious; we even liked to throw around well-felt imitations of it during drunken and smoky evenings, which in no way altered our deep respect for him," said Brunet. "I will always remember his fiery speeches. They were very mobilizing despite our irresistible urge to fool around when his passion caused the pot to boil over. When 'cyclo-frustration leads to action' [...] we start pedalling!" wrote Brunet on social media in 2022.

Apart from his poetry—in English, French, and Spanish—Silverman was a regular contributor to MàB's newsletter and to the US-based *Bicycle Network*; a columnist for *Vélo Mag*; an occasional contributor to the anarchist magazine *Open Road*; a frequent blogger; and the writer of numerous guest editorials, press releases, and letters to the editor.

Starting with Vancouver's Habitat Conference in 1976, Silverman began travelling to conferences in various cities to learn and speak about the merits of urban cycling. In 1981, he was invited by Lord Mayor Ken Livingstone to speak at the Velo City Conference in London, England. In 1982 he was speaking in Kingston, Ontario, at traffic-calming information sessions and at the International Ecology Meeting in Winnipeg, Manitoba. Next year it was the Pro Bike Conference in Miami, Florida. In 1984, Silverman was at the Energy Probe Annual Meeting in Toronto as well as the Federation of Cyclists and Elder Hostelers in Minneapolis.

In 1989 he spoke at the Philadelphia Bicycle Coalition, as well as the Washington Area Bicyclists Association. In 1990, Silverman spoke at the Cleveland Bicycling Association in Ohio and attended the Conference on the Environment at Queen's University in Kingston. In 1992, he attended Conférence Vélo Mondiale Pro Bike—Velo City in Montreal. Silverman was in Havana in 1994 for the Bicycle, Transport of the Twenty-First Century Conference, followed by the Velo City conference in Basel, Switzerland, in 1996. He was in Cali, Colombia, for the International Conference on Bicycling Transport in 1998 while 1999 saw Silverman at the Lobbying for Preserving the City conference in Edmonton, Alberta. By the time he spoke at the Car Free Cities Conference in Lyon, France, in 2001, he had attended and spoken at seventeen such events.

Denied Entry at the US Border

The most eventful trip that Silverman undertook as a speaker was that time to Minneapolis in 1984. Crossing the border by train en route from Toronto to Chicago, he was singled out by immigration officials in Port Huron, interrogated, and deemed an "undesirable alien."[15]

Somewhat like when Silverman was deported from Cuba in 1964, he was caught at the border carrying "subversive" literature. In this case back issues of

Crossing the border by train en route from Toronto to Chicago, he was singled out by immigration officials in Port Huron, interrogated, and deemed an "undesirable alien."

the MàB newsletters featuring an unflattering cartoon of President Reagan in a bathing suit and the book *Autokind vs. Mankind* by Schneider. A letter from the Minnesota Coalition of Bicyclists inviting him to speak at the University of Minnesota did nothing to mitigate his case. After being sent back to Canada, Silverman found that there was no public transit to the next nearest border post. He ended up hitchhiking from Sarnia to Windsor and re-entering the United States in Detroit, this time without issue.

Silverman also served as an ambassador for the bike movement and had a reputation that went well beyond Montreal. Brunet also recalls a trip Silverman organized to New York in 1979, "As young eco-leftist activists, we discovered a man super turned-on and super-connected to American progressive networks, Bob really impressed us. He introduced us to some really cool people from all over New York that we bonded with" wrote Brunet on social media.

Who Is this Lumberjack?

Michel Labrecque of VQ sometimes accompanied Silverman on his trips abroad. "Bob had his ego; he was known internationally, a lot even. I was at the creation of the European Federation of Cyclists in London, we helped to create Pro Bike in the USA, Bob was known in the milieu."[16] Another official from VQ, Jean-François Pronovost, relates how international cycling advocates at various conferences in the US and Europe were always asking him about Silverman.[17] Similarly, Nick Peck—a bike activist from western Massachusetts—recounts wanting to attend a bicycle conference in Havana, Cuba, in 1994. He called *Bikes not Bombs* in Boston for information and was told to contact Silverman in Montreal about attending the conference. Despite such an impressive notoriety, Silverman was also capable of very unconventional behaviour, as also related by Michel Labrecque:

> I presented Bob [in a checkered shirt]—the great Montreal cycling activist—to the mayor of a commune in France. Bob started off with a bizarre French poem, the mayor looked at him as if wondering "who is this

lumberjack?" Bob was not dressed very smartly. When Bob spoke with his inimitable accent, he was polite [...] his voice grew louder and louder as he went along.[18]

The background decor for this presentation was very formal with a lot of gilding; it could have been a movie scene.

Vietnam and Cuba

SUFFICE TO SAY that Silverman was very active in opposing the Vietnam War; after the US withdrawal, he visited for cyclo-tourism. Silverman "bubbled" with enthusiasm, telling the *Gazette* in 1988 that he would lead the first organized tour for foreigners of that country since the Vietnam war ended, with the Mekong Delta as his main destination. My Tho, Vin Long, Can Tho, and Long Xuyen were other destinations during a two-week trip, which cost $2,800 per person. The bicycle caravan that he led was followed by a minivan and baggage truck. It is unclear how Silverman obtained permission from the Vietnamese government to freely visit this country where travel was difficult for Westerners at the time.[1]

Journalist Pierre Foglia wrote about Silverman's trips to Vietnam, recounting the millions of bicycles on the streets of Saigon, which he described as "a Tour de l'Île 365 days a year." Somewhat like Cuba, Vietnam was a cyclist's paradise at that time, boasting more bicycles per capita than anywhere on Earth. Silverman has written about how, during the Vietnam War, the People's Army of Vietnam (PAVN) used bicycles to carry supplies to its frontline fighters. In the early days of the Ho Chi Minh Trail, bikes were often used to transport arms and equipment from North to South Vietnam, though trucks ultimately replaced bikes, according to Tucker in his *Encyclopedia of the Vietnam War*.[2]

Silverman sometimes used a Vietnamese name, *Xe-dap Bob* ("Bicycle Bob"). While he told the *Gazette* in 1988 that he was quickly learning the language,[3] in 2020, he told us that he did not speak Vietnamese. Silverman also told the *Gazette* that he planned to marry a Vietnamese woman and—disenchanted with consumerism and cold winters—to never return to Canada. But he did come back and did so single. However, the cuisine from that country remained his favourite.

Since the late 1980s, there has been an explosion in the number of motorized vehicles in Vietnam—especially scooters. Vietnamese auto maker VinFast is now exporting electric cars to the US and Canadian markets.[4] Consumerism is rampant there now, too.[5] This transformation must have been to Silverman's chagrin. In the 1980s, he wrote several articles in Vietnamese publications, urging that the number of cars there be limited to a strict minimum.[6]

Figure 20.1. Silverman in Vietnam.
Source: MàB Archive.

Return to Cuba

Silverman returned to Cuba for several bicycle trips, perhaps to lead bike tours there as early as the mid-1970s.[7] Guy Montpetit recalls travelling there in the 1980s with Silverman and Morissette to deliver a container full of second-hand bicycles. But it was notably in the 1990s when Silverman returned to the island. Cuba was then in its "special period" of economic hardship, subjected to severe gasoline and diesel rationing. Almost overnight, Cuba's oil supply was reduced by some eighty percent.[8] This was caused by the collapse of the Soviet Union—and the end of subsidized Soviet oil coming to Cuba.

Some say that the Soviet collapse was accurately predicted in the book *Revolution Betrayed* (1936), meaning that Silverman's hero, Leon Trotsky, can also be considered a "prophet before his time." Adding to Cuba's woes, the US government severely tightened the embargo it had put in place in 1962. The 1992 Torricelli Act and 1996 Helms–Burton Act imposed sanctions on non-US companies trading with Cuba. US diplomatic relations with Cuba were only re-established in 2016, under the Obama administration, but trade sanctions were then tightened again under President Trump.

In efforts to save Cuba from economic collapse, authorities there embraced bicycling to an extent almost never seen anywhere else. Cuba purchased 1.2 million Flying Pigeon bicycles from China during this time as well as producing another half a million bikes domestically.[9] Castro's government converted five bus factories to manufacture bicycles, educated riders on how to ride, posted bicycle signs, dealt with cross-harbour bicycle ferries and shuttles, and encouraged workers to do job swaps so as to reduce the length of commutes. It is unclear how many bicycles were previously in Cuba, but in 1990 the island had about eleven million inhabitants. Probably more than one person shared each bike. The scarcity of cars on Cuban roads only added to the island's appeal as a "paradise" for cyclists. While still sympathetic toward the Cuban Revolution, it was an older, wiser Silverman who saw the island through new eyes. In early 2020, Silverman recounted how during the early 1960s in Cuba, it was fairly easy to get a car. "I didn't realize the destructive capacity of cars," he said, using terminology usually reserved to describe weaponry.

Silverman continued, "Fidel [Castro] thought it would be good if more Cubans had cars." Since leaving Cuba in 1964, Silverman had become familiar with writings by Ivan Illich, suggesting that "participatory democracy demands low-energy technology, and free people must travel the road to productive social relations at the speed of a bicycle."[10]

Beyond wanting to ride his bike there, Silverman often brought gifts to the island. He also teamed up with American bike activist Nick Peck to purchase and bring a precision medical instrument to the island. As Peck recalls, a pulse oximeter then cost some $500. They flew from Mirabel Airport in Quebec with the instrument in their luggage.

"This instrument had only recently been perfected and miniaturized in the USA, fitting onto a patient's finger; it indicates the level of blood oxygen levels. This can provide real time readings while the patient is being operated on," explains Peck. Havana-based oncologist Dr. Gilberto Fleites had requested the instrument. Upon receiving the pulse oximeter, he exclaimed: "This is incredible! Only little people give us stuff. This pulse oximeter is only the second one in Cuba!" Fleites later sent Peck an email that was used for a fundraiser in Stockbridge, Massachusetts, to recuperate what he and Silverman had paid for the instrument.

"I got back my half of the money disbursed, thanks to some wealthy ladies. I gave the rest to Bob," recounts Peck.

Another American activist who pedalled with Silverman in Cuba was John Dowlin of the Bicycle Coalition of Greater Philadelphia. During a time of fuel shortages, bicycles played a big part in keeping people and goods moving in Cuba. For some, like Silverman, this only added to Cuba's charm; bicyclists could then ride down the national highway and barely see a car. However, some commentators, such as Manuel Franco, suggest that the country's population was verging on malnutrition.[11]

In April 1993, Silverman attended an international symposium on urban cycling, presented in Havana. Silverman was asked to speak at the Bicycle, Transport of the Twenty-First Century Conference in Havana. A banner over the stage read *La bicicleta llegó para quedarse* (The bicycle is here to stay).[12] One of the champions of Cuba's embracing bicycles during this period was Gina Rey, a renowned Cuban architect. Silverman wanted to meet with her in 1993, but she was apparently wary of the eccentric Canadian and kept him waiting a long time before cancelling the meeting. Silverman took all this in stride, apparently holding no malice. Almost twenty-five years later, Rey told another author that, during the special period, the 2.3 million inhabitants of Havana shared almost one million bikes, this number had since fallen to perhaps 100,000. Rey cited lack of road safety and the disappearance of bicycle lanes, as well as other policies that prioritize motorized transportation.[13] This situation makes a mockery of the banner at that 1993 conference. It also underlines the importance of continued government support in promoting a bicycle culture.

Silverman took another bike trip in 1997 with seventeen North Americans and seven Cubans. His description of this 1997 Cuban trip reads in part:

> The bike trip was lyric. It was like a beautiful dream. It was aesthetic in the extreme, unworldly; a short glimpse of paradise, rural Cuban variety. [...] From January 13 to January 20, we bicycled together on the mountain roads of Pinar Del Rio Province west of Havana. On the first evening we stayed in the Dos Hermanos campgrounds surrounded by mogotes, mountains of about 1,000 feet which rose vertically from the valley floor. When first painted (in the early 1900s), art critics of New York said that they were fakes for "nothing on Earth could be so beautiful."

"The highlight of course was the daily bicycling on virtually car-less roads which, additionally, were rather good. We would encounter about two cars a day. So there was no fear in our riding. We were expansive beyond belief as we feasted on the constant beauty on all sides."

"On the fifth day we encountered an amazing waterfall which cascaded from the rocks about 100 feet above. We took cold showers and swam in a pool of cold water at the base of the cliff in delirious, incredulous, stupefying joy." Peter

McQueen, a MàB member and now city councillor, was on that same trip; he added a different perspective to this incident:

"One time we stopped to swim at a waterfall. We had been riding all morning and were hot. But for the Cubans, it was winter and they were not keen on swimming at the waterfall."[14]

"Bob got up on a rock in front of the falls and began giving a speech that went on for some time. The Cuban commander of our group ordered one of his people to get behind Bob and make sure he didn't fall off the rock. The poor Cuban guy had to stand under the cold waterfall while holding onto the waistband of Bob's swimsuit. Bob seemed only vaguely *cognoscente* of this."

"Visitors and Cubans were laughing at this spectacle with Silverman giving a speech in rudimentary Spanish, using Communist terms reminiscent of the early 1960s."

"They were not laughing at him in a mean way. Bob has an incredible spirit that is funny and admirable. He was helping the revolution."

***

Silverman also describes visiting schools to present pens, pencils, and notebooks—in short supply on the island—to the Cuban school children.

"On several occasions I gave the oral presentation as I speak Spanish well," wrote Silverman. "In return the children sometimes sang a song for us. I brought an extra volleyball and net and had great pleasure when I publicly presented it to the staff at the Vinales campgrounds. I insisted that the volleyball equipment was for the use of all campers, not just for the best players."

"We had a truck to accompany us so when tired or ill, we would [hop aboard] the truck. I did it a few times to avoid the steeper hills." Others on the trip remark that Silverman was nonetheless in pretty good shape for a cyclist in his mid-sixties. Silverman and company also visited doctors, community organizers, bike shops, and an alternative health centre in the mountains. Silverman was very impressed with Cuban health care. Cuba is an anomaly, an

> Silverman was very impressed with Cuban health care.

impoverished nation with very good public health care and life expectancies (79 years), exceeding that of the United States (78 years), Mexico (77 years), or Brazil (75 years).[15] This is despite Cuba's per capita GDP being about one-tenth that of the United States and about half of that of Mexico or Brazil.

★★★

Silverman also talks about receiving a visit from the Cuban doctor Gilberto Fleites while in Havana. He had met Fleites two years previously when giving a conference on natural vision improvement. Fleites credits Silverman for saving his father's life after a heart attack and then kidney failure. Apparently, kidney failure was a side-effect of the pills used for treating the heart condition.

"I brought Gilberto *The Confessions of a Medical Heretic* by Dr. Robert Mendelsohn. There is a chapter in the book about the harmful side-effects of many drugs. This blew Gilberto's mind and he investigated the side-effects associated with the heart pill his father had been taking and noted the kidney danger. Then he and his father were able to persuade the Cuban cardiologist to stop the pills."

"Now [Fleites's] dad has completely recovered and jogs and bicycles every day," wrote Silverman, presumably in the late 1990s. "The father was a famous Cuban doctor who, unlike most doctors, stayed after the victory of the revolution. So I was very glad to be able to help these two amazing Cuban doctors just by bringing them a great book." Many Cubans did in fact leave after Castro's revolution. On his more recent trips there, Silverman remarked how the skin colour of the average Cuban had grown darker because of the numerous lighter-skinned—and wealthier—Cubans leaving.

Silverman and Politics

IN 1984, Silverman ran as a candidate for the Green Party of Canada (GPC), the first time the GPC presented a slate of candidates across Canada. He ran in the Laurier riding, but diverged from the party platform in calling for the abolition of Canada's military. David Berger of the Liberals easily won the riding while Silverman finished in sixth place, gathering 2.79 percent of the vote. Silverman maintained his ties with the GPC for a number of years; he recalled later sharing a stage with Elizabeth May, who led the party from 2006 to 2019. During the 2014 Quebec provincial election campaign, the Quebec Green Party made unsuccessful attempts to recruit Silverman as a candidate; he bowed out for health reasons.[1] Despite being a long-time Trotskyite, Silverman has never been a candidate for the Revolutionary Communist Party of Canada, which espouses Trotskyism.

"I felt more at home with the Greens than the Trotskyites," recalled Silverman in 2020.

Silverman also sometimes endorsed political candidates, most notably Michel Labrecque during his unsuccessful run for a council seat during the 2009 Montreal municipal elections. Labrecque was defeated by Luc Ferrandez, who became the borough mayor of Plateau Mont Royal and was a strong bike infrastructure promoter during his tenure.

Bob, the Anarchist

Silverman often described himself as an anarchist, a term that has different definitions. Given that he ran twice as a political candidate, Silverman was not espousing the violent overthrow of all governments, but rather citizen initiatives to supplement official or spur governments into doing the right thing. Silverman has been very involved with citizen initiatives such as the clandestine painting of unofficial bike lanes and repairs to the Jacques Cartier Bridge sidewalks. All this points to low expectations of governments and high expectations of the populace, if properly organized.

Silverman wrote an article in *Open Road*—the most widely read anarchist newsletter from 1976 to 1990—about the anarchist elements in the Montreal bicycle movement. It subsequently became the most popular article ever published in *Open Road* and was translated into more than twenty languages.

"[Bob] was happy when I told him that it was the most popular article ever," recounts Norman Nawrocki, who reported for *Open Road*. "He really captured peoples' imagination."

Anarchists in Political Office?

Is it a contradiction to see an anarchist running for political office? Not according to some. The architect of anarcho-electoralism is Murray Bookchin who believed that anarchists elected to office would have a different agenda. During the Spanish Civil War, some anarchist militants became ministers in the Republican government, believing that this administration had been cleansed in some fashion because of their anarchist backgrounds.[2]

Sex and Drugs and Rock and Roll?

Silverman came of age at the beginning of the sexual revolution and as the alternative counter-culture gained popularity across North America. He was inspired by San Francisco's City Lights Bookstore, which was associated with Charles Bukowski and Timothy Leary, linked to alcohol and LSD, respectively. But Silverman did not make heavy use of either.

"Bob didn't do a lot of drugs," maintained Terry Regan who knew Silverman well for over thirty years.[3] "He took some LSD, was not a big drinker, smoked a little bit, and was sometimes a woman-chaser."

"We often went drinking at Henri Richard's tavern,[4] but Bob wouldn't have too many beers," continued Regan. Regan's description seems to be corroborated by Silverman's cautious style of bike riding, something that would jibe with not taking too many risks in other aspects of his personal life. In regard to relationships with women, Silverman may have had a fetish for women's wrestling. This rather obscure sport is typically performed topless. He once wrote an admiring poem to former Belgian champion Beatrice Goffin, whom Silverman described as "a friend."

Instead of rock and roll, Silverman said his preferred music was classical, especially Vivaldi.

★★★

Montreal's "gay village" has migrated east of Berri Street in recent decades, but Silverman's Seven Steps Bookstore was located in the centre of the gay village of 1960. This seems to have been a non-issue for Silverman. He has criticized Fidel Castro, one of his idols, for not being more tolerant of Cuban homosexuals. Silverman also praised Claire Morissette, among many other perceived virtues, "for being androgynous."[5]

Silverman, the Cyclist

Silverman was unconventional in many ways, and this extends to his use of bicycles. While many cyclists obsess about technical aspects of their bikes, Silverman seemed indifferent to such things. He could have difficulty telling his bike from others despite obvious differences in brand names, frame colours, and accessories. He acquired many of his bikes second-hand.

Even when living precariously, he kept three bicycles: a good one for the summer, a "clunker" for winter riding, and an (adjustable) folding bike that could be lent to guests. Later, after moving to Val-David and living in a more affluent manner, the backyard shed was filled with his bikes, which he would gladly loan to guests.

He was a winter cyclist before there was a term for such things, going about on his bicycle in the coldest weather. In his younger days, Silverman was an avid skier and he saw winter biking as a similar sport, "only more fun." Regarding the use of bike helmets, Silverman wrote: "Obviously, it would be better and safer if bicycle riders wore helmets. I always do. But imposing its use and fining those not wearing them is another matter. Education, not coercion, is the best path here."[6] Despite his claim of "always using a helmet," there are photos of Silverman on a bike without a helmet.

The MàB maintained that mandating the use of bike helmets discourages cycling. In an article Silverman wrote in 2000,[7] he pointed to how a helmet law in Australia led to a thirty percent reduction in the number of cyclists there. Silverman also noted a study by Hillman published in the *British Medical Journal*[8] indicating that cyclists, on average, tend to live two years longer than the general population. Analysis of the risk of injury or death from cycling was factored into these results, indicating a significant net health benefit. It follows that helmet laws could thus be detrimental to public health if they diminish the number of cyclists. While jurisdictions in North America often mandate cyclists to wear helmets, such regulations are rare in Europe. Silverman was generally a prudent and responsible cyclist, though not always coming to a complete stop at stop signs.

There are also photos of Silverman wearing a gas mask—of the type used by troops in the First World War—while riding his bike. It is unclear whether this was out of genuine concern for his health and not wanting to breathe exhaust fumes, or as a protest against cars, or both. Whatever the case, the gas mask cannot have helped his vision.

How Silverman, whose eyesight was very poor, managed to ride his bike in busy traffic for so many years without serious injury remains a mystery. Does it lend credence to the notion that Silverman's unconventional vision therapies actually worked?

The Anti-Car Crusader

Silverman's inspiration came from many authors he has read, notably Ivan Illich. Urbanist Jane Jacobs, another author he admired, wrote in *Dark Age Ahead* that "[it was] not TV or illegal drugs but the automobile [that] has been the chief destroyer of American communities."[9] Silverman's father was no fan of his son's anti-car crusade, claiming that he "was taking away jobs from auto workers."[10] This might have been a backhanded compliment, suggesting that Silverman actually had had the power to tackle the mighty car industry. In a 1976 interview, Silverman compared cars to slums and napalm bombs as "things that do not have a right to exist" and claimed that MàB is a "world leader" in combating cars. He compared his group to a US association, Zero Automobile Growth, which advocated for reducing the number of cars in the United States.[11]

Silverman was also very impressed by a presentation that lawyer Bradford Snell made to a US Senate subcommittee in 1973 entitled "American ground transport: a proposal for restructuring the automobile, truck, bus, and rail industries."[12] This presentation accused automaker General Motors (GM) of acting like a "sovereign economic state" over previous decades. Together with partners such as Standard Oil and Firestone, GM allegedly worked actively to sabotage public transit across North America. The purported motive was to replace streetcars with buses and replace buses with cars, greatly increasing GM's revenues. Silverman has written about how "one bus can eliminate 35 automobiles [...] one train can supplant 1,000 cars or a fleet of 150 cargo-laden trucks." The profit motive here is obvious, but apart from corporate revenues, this is a move toward more polluting and higher energy consumption transport.

Snell's work laid the groundwork for a conspiracy theory that big business deliberately ended the streetcar era in most North American cities.[13] For example, Montreal's streetcar network was decommissioned in 1959, replaced by buses. While this theory is not universally accepted, Silverman certainly subscribed to it, pushing the idea in many conversations. Silverman also pointed out GM's role in establishing dedicated highway funds in the United States. From 1945 to 1970 some $156 billion was disbursed, leading to the construction of hundreds of thousands of miles of highways. During this same period, only sixteen miles (twenty-five kilometres) of subway were built in the United States. In situations with no viable alternative transportation methods, millions of people are thus forced to drive to work or school or for other purposes. Huge tracts of land are also consecrated for roadways, parking lots, etc.

When Silverman wrote about traffic fatalities, he used terminology such as "destructive capacity" to describe the carnage caused by cars. Many more suffer indirect health effects from cars such as respiratory illnesses caused from tailpipe emissions or obesity caused by lack of exercise; all this has been confirmed by scientific research.

Others still are put into debt trying to finance car purchases, insurance, fuel, maintenance, and parking costs. Referring to the aggregate appetite cars and their infrastructure create for steel, oil, rubber, glass, asphalt, and cement industries, Silverman contends that "there could be no better vehicle to advance corporate values in the whole society than the automobile" (see The Cost of Cars section in the Annex). Silverman also pointed to the lack of social contact with fellow travellers that car drivers experience, compared to pedestrians or cyclists who can easily stop and start long conversations with people they meet.

***

Terrence Regan told us of "Silverman's dirty secret: that he drove a taxi in the mid-1960s," an experience he did not seem to enjoy. During his bookstore days, Silverman also drove a blue Volkswagen Beetle, viewed by some as the "un-car" of its time. Silverman attempted suicide and nearly died due to carbon monoxide poisoning from a car tailpipe, an experience told and signalled in the title of his poem, "Killed by a Car." Edith Rosenkranz—the apparent love of his life—was killed in a 1972 car accident. Although she had already left him for another man, her death profoundly affected Silverman.

Given all the above, it is no small wonder that Silverman's Cyclists' Manifesto (see the Annex) calls for "cars to be replaced by bicycles in the long-term." This manifesto clearly presents cars as the problem and bikes as the solution. It is also no wonder that Silverman and colleagues protested the Montreal Auto Show, an event that markets and glorifies cars. Silverman was unabashedly anti-car. Silverman stopped driving a car in the 1970s and resolved to never again embark in one again. Over the years, especially as he became less mobile on a bicycle, Silverman relaxed this resolution. He also later altered his demand about "cars to be replaced by bicycles," specifying that he meant in urban settings.[14]

Speaking in 2020, Silverman suggested that these arguments against cars are even stronger today. "We didn't know then [in the 1970s] about climate change."

Some obituaries for Silverman in early 2022 declared that he "achieved everything he asked for," but this is not quite true. Silverman's first *yahrzeit* (anniversary of his death) almost coincided with the 2023 Montreal International Auto Show, an event that he once promised "to drive out of town."[15] The 2023 edition was held at Palais des Congrès after a two-year hiatus due to the COVID-19 pandemic. Attendance was down to fewer than 150,000 attendees, or about seventy-five percent of pre-pandemic shows, prompting concerns about whether the event was still viable.[16] Many visitors were disappointed because there was much less to see compared to previous editions, with only a single floor of exhibition space instead of the usual three. Consequently, many visitors also vowed not to return in 2024.[17] Electric cars were front and centre, touted as "environmentally friendly," but Silverman would never have bought that propaganda. Perhaps he would have been pleased to know that a virus might have mortally wounded an event he so reviled. Similarly, Montreal is not (yet) a car-free city, nor has justice been achieved for the Palestinians. Additionally, his goals of challenging conventional medicine were largely unmet. Silverman had the *chutzpah* to often strive for things that others considered hopelessly ambitious, and he was surprisingly successful. Given enough time, would he have achieved all his goals?

Our Own Experiences with Silverman

One of John Symon's most enduring memories of Silverman is the two of them attempting to pedal part of the *Route verte* from Sainte-Thérèse to Laval one afternoon in 2009, verifying if that part of the network was complete. Silverman, in his mid-seventies, was twenty-five years Symon's senior but easily able to keep the pace. Despite his eye problems, he had no trouble finding the bike path as it twisted and wound through unfamiliar suburbs. There was one section of a bike path that was rather secluded; Silverman immediately noted that this might be a problem for female riders who can feel more vulnerable. "Bike paths are only truly successful when women feel safe riding them," he proclaimed. The most remarkable, however, was his enthusiasm. "We made it!!" Silverman loudly exclaimed as we finally reached the city of Laval on this bike path; Lewis and Clark were probably more subdued in 1805 when they finally saw the Pacific.

What Made Silverman Tick?

For more than half a century, Silverman was a tireless community activist. Most of that time, he was unpaid for his work. Where did his energy come from? Some commentators noted that in his latter years, when Silverman was old and tired, his speeches picked up in tempo as he went on, as if Silverman drew energy from the crowd around him.

"He had boundless enthusiasm, there was a lot of joy in this gentleman," recounts Marianne Giguère, the Montreal city councillor responsible for active transport. "When he talked about his struggles, his difficulties, he never presented things from a negative point of view, but always a positive angle; how beautiful it would be. I knew him as an old man, but I don't see how he would have changed: always humorous, even his lexical approach was festive with lots of smiles."

Yvon Dinel, who was in the MàB from 1984 to 1990, described Silverman as: "having a very particular laugh: he almost cried, impressing others in discussions. I was in my twenties and surprised to see a guy of my father's age who was so committed and radical with poetic political ideas." Silverman was a Jew who demonstrated in support of Palestinians. He was an anglophone Montrealer who invariably spoke French. Ray Gottlieb describes Silverman as the embodiment of Thomas Paine's words: "My country is the world, and my religion is to do good." Silverman's favourite quotation, however, is from H. G. Wells, "Every time I see an adult on a bicycle, I no longer despair for the future of the human race."

There is some mystery about the origin of this quote attributed to Wells. While he was a cycling enthusiast, it is unclear when or where Wells wrote it. The first recorded occurrence of the quote in print can be traced back to a 1988 letter-to-the-editor published in Bicycle USA magazine. Silverman was the author of that letter!

It is unknown whether Silverman—a voracious reader and former bookstore owner—discovered a quote by Wells overlooked by others; if he embellished something said by Wells; or simply fabricated the quote. But we like it and are using it here.

The Visionary with Poor Vision and Other Contradictions

All of us have contradictions; for Silverman a most notable one involved his vision problems that he suffered from for most of his life. In the end, he was almost blind as a result of macular degeneration, cataracts, presbyopia, and "birdshot" chorioretinitis. Yet even in his seventies, Silverman regularly cycled on busy streets and apparently was unscathed by injury.

France Lebeau, a riding companion who feared for his safety, suggests that Silverman memorized the layout of streets where he frequently rode, a technique some blind people use for where they walk regularly. This may be true, but it does not explain how he could avoid cars, pedestrians, and other moving objects along his way.

"Age-related macular degeneration (AMD) is a disease that affects a person's central vision. AMD can result in severe loss of central vision, but people rarely go blind from it," according to the John Hopkins Medicine website.[18]

"A cataract is a clouding of the normally clear lens of the eye. For people who have cataracts, seeing through cloudy lenses is a bit like looking through a frosty or fogged-up window. Clouded vision caused by cataracts can make it more difficult to read, drive a car (especially at night) or see the expression on a friend's face," according to the Mayo Clinic website.[19]

Presbyopia is defined as "a visual condition which becomes apparent especially in middle age and in which loss of elasticity of the lens of the eye causes defective accommodation and inability to focus sharply for near vision," according to Merriam Webster's online dictionary. Those afflicted can often see well at a distance, but not up close. And "farsighted" was a very good adjective for Silverman, described by some as "ahead of his time."

Symptoms of "birdshot" or "shotgun" chorioretinopathy include floaters, blurred vision, photopsia (flashing lights in eyes), loss of colour vision and nyctalopia, also called night-blindness. In an eye examination, light-coloured spots on the retina are seen. The name of the condition comes from those small light-coloured spots, reminiscent of the scattered pattern of pellets from a shotgun. All the above conditions can be age-related according to conventional medicine, but there are other risk factors. Silverman wrote that he developed chorioretinitis as a young child from to the emotional shock of seeing his disfigured paternal grandmother, claiming that this shock perforated both his retinas.[20] Without giving any references, he cited how some Cambodian women became blind from the emotional shock of seeing their husbands or children tortured.

Some people might be skeptical of Silverman's explanation of how he developed birdshot chorioretinitis, but one expert finds it reasonable. Ray Gottlieb, a retired optometrist (University of Berkeley, 1964) with a PhD in Humanistic Psychology/Human Sciences (Saybrook University, 1978), knew Silverman well. The two became friends after meeting at the North American Symposium on Natural Vision Improvement in Virginia Beach in 1999. While they sometimes discussed Silverman's vision problems, Gottlieb was not Silverman's optometrist.

"Silverman's chorioretinitis could have been psychogenic or psychological," said Gottlieb. "This sort of explanation is becoming more mainstream. There's more and more evidence about how such things can affect our physical and mental health. But I never heard Bob mention his grandmother in connection with this."

Gottlieb is also not too surprised by the apparent paradox of Silverman not recognizing friends from a very close distance, yet still being able to safely ride a bicycle in traffic. "It is not unusual for patients with such vision problems to have ups-and-downs; lighting can be a big factor and on a dark day they will not see so well."

Gottlieb writes that he eliminated his own myopia using Bates natural eye-improvement methods and prevented the onset of his presbyopia using an approach he invented: "The Read without Glasses Method." Such methods are not accepted by conventional medicine.[21] The Bates Method "defies the traditional belief that vision problems are genetic or age-related and therefore unavoidable. Ophthalmologist William H. Bates has shown that eyesight is highly variable and can be improved as much as it can be worsened by conscious choice and unconscious habits," according to the Association of Vision Educators.

Gottlieb, who lives in Florida, visited once with Silverman in Val-David, and the two often spoke by telephone. Silverman was enthusiastic about having Gottlieb's presbyopia reduction chart translated into French, Russian, Spanish, and Vietnamese. Another paradox was Silverman's apartment in Val-David, which was essentially an art gallery, decorated with dozens of colourful paintings. Some former colleagues from Montreal expressed surprise at Silverman's good taste. Others asked how somebody who was almost blind did this? And why? Part of the answer might be Silverman's belief in something called *Syntonic Optometry*, which is described on Ray Gottlieb's website as "the biological and psychological impact of light and colour and how it is used as a therapy to protect, preserve and promote visual and mental capacities."[22] Silverman's Val-David apartment was also spacious and well-lit. Perhaps for those reasons, mosquitoes and other biting insects did not seem to come into Silverman's apartment despite his leaving the balcony doors wide open during "blackfly season" in May and June.

Silverman was a strong believer in some unconventional remedies for vision problems. One of the more memorable of these were eyeglasses made of mesh; he would walk around in public wearing what looked like fly swatters on his face. The reader will appreciate Silverman's courage of his convictions to so readily do something that made him look quite ridiculous.

Every morning, he repeated as a mantra "there is nothing wrong with my eyesight." Was it mind over matter?

Being a strong believer in alternative remedies for vision improvement and emotional healing did not necessarily preclude Silverman from availing himself of modern medicine; he may have had cataract surgery around 2008. Silverman also promoted Vita-Lite light bulbs, which replicate the light spectrum of sunlight, selling these as a sideline. Ostensibly, this was another activity that supplemented his modest income. The only problem was that Silverman often gave the thirty-dollar lightbulbs away for free, reminiscent of how he encouraged customers at his bookstore not to buy books, but simply borrow them.

Silverman has given conferences on vision improvement. In this regard, he was a follower of both Gottlieb and of Aldous Huxley. Readers might be more familiar with Huxley as the author of *Brave New World*, but he was also an advocate of the Bates Method, writing about it in his 1942 book *The Art of Seeing*. The Bates Method, and associated eye exercises, are not endorsed by the scientific community.[23]

Silverman's resumé also lists a diploma in vision improvement given by the Jane Goodrich Institute in Queensland, Australia, in 1991. (Jane Goodrich is also known as Janet Goodrich.) The Jane Goodrich Method for eye improvement promises that people can learn how to see clearly naturally without glasses, contact lenses, or surgery.[24] After visiting Australia, Silverman wrote this poem:

> MY MOTHER SAID
> "Get a degree!"
> So you'll have
> some security!
> a place on the hierarchy!"
> So, now,
> I've got my Ph V.
> a degree
> recognized by only Janet and me

Silverman claimed that his optometrist confirmed a marked vision improvement following use of such unconventional methods.[25] One associate notes that Silverman "had a lot of trouble with his vision. But he worked assiduously at it, putting his heart and body into it. Nothing would discourage him, no matter the resistance."[26] Silverman's vision problems might also help explain his unusual character. Apart from the determination and discipline alluded to above, there may have been something else. In a curious passage in his writings, he once thanked his grandmother for ensuring that he will never get "tunnel vision, a narrow overspecialization, encouraged by the school system and so destructively common."[27] We get only this tantalizing tidbit, there is nothing more.

As for being a visionary with poor vision, the ability to imagine and conceptualize things can be independent of one's eyesight. One of the world's greatest composers, Ludwig von Beethoven, was completely deaf by about 1814 yet continued to compose beautiful musical almost right up until his death in 1827.

The Reincarnation Paradox

Despite being raised in a Jewish tradition, Silverman believes strongly in reincarnation, a concept usually associated with Buddhism and other Eastern religions rather than Judaism.[28]

"Silverman started believing in reincarnation, saying he used to be a poet in seventeenth-century Spain," recounts Dimitri Roussopoulos. "I would meet Bob socially and listen politely to what he told me. It was part of his persona."

Roussopoulos has known Silverman for over sixty years and has many positive adjectives to describe his friend. But telling others matter-of-factly that you are the reincarnation of a Spanish poet who has been dead for five hundred years is not typically normal, socially acceptable conversation. Silverman, however, was uninhibited about such things. Another paradox is that those who believe in reincarnation often also tend to believe that "unborn souls choose their parents."[29] Yet it is difficult to reconcile this notion with Silverman's "choice" of father.

Silverman, a Jew, also joined a Montreal Mennonite congregation, not for spiritual reasons, but rather ideological ones. He appreciated their pacifism and how this church sent humanitarian aid to North Vietnam during the war. Perhaps even more so because the role of pastor was rotated through the congregation, not unlike how Silverman liked to see volleyball teams rotate through the various positions.

What Does Astrology Suggest?

Chinese astrology, which functions by birth year, describes the behaviour of those born under the sign of the rooster (in 1933) as "no matter how difficult something is, they won't give up."[30]

According to Western astrology, which functions by birth date, Silverman should share personality traits with others also born on November 30. This list includes Sir Winston Churchill and Abbie Hoffman. Churchill warned the world of the dangers of Nazi Germany, then showed tremendous determination to win the Second World War against what initially seemed like hopeless odds. All this echoes in Silverman's determination to advance cycling against similarly daunting obstacles. Churchill ultimately won against the Nazis, only to lose the 1945 election. Silverman also had a pattern of achieving the impossible, then losing control. Both became brilliant orators despite neither being a stellar student at school. Both were described as "fearless" and did military service in Cuba early in their respective careers. Silverman espoused the "Four Vs" of *Vélorution*, volleyball, Vietnam, and vision improvement while Churchill simply preferred the V of victory. But by far the closest parallel is with Abbie Hoffman.

Comparison with Abbie Hoffman

Born three years after Silverman, Hoffman similarly came from a middle-class Jewish family, growing up in northeastern North America, in Massachusetts. Hoffman was outspoken in opposing the Vietnam War and was labelled the "court jester of the counterculture" for his theatrical and comical stunts.[31] One of these included disrupting the New York Stock Exchange by throwing real and Monopoly money down on the traders.

Hoffman organized for a pig to run as a Democratic Party presidential nominee in 1968. Another stunt included trying to convince soldiers guarding the Pentagon that Hoffman could make the building vibrate, turn orange, and levitate. For this, he had help from poet Alan Ginsberg. Silverman, of course, was also known for his theatrical and comical stunts; perhaps he was the "court jester of the bicycle movement." Both men were arrested for civil disobedience and went to jail for it. Both were very good at attracting media attention.

Silverman, as a bookseller, displayed a flair for marketing, but lent his books for free and once let a shoplifter go unreprimanded. Hoffman, as an author, wrote *Steal This Book* (1971),³² which was rejected by thirty publishers before becoming a bestseller, despite almost no publicity. Hoffman also authored several other books, including *Revolution for the Hell of It* (1968). Revolution was a big recurring theme in Silverman's life as well as its anagram, Vélorution. Hoffman also preached frugal living, something that Silverman lived for most of his life. Both were committed environmentalists. One reviewer claims that "Hoffman pioneered the use of humour, theatre, and shock value to drive home his points."³³ The same is obviously true of Silverman. Hoffman, a Marxist, co-founded the Youth International Party (Yippies). Silverman, a Trotskyite, co-founded le Monde à bicyclette. About the same time that Silverman, dressed as Moses for a cyclodrama, pretended to part the waters of the St. Lawrence River, Hoffman was a fugitive, living under an assumed identity upstream on the same river in Fineview, New York.

Both married twice. Hoffman had children while Silverman did not. Hoffman, who was bipolar, eventually committed suicide in 1989. Silverman made at least one suicide attempt.

Comparison with Don Quixote

Silverman indicated that he liked the comparisons to Don Quixote, the fictional protagonist of Miguel de Cervantes' *The Ingenious Gentleman Don Quixote of La Mancha*, first published in 1605. This character, also appearing in film as *The Man of La Mancha*, famously charged forward on his trusty steed to do battle with windmills. Quixote, the assumed name of Alonso Quixano, was a Spanish nobleman who read too much and subsequently lost his mind. He set out on a mission to serve his nation and restore chivalry, with his trusty companion, Sancho, at his side.

Don Quixote is often labelled as the first modern novel and is considered one of the greatest works ever written. It also holds the distinction of being one of the most-translated books in the world. In opposition to reality, *Don Quixote* offers a knightly story. First published as a comic novel, it was better received after the French Revolution because of its central ethic of the individual displaying courage and idealism and fighting for their beliefs in a world of inequality and disenchantment. The world depicted in Don Quixote is almost insane, and the chivalric battles of its main characters are just a comic sham in reality.[34]

Silverman, the Movie

Two documents suggest that consideration was given to making a movie about MàB; one is a letter and the other is a script. Silverman wrote a letter to actor Dustin Hoffman, trying to interest him in playing Silverman's role in a movie about the MàB. Hoffman played leading roles in movies such as The Graduate (1967), Midnight Cowboy (1969), Little Big Man (1970), Papillon (1973), and All the President's Men (1976). The Silverman movie never materialized, however.

That typewritten letter from Silverman to Hoffman, dated November 5, 1984, includes a short introduction of the work done by him and by Claire Morissette. After that, the letter reads: "We are now working on a movie script and think that you should play the central character in the movie: Bicycle Bob." There was no suggestion of who might play Morissette.

The letter chronicles Silverman's life as he goes from suicide attempt to bookstore to Cuba to Israel and back to Montreal. Bikes then make an appearance, soon followed by "criticism of conventional psychiatrists, use of alternative therapies such as rebirths, and eyeglasses for vision improvement, etc," as Silverman wrote in the letter. In short, many topics are crammed in.

Silverman's 1984 letter also makes mention of "the Bay of Pigs Crisis as seen from Cuba," apparently confusing the 1961 Bay of Pigs event—which he missed—with the 1962 Cuban Missile Crisis—when he was in Cuba.

"At one point, a Hollywood producer wanted to make a movie about Bob, and tapped Dustin Hoffman to play his character role. The producer then got cold feet, mainly because he didn't think it was possible to easily sell a movie filmed in Montreal," said Jacques Desjardins speaking at the Centre d'histoire de Montréal in 2015, marking the fortieth anniversary of MàB.[35] Some of Silverman's contemporaries think that the movie was a hoax: "I always thought that was bullshit," said Terrence Regan. Others, such as Desjardins, insist that the movie concept was real.

A 1981 article in the Gazette names the Hollywood producer as Lamont Johnson, claiming that he stumbled across the MàB while in Montreal researching another topic.[36] Johnson was the winner of two Emmy awards, one for directing Wallenberg: A Hero's Story (1985) and another for Lincoln (1988).[37]

Johnson apparently returned to Montreal in about 1982 with contracts to sign for the movie. The movie's budget was six million dollars, meaning that it had to make back at least as much. The marketing people perhaps then suggested that such a movie did not have much potential outside of Quebec and was thus, unlikely, to be profitable. The MàB archive contains a typewritten script of "The long bike path of Bicycle Bob," an outline of which lists fifteen point-form items in the following order: "Moses, Rebirth, Suicide, Cuba, Bookstore, Israel, Back to Montreal, Claire (including Chanson), Velo-baby, Street Painting, Subway & Court, Frog-cycles & mayor, Anti-car, Die-in, and Final Parade." The script looks like Silverman's work. Many of the above themes are readily understandable, but it is unclear what the "Frog-cycles & mayor" or "Final Parade" pertain to. It is surprising that Silverman lists his suicide attempt so prominently on this list.

"Rebirth" here could have a double meaning, pertaining to Silverman's rediscovery of cycling in 1969, but also pertaining to an alternative therapy technique that can allegedly be used to treat various conditions: self-destructive tendencies and patterns; post-traumatic stress disorder (PTSD); depression and anxiety; chronic pain; mental distraction and attention deficit hyperactivity disorder (ADHD); behavioral issues in children; low self-esteem; and addictions.[38]

It is unclear if Dustin Hoffman ever saw the letter. France Lebeau, the MàB archivist, says she never saw any evidence of a response from the actor. Silverman did not have the personality for mundane and dreary tasks such as sorting and filing, so he accumulated decades of press clippings, correspondence, photos, notes, etc., in an unorganized fashion. Perhaps somewhere there is further documentation about the Silverman movie.

The Influence of Silverman's Education

During the 1970s and 1980s, other bike groups were also active in Boston, London, Melbourne, New York, and San Francisco. An interesting comparison can be made between the cycling movement in Montreal and those in other major cities during the same period. As Jacques Desjardins said: "Without any money, MàB often got onto the front page of daily newspapers. We were on Radio-Canada, and CBC Radio for ten minutes daily. It was incredible for the 1970s. While bicycle activism was happening in many cities, the Montreal movement was more artistic and imaginative. I know this, after going to New York City and to Amsterdam."[39]

The presence of Silverman—with his interests in poetry, painting, and theatre—in MàB probably explains the more artistic and imaginative methods used by activists in Montreal. The apparent result is that Montreal is considered to be the foremost city in North America for cycling in 2020. For this, we can partly thank Silverman's education—both formal and informal. As noted, Quebec's artistic community was prominent in the 1950s, initiating what would become the Quiet Revolution. Painters, songwriters, and poets helped dethrone the Catholic Church and conservative politicians who held the province in the Great Darkness. Silverman deployed some of these same tactics for his Vélorution.

Although Silverman never completed his degree in liberal arts, he certainly appreciated the fine arts. This appreciation probably helped inspire him to emulate Moses or Icarus demanding a way for cyclists to cross the St. Lawrence River and to effectively do so with street theatre. Beyond that, he had a lot of political savvy. Abraham Weizfeld notes that "Silverman was not well educated but had great clarity of thought that enabled him to achieve great things [...] Bob was rational, directed *chutzpah*. As a political organizer, he knew what he was doing."[40]

While protests and demonstrations are old hat for unruly Montreal,[41] MàB took these to another level with cyclo-demonstrations. Following Silverman's recipe, a very small group of demonstrators could make a big impact on the next day's newspaper headlines and ultimately on public opinion. All this was done peacefully though civil disobedience was sometimes on the menu. Silverman had a flair for creating images that symbolize and emphasize the contradictions and highlighting the ridiculous in his adversary's views.

"I am the guy who started the street theatre," said Silverman.[42] "But the inspiration for die-ins came from Australia." Silverman, largely because of his contacts with John Dowlin from the Bicycle Coalition of Greater Philadelphia, was very aware of bicycling activism trends internationally. MàB may have been the second group worldwide to use die-in demonstrations; it certainly refined the idea. Street theatre was the medium, but Silverman also knew what to put as content. As per Morissette's poem, Silverman heaped scorn and ridicule on his adversaries, pointing out their contradictions and hypocrisies.[43] But contradicting himself, Silverman told us: "Not all that much preparation went into organizing the cyclodramas," while telling Andy Riga of the *Gazette* that "each event was meticulously planned."[44] When we challenged him on this inconsistency, Silverman offered this: "We got better at it. The cyclodramas took less planning as time went on."

Silverman's street theatre events often involved procuring or making elaborate costumes and stage props: the Moses costume and Icarus's winged bicycle come to mind. Scripts and pamphlets were devised, often in Canada's two official languages. Roles were choreographed in order to quickly make a coherent message. Very specific locations had to be scouted out, thinking about public access, visual backdrops, and sometimes public safety. Die-ins on the

> As per Morissette's poem, Silverman heaped scorn and ridicule on his adversaries, pointing out their contradictions and hypocrisies.

street often involved a sympathetic motorist staging a fake mechanical problem to block traffic and protect protestors. All this points to meticulous planning.

"We ensured the blocking of cross streets by one or two cyclists at each street in constant rotation," as one MàB describes the die-ins. "Drivers honked their horns, shouted at us or tried to sneak past. But we remained calm and jovial, trying to make them wait or convince them."[45]

In fact, Silverman described MàB's first die-in on Park Avenue in the Mile End district as unsuccessful because the wrong location was chosen: "In front of the YMCA on Park Avenue was the wrong place; outside of the old Eaton's (Sainte-Catherine West at Robert-Bourassa Boulevard, downtown) was the right place. The cyclodrama (die-in) went very well there and was better organized. We passed out flyers inviting the public to 'come die with us.'"

In referring to the unsuccessful die-in on Park Avenue, Silverman confided that "a lot of car drivers are crazy. A car almost hit people participating with the cyclodrama." On Ste Catherine Street West was a successful downtown location a one-way street where congestion slowed down traffic, making it easier to block the vehicle flow there. Silverman himself was not always present at all MàB cyclodramas and some of the group's actions might have been spontaneous, led by small cells. After all, this is the type of organizational structure (or lack thereof) of which an anarchist like Silverman would have approved. Another of Silverman's inconsistencies was when he declared to have "no special advice for similar groups today." He then drew up a list of remaining cyclofrustrations: scarcity of winter cycling routes; lack of bus racks on Montreal buses; and no bicycle access across Mercier Bridge—as causes to fight for. To draw attention to these causes, Silverman suggested holding parades and publishing a newsletter. He then added that publishing a newsletter—entitled *Vers une Ville Nouvelle*—was probably the most challenging activity that MàB undertook. Presumably this is because of all the tedious clerical work involved in publishing a newsletter.

The comment about him climbing a hill on a one-speed bicycle jibes with the authors' experiences of bicycling with Silverman. He was always in good shape for his age, but for some reason, ignored or eschewed new technology on bicycles; perhaps trying to idealize bicycles in their simplest form as Ivan Illich wrote about them. Yet Silverman was not a Luddite in other spheres and widely used electronic media to spread his messages.

Achieving the Impossible, then Losing Control

A recurring theme in all Silverman's activities—the bookstore, the bicycle movement, and participatory volleyball—is that Silverman proved himself a brilliant visionary in achieving something that initially seemed impossible. But in each case, he ultimately lost control of what he initiated.

"The MàB was very effective in capturing the imagination and helping people to see the potential. The group wanted to change the world, but lacked the administrative skills to do so," says Zvi Leve, a close associate of Silverman's.[46] This reflection probably most aptly applied to Silverman himself.

Silverman had a lot he could be boastful about but remained surprisingly modest. In his later years, Silverman often used the word "insane" to describe his actions of previous years, especially during the bookstore period. Despite numerous and generally glowing compliments from many contemporaries, sadly it seems to be his father's rejection of him that made the greatest impression on Silverman.

Claire Morissette's poem dedicated to him asks Silverman "to look at all of his thousands of fans," but in his later years, he seemed not to notice them. He was more preoccupied with his family's rejection of him, wanting this biography written to set the record straight so that his family would understand.

Milton Park Days

MILTON PARK is a neighbourhood just to the east of McGill University and is a portmanteau of Milton Street and Park Avenue. Once an affluent part of town, home to many of Montreal's business elite, the area fell into decline in the latter half of the twentieth century. By the early 1970s, a massive demolition of the area's greystone low rise mansions was proposed.[1] "[The] plan was to tear down everything but the institutions [i.e., hospitals and schools] and construct a new, shiny, modern city: high-rises, offices, and commercial buildings. The Drapeau city administration was thrilled, the residents were alarmed, and the Milton-Parc Citizens Committee was born," wrote Lucia Kowaluk,[2] describing these events. The same Dimitri Roussopoulos who introduced Silverman to political activism in 1959 was prominently opposing the demolitions.

"Bob was active with the Milton-Parc Citizens Committee during the struggle to save the neighbourhood," says Roussopoulos. "In 1972, he was arrested during a demonstration with 59 others when we occupied the offices of the developer on Park Avenue [...] Bob was one of the first ten who went on trial, along with myself. The McGill Daily published a wonderful photo of the ten of us, with our lawyer. The charge was 'public mischief,' which can carry a five-year jail term [...] The jury found us not guilty. Thereafter, charges were dropped against the others." Some demolition occurred to make way for the thirty-storey La Cité tower, which includes an office building, two residential towers, and an underground mall with a cinema. There was also a hotel later converted into student housing for McGill, but subsequent phases of the project were ultimately abandoned. Popular opposition to the project also spawned the Cooperative Housing Milton-Parc (CHMP), today the largest housing co-operative in Canada. This movement to save the greystones and create a housing co-op was active the same time as MàB was formed and used many of the same methods, including civil disobedience.[3] Phyllis Lambert and her Heritage Montreal group were also central in saving Milton Park from the wrecker's ball.[4] An associate of Silverman's from Save Montreal, Lambert is also a notable community activist and "the black sheep" of the Bronfman's, a very rich local Jewish family. A large mural erected in her honour in Milton Park includes a quote from Lambert: "Flourishing cities are run with democratic fairness where we can smell the flowers and hear the birds [our translation].[5]" Similarly, Morissette once described her ideal city as having "parking meters replaced by trees, trains instead of bridges blocked with cars, fountains at intersections, gardens replacing parking lots, parks in alleyways, and trees planted alongside and sometimes in the street."[6] Photographs from the MàB actions in the 1970s and early 1980s often show streets scenes with backgrounds almost devoid of vegetation, especially in Plateau Mont Royal. Since then, many trees and flowers have been planted there. As an early member of Save Montreal, Silverman also played a role, alongside Lambert, in this greening of the city.

★★★

Silverman had been living precariously before moving to La Petite Hutchison,[7] part of CHMP on Hutchison Street between Pine Avenue and Prince Arthur Street. A minimum of fifteen percent of the housing units are subsidized in agreement with the Canada Mortgage and Housing Corporation (CMHC), a Canadian crown corporation. Rents were thus capped at thirty percent of the tenant's annual income. For Silverman, this meant decent quality housing at affordable rents.

Perhaps more importantly for Silverman, at 3689 Hutchison, he was only a few steps away from the Jeanne-Mance outdoor volleyball courts. It is also a few minutes from Silverman's old high school and from McGill University. While never a student at McGill, he spent much time on the campus. The coffee shop at 201 Rue Milton Street where he celebrated his fiftieth birthday by reading his own poetry to friends is still there, though it is now a popular pizza restaurant. In short, this was Silverman's 'hood.

Naessens and Dismantling the Spaghetti Interchange

Silverman, a long-time advocate of alternative medicine, spoke in defence of Gaston Naessens, a biologist from France who lived in Sherbrooke, Quebec. Called "the Galileo of the microscope" by supporters, Naessens invented a new type of microscope for studying blood,

Silverman, a long-time advocate of alternative medicine, spoke in defence of Gaston Naessens, a biologist from France.

which led him to develop unconventional remedies to which he ascribed almost miraculous curative powers.[8]

"With a non-toxic serum he calls 714-X, Naessens has achieved complete remission: over a thousand cases of cancer and dozens of (cases of) AIDS. (But) instead of receiving the Nobel Prize, Mr. Naessens faces three sets of civil and criminal charges brought against him by the [Collège des médecins du Québec], including 'illegal practice of medicine,' 'fraud,' and most serious, 'criminal negligence contributing to death.' He could face heavy fines or even a prison term," wrote Silverman.[9] While there is strong anecdotal testimony in favour of 714-X, this does not constitute scientific proof nor have any clinical trials validated Naessens' claims. The criminal negligence charge was apparently related to one patient on 714-X who died after refusing treatment with conventional medicine.[10]

In 1989, Naessens was arrested by police in Sherbrooke, leading to a highly publicized trial in which Naessens was ultimately acquitted. However, access remains restricted to the 714-X serum, which is available by prescription through Health Canada's Emergency Drug Release Programme, but remains banned by the Food and Drug Administration (FDA) in the United States.[11]

***

Silverman also spearheaded efforts to tear down the "spaghetti-like" traffic interchange of Park and Pine avenues, a massive concrete structure more fitting of an interstate highway exchange than the intersection of two inner city roads.[12] That interchange was ultimately demolished in 2006. Silverman also worked to make Hutchison Street the first in Montreal to observe "Car Free Day," a worldwide event promoting alternatives to private vehicles.[13]

An Exemplary Member of the Co-op

Tenants of CHMP were expected to participate actively in co-op activities. During this time, Silverman was described as "an exemplary member of the co-op," working primarily on the co-op's external relations committee.[14] This notably meant liaising with the city and with other co-ops.

Being an exemplary member of the co-op did not necessarily mean that he kept his apartment tidy. One visitor described his place as saying "Bob had serious organizational challenges. He couldn't organize his clothes in a drawer. There were piles of information papers lying around. He was not able to pare down and eliminate things he didn't need."[15]

Meeting Ivan Illich

It is unclear if Silverman encountered his hero Ivan Illich at the 1976 Habitat conference in Vancouver. Certainly, the two spoke in 1994 when Illich came to speak at the Fourteenth Annual E. F. Schumacher Lecture at Yale University in New Haven. Silverman and his friend Nick Peck sat together in the front row during the speech. Afterwards, they chatted and Illich thanked Silverman for his work promoting bicycles.

Creating Oxygen Park

While Silverman was living in la Petite Hutchison Co-op, there was a small patch of land covered with asphalt on Hutchison Street, just north of Prince Arthur Street West with three linden trees growing on it. The privately owned piece of land, in Silverman's opinion, "was too small to do anything with." In the middle of the night, Silverman and other individuals, including Tooker Gomberg of MàB, tore up the asphalt in true anarchistic fashion, creating what they called "Oxygen Park." Nobody gave the group permission to create this park on private property. Justifying his actions, Silverman wrote: "Previously the space was a dangerous taxi shortcut. On several occasions a child playing there was nearly struck by a taxi."[16]

Silverman described the conversion of this area to greenspace: "at least fifteen neighbourhood children participated regularly in the construction by carrying asphalt and spreading earth as well as numerous adults from nearby and throughout the city [...] The Committee for the Construction of Park Oxygen paid out $1,000 for earth, sod, fine crushed gravel and paying to have the remaining asphalt removed." In September 2000, a party was organized to celebrate this new park involving singers, jugglers, dancers, and poets. Since Silverman carried out these actions, there has been recognition of how mini green spaces help mitigate urban heat islands and regulate storm waters. Sadly, this new park only lasted a few years before the local borough council authorized a developer to build on Oxygen Park.[17] And this was a supposedly "green" administration of Projet Montréal under borough mayor Luc Ferrandez.

"Unfortunately our administration gave a green light to building condo towers there," recounts municipal councillor for the area, Alex Norris. "But Oxygen Park was the inspiration for creating new greenspaces in the area. We also renovated the nearby Yvonne-Maisonneuve minipark." Norris says that he explained the dilemma to Silverman; the cost of compensating the developer was prohibitive for such a small area. Instead, the borough used its funds to make bicycling easier and safer everywhere. As Norris puts it, "Bob understood." But at least one unnamed co-op resident, interviewed years later, did not seem to understand. He spoke instead of "Projet Montréal selling out to the developer."

De-Paving Paradise

Today there is an organization in Toronto called Depave Paradise, which is a project of Green Communities Canada. It sponsors actions very similar to those Silverman undertook at Oxygen Park, typically converting unused parking lots into mini greenspaces. "Depave sites all across Canada have beautified communities, and created a real sense of belonging, motivating further environmental action and stewardship, and educating the public about stormwater issues in the process," reads an excerpt from their website.[18]

> ODE TO OXYGEN PARK
> It's only
> a bit of land
> in the heart
> of the city
> but it is profound
> and even sacred
> for it was polluted
> and dangerous
> whilst mad machines
> terrified small children
> usurped their playgrounds
> to save a minute
> we could not accept these perversions
> as our children's lives are precious
> so, in wrath
> we excavated their asphalt
> blocked the speeding danger
> with the asphalt's heap
> covered up the noxious substance
> with friendly earth,
> and covered up the pile
> and liberated land,
> with greenest grass
> now it's here

for all to see
to play and eat
or just pass through
where months before
only crazy taxis flew.

A Jew in Support of Palestinians

SINCE THE 1960S, Silverman professed sympathy for the Palestinian cause and has been active with the group Independent Jewish Voices (IJV) as well as with PAJU (Palestinians and Jews United). He was strongly influenced by writers such as Maxime Rodinson and Jean-Paul Sartre who described Israel's occupation of Palestinian territory as "colonialism." Silverman regularly picketed the Israeli consulate in Montreal, protesting the occupation of the West Bank since the 1967 Six-Day War. He also wrote articles supporting the Palestinian position. Silverman helped initiate the Jewish Alliance Against the Occupation, which later became the Alliance of Concerned Jewish Canadians. This latter group may have since merged with IJV.

"Supporters of these movements felt a responsibility to form an opposition to the Zionists in Israel," explains Abraham Weizfeld, an activist who worked closely with Silverman on this cause. "The Zionists are not representative of the Jewish Diaspora."

Visiting with Yasser Arafat

In 2000, Silverman was part of a delegation travelling to the West Bank: East Jerusalem, Jericho, Hebron, Gaza, and Jenin. During this trip, Silverman met Yasser Arafat, then leader of the Palestinian Liberation Organization (PLO) in Ramallah, as well as his brother Fathi Arafat. Arafat notably received the Nobel Peace Prize in 1994, jointly with Israeli prime minister Yitzhak Rabin and Rabin's minister of foreign affairs, Shimon Peres, for work on the Oslo Accords, attempting to secure peace between the PLO and Israel. Terms for these accords notably included Israel and the PLO recognizing each other and resolving their differences without violence. There are many reasons why the accords ultimately failed; most notably because Rabin was assassinated in 1995. Then in 1996, Benjamin Netanyahu, who opposed the peace accords, became Israel's prime minister.

Arafat probably believed that by surrendering 78 percent of historic Palestine, a Palestinian state could be created in the remaining 22 percent. But Israeli settlers continued to pour into the part that was supposed to be Palestinian. In 2002, Israel decided to build a 710 km wall to separate its people from the Palestinians; while still not completed, this wall remains a very divisive issue. Palestinians staged the second Intifada uprising from 2000 until 2005. It was in the context of this second Intifada that Silverman said: "There were a dozen of us who visited with Yasser Arafat. Everything in Ramallah was shot up to hell."

"Arafat was a nice guy, he said to us: 'just tell them you were here; tell them the truth.' Arafat called upon the Canadian government to intervene in the conflict and send a peacekeeping force. Then we shook hands and said *masalam* [goodbye]."

Silverman described Arafat as appearing "old and tired." In 2004, Arafat died under mysterious circumstances. Some suggest that he was poisoned by Israeli agents. Silverman and his delegation also met Israeli civil rights groups, lawyers, and conscientious objectors, as well as Palestinian feminists and ecologists. Among the environmental issues in this region is Israel's disproportionate water consumption that Palestinians consider "stealing of water."

Meeting with Arafat—viewed as a terrorist and war criminal by some—did not make Silverman popular within Montreal's Jewish community. For that and his other pro-Palestinian stances, Silverman said: "I got death threats and my sister didn't talk to me for [a] year and a half," as Worton wrote in the webzine, *Montréal Serai*. After the failure of Arafat's PLO to secure peace for the Palestinian people, and his death in 2004, the militant Hamas movement rose in power, ultimately gaining control of the Gaza strip in 2007.

Jews Speak Out against the Occupation

Shortly after returning to Montreal, Silverman co-authored "Jews Speak Out against the Occupation," an open letter condemning Israeli policies toward the Palestinians as published in the *Gazette* on November 4, 2000. That letter concludes with "We who are Jewish must demand an end to the war on the Palestinians, a proper respect for the UN resolutions recognizing the rights of Palestinians, end Israeli occupation of the West Bank and Gaza, a guarantee for Palestinian self-determination, and the dismantlement of the Israel-style apartheid system. It is not in our interests that we continue enforcing unjust conditions that perpetuate resistance and bloodshed. Solidarity with the Palestinian people is also in effect, solidarity with the Jewish people."

Three dozen prominent Jewish intellectuals signed this document. About half of the signatories were from Quebec, the rest being from Israel and the United States. Weizfeld used his connections to have Noam Chomsky, well-known MIT professor and social critic, sign. Strangely, Weizfeld, a close confidant of Silverman's, also claims that the two never spoke of his meeting with Arafat. Weizfeld only learned of that meeting when he was interviewed for this biography.

Silverman's position towards the Palestinians was tantamount to treason for many Jews in North America. Israel represents the Promised Land for them, a haven after having survived the Holocaust. But for Palestinians, the creation of Israel in 1948, which they call the *Nakba* ("disaster" in Arabic), meant the loss of their homeland and ongoing injustice. Some choose to overlook this injustice in the name of solidarity with Israel, but not Silverman. Palestinians sometimes call themselves "victims of the victims."

Moving to Val-David

SILVERMAN left Montreal in 2002 to spread the Vélorution to Salamanca in Spain. He returned to Canada for Tooker Gomberg's memorial in 2004; his protégé's suicide must have been a big shock. Then, in 2005, Silverman settled into a large loft in Val-David, a village of some five thousand inhabitants in cottage country about an hour north of Montreal. Set among forested hills with many lakes nearby, the village has a reputation for outdoor sports, such as skiing and rock climbing. It is also known for its artistic community and anti-conformist spirit. Silverman also became involved with a movement to provide social housing in Val-David and efforts to protect low-cost housing in a sector nicknamed Guindonville.

The loft, located at 2627 Chemin de l'île, was owned by Guy Montpetit, a renowned Quebec painter with whom Silverman had become friends. Montpetit who has notably created large-scale public art murals, was inspired by Paul-Émile Borduas, author of the 1948 *Refus Global* document that sparked Quebec's Quiet Revolution.[1] Montpetit and Silverman were previously acquainted, perhaps through their mutual friend, Armand Vaillancourt. As Montpetit puts it: "With his theatrical demonstration techniques, Bob got the attention of the public and decision-makers. He denounced how dangerous the city was for pedestrians and cyclists. His approach to urban renewal has earned him the admiration of several urban planners at McGill University. I knew him at the time of the first sit-ins of le Monde à bicyclette. I found his approach brilliant and he inspired many artists."

"I had designed a big house which was a potential workshop," continues Montpetit. "It was as if you lived in Old Montreal, a place where you could invite artists. When Bob saw it, he said: 'that's what I want!' I discovered how awesome he was: he didn't live for himself, but for others. He wanted people to be happy, less withdrawn."

Reasons for Moving

Some friends expressed surprise about his move to a small town. In 2004, Silverman articulately defended his choice of moving to Val-David, writing to the local newspaper, *Ski se Dit*, to enumerate the reasons.[2] These included the presence of a good bike path connecting to other towns, a volleyball court, street

Figure 24.1. FRAPRU protest.
Source: MàB Archive.

signs that are easy to read for the visually impaired, poems in the local newspaper, possibilities for kayaking on the river, and decent bus service to Montreal. In the first few years, Silverman could easily bicycle in season to the village centre about five minutes away. Not only did he initiate volleyball games among the senior artists, but he could also enjoy Vietnamese soup (pho) at his favourite bistro, the *Mouton Noir* (black sheep). The compact downtown area hosts many businesses and services.

"When Bob arrived here, he decided to form a volleyball club among senior artists," says Montpetit. "It was very original, the artists have a hard time talking to each other because they are competitive, they met for leisure to discuss: it worked for a few years. He called it: his geriatric games."

"He was funny and extremely brilliant. The volleyball was ingenious: people played sports to relax and became more open-minded," continues Montpetit. "Bob wandered around the town, we had jazz concerts on weekends, he became a tradition in Val-David restaurants." Montpetit also remarked how Silverman could look like a tramp; someone who had lost their way.

Filling the Loft with Artwork

The decor in his spacious and bright apartment was dominated by some one hundred pieces of art, including seventy oil paintings hanging from his walls. For the most part, the colours were vivid, adding gaiety and joy. The most foreboding painting is the portrait of Silverman as painted by Godfrey Stephens circa

1961, depicting him covered with screws. Among the items that Silverman brought with him were items dating from the Seven Steps Bookstore/Ember Coffee House days. Silverman soon began collecting paintings, prints, and sculptures from local artists to fill the walls of his loft. Apart from Montpetit, featured artists included Francois Cliche, Agnes Guay, Normand Ménard, Natalie Natalie (Liluushka), Lyne Pinard, Godfrey Stephens, Eric Van Ham, and Robert Venor. Silverman encouraged people to use his loft, which he baptized "Galerie de l'âme [gallery of the soul] chez Robert," for poetry readings, vernissages for artists, play readings, chanting, meditation, and more.[3] Was this the rebirth of the Ember?

"Robert Silverman is opening his gallery to host many more such events, welcoming and sharing his love of the arts," read text that he posted on the blog.[4]

Anna Louise Fontaine, a local poet, found Silverman to be a fascinating man. "He was interested in international news. He was lucid, without those compromises that often excuse exploitation and political nonsense. He never lost his protesting ardour. I knew him at a time in his life when he had mourned his sight. But he remained a *bon vivant*, he liked to party and eat well."

"Moving to Val-David slowed his life down. It meant that art could be his passion," recounts his friend Angela Bischoff. Silverman was also able to afford domestic help to keep his place well organized. His new-found affluence was presumably due to the fact that, while Silverman lived very modestly most of his life, he ended up receiving a pension of five thousand dollars a month from his family, besides what he had already inherited from his mother.

The Bike Path into Town

Silverman's loft was on a small island in the Rivière du Nord, accessible at one end via a car bridge and the other end via a small footbridge leading across the river to the P'tit train du nord bike path. This 200 km bike path, built on a historic former train track from St-Jerome to Mont-Laurier; it is part of Quebec's 5,300 km *Route verte* cycling network and also part of the 17,000 km multipurpose Trans-Canada Trail. Cyclists pedalling from the Pacific to

"Robert Silverman is opening his gallery to host many more such events, welcoming and sharing his love of the arts."

the Atlantic or vice-versa would commonly ride within a stone's throw of Silverman's apartment. This much is very appropriate.

One day, on this bike path, Silverman was near the old Mont-Tremblant train station, according to Marie-Josée Legault, his former home support worker. "A man on a recumbent bicycle stopped and Robert got up because he was fascinated by this bike. They started talking and when the man realized who he was talking to, he was overwhelmed. He insisted that I take a photo of him and Robert. He was with a star!"

Legault also relates how Silverman had a big impact on her life. "Robert was a pillar for me. Thanks to him, I left my job as a home worker to live from my passions. He taught me that it is important to know happiness."

Getting Away from Car Pollution

What is strange however, is that, born and raised in Montreal, Silverman seemed to be the embodiment of a city person. When asked in early 2020 why he had moved from Montreal to Val-David, he wondered out loud: "Was it a mistake?" Then he added "I got away from the pollution caused by cars."

Silverman often wrote in earlier decades about health problems—especially respiratory issues such as asthma—triggered by car emissions. Norman Nawrocki, a close neighbour in Montréal, believed that the move north "was for his health." In his later years, Silverman was less mobile and often complained of the cold. As with many rural locations, it can be difficult to get around in Val-David without a car, especially in winter. But he did take rides with friends who offered lifts in cars. Staying on top of world events, Silverman often followed Al-Jazeera, the state-owned international media broadcaster of Qatar.

Che Guevara Still with Bob

Silverman admired "Che" Guevara, sometimes watching documentaries about him. His apartment also had a large poster of "Che," but Silverman eventually took it down to avoid offending some people, recounts Reesa Roumel, his caretaker from 2013 to 2019. It is unclear who in particular was offended by Guevara, but this Cuban revolutionary hero remains a controversial character. Ho Chi Minh and Ivan Illich were among Silverman's other heroes, together with Claire Morissette. One of Guevara's famous quotes is "always be capable of deeply feeling any injustice committed against anyone, anywhere in the world. This is the most beautiful quality in a revolutionary." And this quote seems to embody much of what Silverman was about.[5]

Around 2009, Silverman and John Symon went up to visit friends on Lake Ouareau. There they learned how a very wealthy neighbour was using his economic clout to try and deny their friends access to the beach. Nobody was more upset about this than Silverman. Eventually he stopped reading because of his failing eyesight. While the Canadian National Institute for the Blind (CNIB) sent him audio books, Silverman claimed that they were mostly "garbage." He said that "normal people" read "normie" books, filled with fluff; most of these titles would be sent back to the CNIB, but every so often a good book would turn up. Silverman had an electronic book reader and would read that way. He also had a Text-to-Speech (TTS) program for reading articles online. Roumel explains: "Sometimes my voice would give out after reading for too long. With TTS, you can choose the voice you want to hear, the speed, etc."

"After I left, he told me that he missed his 'brain exercises' and asked me to please send him articles."

"I hired a housekeeper and a top vegan chef who made amazing food for Robert on a weekly basis," Roumel adds. "Robert had his crabby days, but he always made me smile." Silverman described his chef as "a wonderful woman" who was making him "eat well." This regimen of care was expensive, however. While the CLSC Sainte-Agathe-des-Monts[6] provided some nursing, Silverman paid for additional services out of his own pocket.

"He had a small inheritance over and above his pension," says Roumel. "One luxury that he afforded himself was buying the latest reading glasses. But two weeks later, I would find them forgotten in a drawer somewhere." In this interlude of financial security, Silverman spoke about how he "used to hate money, but was now loving it."

When asked who his closest friends are, Silverman responded by listing people he has met since moving to Val-David. The town's population is about ninety-three percent French speaking. People who met Silverman after his move north called him "Robert" (pronounced in a French fashion) as he requested. Until about 2017, Silverman often travelled to Montreal, especially to attend cycling events in the city. This was the case for MàB's fortieth anniversary in 2015, held at the former *Centre d'histoire de Montreal* museum in Old Montreal. He spoke there, detailing the history of the group he co-founded. There is a strange irony with the man who once dressed as Moses celebrating such a fortieth anniversary; according to Scripture, the original Moses and his followers spent forty years in

Figure 24.2. Jacques Desjardins and Bob Silverman in 2015.
Source: John Symon.

the wilderness before arriving in the Promised Land. By 2015, so much had changed that Montreal was indeed starting to resemble Silverman's vision for it.

Friends and colleagues typically recount visits made to Silverman's Val-David abode. John Symon is among them, and was warmly received there. In 2015, Zvi Leve and British writer Carlton Reid rode around Montreal with Silverman on a cargo bike while he marvelled at how the city had changed. Again, many of those changes reflected Silverman's vision for Montreal.

Figure 24.3. Carlton Reid and Bob Silverman.
Source: Zvi Leve.

Nearing the Finish Line

SILVERMAN'S HEALTH deteriorated in his later years. He suffered a heart attack and then a stroke in 2017 and he complained of being nearly blind. He suffered from some undiagnosed urinary problem that might have been cancer. And then there was dementia.

"Living is not so much fun as it used to be," Silverman once said to us about growing old. With dark humour, he quickly added: "But you're invited to the funeral!"

Talking about Euthanasia
Always outspoken, in a 2016 video, he claimed to be talking to his physician in the near future about euthanasia, something he describes as "a liberation," and "a relief" from the pain he suffers. Technically, he was referring to physician-administered euthanasia (PAE) or physician-assisted suicide (PAS). Despite such public announcements, ultimately Silverman never carried through with this.

Contemplating Suicide
In 2017, British author Carlton Reid dedicated his book *Bike Boom* to Silverman. "The book was dedicated to him and the other (forgotten) heroes of international cycle advocacy. And international they were, meeting at various events such as early Velocity events and the like. The groups inspired each other, with die-ins, etc," according to Reid.

"Bob and Claire had international profiles at the time but, sadly, people forgot about these heroes. Bob very much appreciated he was being remembered."

Writing back to say that discovering the bicycle in the 1960s gave him a reason to live, Silverman noted that failing health had recently made riding a bike impossible.

He had been contemplating suicide, but after reading the book's dedication, changed his mind.[1] But in late 2020, Richard Wutzke found a dazed and bleeding Silverman wandering near his apartment. Perhaps he had fallen into the river? Some indications point to a botched suicide attempt. Whatever the case, it was clear that Silverman could no longer live alone in his Val-David apartment.

Arrangements were made to transfer him to a palliative care home Pavillon Philippe-Lapointe, in nearby Sainte-Agathe-des-Monts. True to his nature, within two days of arriving, Silverman asked the administration to set up a wheelchair volleyball activity.[2] Silverman spent almost eighteen months in palliative care, hanging onto life with tenacity.

Epilogue and Homages

WHILE IN PALLIATIVE CARE, Silverman remained aware of world events, intently following political news until Joe Biden's victory over Donald Trump in the 2020 US presidential election. After that, he didn't seem to care anymore. "A bowl of ice cream for dessert outweighed any political considerations," Silverman's new caretaker Richard Wutzke wrote on Facebook to keep the entourage of his patient abreast of developments.

"Growing old and frail can be very frightening when seen in the mirror of cold hard reality. Dementia may be nature's way to let the imagination soften the landing," was another of Wutzke's Facebook comments about Silverman.

COVID-19 complicated things for those wanting to visit Silverman, though some managed to do so when sanitary measures were more relaxed at different times between the various waves of the pandemic. Silverman defied expectations one last time in not dying quickly, seeming to gain strength physically as time wore on. Wutzke wrote about leaving him on evenings, expecting Silverman to be dead by morning, but he kept strong through 2021. Early 2022 was a different story and Silverman did not rise from his bed after the New Year, passing away on Sunday, February 20, in the mid-afternoon. Congestion in his lungs was the apparent cause of death. The man who perfected die-ins for street theatre exited the stage for real.

Homages to Silverman

Later that same day, Montreal mayor Valérie Plante tweeted: "Robert Silverman was a cycling pioneer in Montreal. An early activist, he helped make cycling safer and promote active mobility. We owe him a lot. My thoughts are with his family and loved ones."[1] There was an avalanche of tributes to Silverman in various news media in the following weeks. *Forbes*, *La Presse*, *The Gazette*, the *Globe and Mail*, and more. *Gazette* journalist Josh Freed insisted that something should be named after Silverman, writing that "I cannot think of anyone who has literally changed the landscape of our city more than Bicycle Bob."

One tribute suggested that Silverman "achieved everything he asked for" while at MàB. While many of his demands have been met, no progress was made on eradicating cars, as the number of vehicles in Montreal increased from about

Figure 26.1. Unofficially naming Saint-Denis Street REV after Silverman.
Source: John Symon.

sixty-five thousand vehicles, when Silverman was born, to some two million in the Montreal region by his death in 2022.[2]

A Public Gathering on Saint-Denis Street

A gathering of supporters took place on March 12 at the corner of Saint-Denis and Roy streets. Some two hundred people assembled in the wind and sleet while different speakers took the microphone, sharing memories of "Bicycle Bob" Silverman. The crowd, with its mix of ages, seemed to represent all "generations" of MàB. City councillor Marianne Giguère (De Lorimier district) said that she visited with Silverman a few years earlier in Val-David, mentioning to him that the REV (Réseau express vélo) express bike path would soon be built on Saint-Denis Street. Silverman responded that this would be "extraordinary!"

His friend and fellow co-founder of the MàB, Jacques Desjardins, spoke about how Montreal needs to recognize the work of Silverman. Both he and Giguère said that efforts to work with the toponymy commission on this had simply proven frustrating. One of the rules is that nothing can be named after someone until a year after their death. Organizer Mathieu Murphy-Perron of Vélorution Montréal, took the microphone next, reminding the crowd that "If Bob were here, he would say 'fuck it! Let's just do this.'" Then bike advocate Karim Kammah climbed a stepladder to post a plaque on the corner lamp post, unofficially naming the Saint-Denis Street REV after Robert Silverman. The crowd cheered!

Apart from the Claire Morissette bike path on de Maisonneuve Boulevard, the REV "Robert Silverman" would apparently be the only other bike path in the world named after a person. This REV is a major north–south bike axis and, since its inauguration in November 2020, it has registered over one million users in less than twelve months.[3]

> The REV (Réseau express vélo) on Saint-Denis Street is a completed portion of a proposed 184 km bicycle path network on the island of Montreal. This network, consisting mainly of protected lanes, is designed to ensure the comfort and safety of cyclists. It is a new type of bike path—sometimes called a "bike highway"—and accessible twelve months of the year. Over much of its length, the REV will replace either car parking spots or car driving lanes, "reconquering the city" as Silverman used to say. Building the REV was supported by both major political parties in the 2021 Montreal elections, but with different visions. Perhaps more importantly, the REV has been enthusiastically received by local merchants who now see it as a way to attract new customers.[4] Initially, some of these merchants opposed the bike path. According to a City of Montreal web post, "the REV will enable achieving the goal of 15% of utility trips by bicycle in the metropolis by 2027."[5]

Exceeding Everyone's Expectations, Including His Own

The following day, on Sunday March 13, some fifty friends—many from the artistic community in Val-David—gathered at LézArts Loco, a cultural center in Val-David, following the monthly Rencontre de Poésie. The crowd was greeted by a well-stocked buffet and, in the performance hall, Bob's ashes on a pedestal. The urn was framed on the right by a bulletin board covered in photographs of Bob at various stages of his life, and on the left by a rather cheerful, gorgeous floral tribute: a blooming bicycle wheel. Despite the COVID-19 measures, nobody wore a mask. The wheel was made by Marie-Josée Legault, who owns a flower business in Val-David, but who was, above all, a beneficiary attendant and home support worker. She took care of Bob near the end of his life.

"I was at his house every day during the pandemic," she said. "We talked, we had fun. I bored him. He had a dedicated cook because he ate vegan. There were always several women around him, a sort of harem."

Silverman's caretaker Richard Wutzke said: "He exceeded everyone's expectations, even his own. The kid with the learning disorder that hindered his ability to write became a poet and an intellectual. The kid who was afraid of baseball invented a novel volleyball game that everyone could play and took over a city park. His apprehensions towards the automobile transformed the streets of Montreal."[6]

Eulogy at Quebec's National Assembly
Another homage followed on March 15 in Quebec's National Assembly when David Birnbaum (MNA: D'Arcy-McGee) addressed the chamber:

> Thanks largely to Bob's offbeat, outrageous, unflinching, and ultimately successful theatrics of persuasion, cycling is now safe and accessible across some 900 km of bike paths in Montreal alone. Back in the '70s and '80s, it took Bob's "Vélorution" to get the wheels finally turning [...] Merci, Bob. May all Quebeckers remember with gratitude how you have helped make their lives a little better. Merci.[7]

From Philadelphia, John Dowlin sent this tribute: "Bob was monumental in our movement for bicycle progress in our cities, our lifestyles and our hearts. He has left an indelible mark on the world. Long live the Vélorution!"

A Mass Bike Ride for Bob

Another gathering to honour Silverman took place on April 30 this time involving a mass bike ride, a die-in, a ghost bike, tossing of a volleyball, street graffiti, speeches, and ending with a book launch in a tavern. This event was organized by the group, Vélo fantôme, which installs ghost bikes—painted white—where cyclists have died in traffic accidents. Members of Silverman's extended family, including his niece Joanne, participated in the speeches and bike ride that day. She joked about how Silverman very publicly gave her a book on tantric sex as a wedding present. Bob's sister, Rona, was among those riding with the group as well as Joanne's teenage children.

After the speeches came a die-in at the same street corner (Robert-Bourassa and Sainte-Catherine) where MàB held such an event in 1976. About one hundred cyclists of all ages lay still on the street and stopped traffic for three minutes while organizers traced their outlines with sidewalk chalk. The two authors joined those lying on the pavement. Afterward, the scene afterward looked like mass traffic fatalities had occurred. Using a stencil, participants painted *On veut des pistes partout* ("we want bike paths everywhere") on the pavement. The group stopped at the Old Port's Clock Tower, within sight of Jacques Cartier Bridge. One of Bob's bikes was there as the group recalled some of MàB's theatrical demonstrations over the years. As the group passed through intersections, volunteers "bracketed" the intersections so that the entire group could pass together. This same technique is commonly used by motorcycle police to allow VIP processions to pass intersections—but this time, the VIP was a *vélorutionnaire*. The book launch was for Marc-André Brouillard's, *À vélo vers une ville nouvelle*, about the MàB.

One last poem:

MY LITERARY STEP
My journey
is now over,
The path ahead
is clear,
the pain forgotten,
Nothing left to fear.

Annex

Definitions and Vocabulary

William Shakespeare is credited with having created up to 1,700 new words in the English language. Silverman was also a wordsmith, having invented a few words and terms while helping to popularize others. This new vocabulary is important to help frame or reframe major topics and is often used to describe events in the pages of this text.

Active transport in this text includes bicycling, but also incorporates walking, jogging, and rollerblading.

Anarcylists: The term makes allusion to anarchists, "a person who rebels against any authority, established order, or ruling power," according to Merriam-Webster Online Dictionary. Silverman described "anarcyclists" as people who concentrate on bicycle liberation, such as bike access to subway systems. Silverman claimed to be able "to name such people all over the world."

Autocracy (or Auto-cracy): This term was not invented by Silverman but he gave it new meaning. The word typically means "a country, state, or society governed by one person with absolute power" as defined by Lexico. But Silverman unconventionally defines it as "a country, state, or society where the automobile has absolute power." "Auto-crazy" might be an alternate spelling.

Autoeroticism: Again, this term was not invented by Silverman and can mean "sexual gratification obtained solely through stimulation by oneself of one's own body." However, Silverman unconventionally gives the term new meaning to describe how automobiles have been transformed into an erotic object and how female sexuality is subjugated to market automobiles.

Autophobe: Someone who is afraid of automobiles. Again, this term was not invented by Silverman, but popularized by him.

Bike lane: While not invented by Silverman, he was one of the earliest users of this term in Montreal, referring to part of the road surface painted to indicate it is for use by bicycles (see "bike path").

Bike path: This was a term not invented by Silverman, he used it to mean "a bicycle lane being a paved surface separated from automobiles by a physical barrier." Silverman also sometimes used "cycle path" as a synonym for bike path.

Bikesheviks: This term makes allusion to the Bolsheviks, a militant, very organized, and ultimately successful segment within the Russian Revolution. Presumably, whatever the Bolsheviks lacked in popular support, they compensated for with remarkable organization and commitment to their cause. Silverman described himself, Claire Morissette, and John Dowlin (in Philadelphia) as "bikesheviks."

Carmageddon: Presumably a play on Armageddon, predicting that the world will end because of the use of private cars.

Carn-nage: The destruction and bloodshed caused by automobiles.

Copenhagenize: That is, prioritizing bicycle and pedestrian transport in an urban setting and on a world scale, Copenhagen serves as a model on this. This is not a word developed by Silverman. Nonetheless, Silverman did much to popularize the underlying concepts. Was it an accident that his second wife was Danish?

Cycloconsciousness: Describes the state of mind of people very conscious of the situation for cyclists. Silverman relates how, when a group of Trotskyites tried to take over le Monde à bicyclette, their two-hundred-page program contained no mention of bicycles. They were thus exposed as not having Cycloconsciousness and their initiative was rejected by the rest of MàB.

Cyclodrama: MàB actions combined demonstrations with street theatre. Silverman points to one cyclodrama involving a pack of cyclists who attached lightweight wooden structures to their bikes, making these bicycles "as big as cars." The cyclists then rode slowly in formation down the street, much to the frustration of car drivers. Silverman dressing as Moses to part the waters of the St. Lawrence River is probably MàB's most famous cyclodrama.

Cyclofeminism: A militant movement using the bicycle as a tool for emancipation. The objective is to give women a greater role in society and expand their rights. This movement was very active in the late 1800s and early 1900s, coinciding with the suffragette movement.

Cyclo-frustration: A human condition caused by the inability to feel the simple pleasure of bicycling due to a lack of urban infrastructure suited to this purpose. It is similar to "cycloconsciousness" in that it is being conscious about the situation for bicyclists and how appropriate infrastructure for them is often lacking. Alternately, the behaviour of motorists, politicians, or bureaucrats is less than conducive for cyclists. Cyclo-frustrations can be a good thing, providing motivation for the bicycle-advocacy movement. Silverman mentioned how on certain well-designed bike paths, there might be no cyclo-frustrations.

Cyclomartyr: Someone who makes great sacrifices to advance bicycling.

Cyclophobia: Fear of cycling or of encouraging cyclists.

Cyclotherapy: This term is used in medical circles to mean a therapeutic strategy for protecting normal cells during chemotherapy. Silverman has appropriated the term to also mean riding a bicycle to cure what ails you. This prescription is equally good for individuals as it is for society. An alternate spelling could be "cycletherapy," which by coincidence some bike shops in various locales have chosen as a name.

Die-in: A type of street theatre where many people pretend to lie dead as a form of public protest. Silverman claimed that the concept originated in Australia, but that he refined it. The authors wonder, however, if Mahatma Gandhi didn't pioneer this technique.

Icycle path: A comical term for a bicycle path covered with snow and ice. But it doesn't have to "B" like that...

Impossibilist: Claire Morissette used this term to describe Silverman, but reverses its meaning. Whereas dictionaries ascribe the definition of "defeatism" and believing "everything is impossible," Morissette obviously implies the opposite.

Lucraphobia: This was Silverman's term for "fear of making money," but it is not in the dictionary. However, the word "chrematophobia" (fear of spending money) is there.

Pelle-t-in: Borrowing from the idea of a die-in, a pelle-t-in is a public snowclearing event done where local authorities refuse to do so, such as on a bike path, usually with the idea of shaming authorities. The term is based on the French word: "pelleter" (to shovel).

Poetico-Vélorutionary: This term describes the rare cycling advocates who put a high priority on giving bicyclists as many rights as the users of other forms of transportation. Within this small group, many are poets.

Vélo-holy rollers: Presumably this term describes dancing, shaking, or other boisterous movements by cyclists who perceive themselves as being under the influence of the Great Spirit.

Velophobia: An irrational fear of bikes as demonstrated by the management of Montréal's transit authority, the CTCUM, or in recent years by Toronto mayor, Rob Ford.

Vélorution: Silverman does not claim to have invented this word but was among its earliest adopters. The reader will appreciate how this word transposes the V and the R from the word "revolution." In French, the word vélo is commonly used to mean bicycle. In socialist thought revolution is needed to usher in real change in society. As such, Silverman traded one battle cry for another.

Revolutionary thinking presumably inspired most of the vocabulary above; psychology accounts for much of the balance, with perhaps one word from the Bible. In 2020, Silverman still professed to be a Trotskyite, believing that "the revolution was just around the corner."

Manifesto of le Monde à Bicyclette
Analysis
Originally an eleven-page typewritten document composed in French by Silverman, we present here an English translation. The French version was published in *Le Devoir* newspaper among other places. The document is surprisingly bold in calling for cars to be replaced by bicycles in the long-term; in fact, the first three of the original eleven pages were devoted to denouncing cars before an alternative—the bicycle—is mentioned. Silverman's document is quite avant-gardiste for 1975 in calling for an extensive system of bike paths and bike lanes when there were none in Montréal. The text is also prophetic, especially in regard to the logistics of its call for communal bicycles more than three decades before Montréal launched its BIXI communal bike program. By 2024, BIXI counted more than 11,000 bikes (including 2,600 electric ones), exceeding the 10,000 that Silverman called for almost fifty years earlier. Silverman wittingly concludes by quoting from the 1848 *Communist Manifesto*, "Workers of the world unite..." and adapting it for cyclists.

THE CYCLISTS' MANIFESTO
Le Monde à bicyclette, May 26, 1975
In Hindu mythology, the god Krishna owned a mighty chariot called "Juggernaut." Every year, Krishna drove his gigantic cart through the streets and his disciples, children, and adults alike, sacrifice themselves by throwing themselves under its wheels.

The automobile killed one hundred and thirty people in Montreal in 1974. Many were injured, some were left crippled. The exhaust gasses are slowly killing us. Fourteen percent of Montrealers suffer from lung disease. In the city centre the rate reaches nineteen percent.

The automobile slows down buses, some of which carry dozens of citizens. The noise it makes dominates the city. It monopolizes urban space: the city centre is disfigured by the excess of land devoted to parking. Its deadly presence prevents our children from playing in the street. It uses huge amounts of gasoline and the oil it uses pollutes our beaches and contaminates fish.

It is excessively expensive. Its purchase has provoked massive indebtedness for many of our fellow citizens. It is inefficient as it is mainly used for trips of less than six miles with a single passenger. Cars spend most of their time being parked before ending up in dreadful scrap piles that disfigure our suburbs.

Because of the car we don't exercise enough and our [Canadians] physical condition is one of the worst in the world.

Even those who don't use cars have to pay the social and economic costs of living in a society dominated by the auto industry, such as wasting millions on highways, millions spent on motorways, the millions spent on the treatment of illnesses and injuries, and especially the destruction of the city's social cohesion, the formidable cultural alienation that half a century of the automobile has imposed on North American city dwellers.

Just as auto pollutes our cities, those who profit from it pollute our airspace and our public institutions. They are forcing governments to defray exploration costs while they pull the chestnuts out of the fire. Syncrude(a Canadian petroleum company) is a good example. Ford and Chrysler largely funded the Canadian Radio and Television News Editors' Convention in Ottawa last weekend.

The car degrades our values, our tastes, our ideals. It not only steals precious material resources from us, but it has robbed us of our integrity as human beings. For this vehicle of death we must substitute the vehicle of life: the BICYCLE.

We believe that the bicycle is the healthiest, the most economical and the most efficient means of transportation; in terms of a higher standard of living, cycling is clearly needed. Of all the vehicles, only the bicycle allows the user to go from door to door.

Staying in the spirit of the bicycle, our movement has the motto: To each his own and let us only rely on our own means. We must seek to persuade those who depend on the automobile to become independent on bicycles. The bicycle is the vehicle of common sense, it conserves energy, it frees the environment, and it is economically beneficial.

Le Monde à bicyclette is a movement that brings together cyclists and citizens who do not accept the deterioration in the quality of life in our city. Everyone suffers from this state of affairs, which explains why our members are recruited from all sections of the French-speaking and English-speaking population, old and young, poor and rich, women and men, workers and students.

We have the support of the Rassemblement des Citoyens de Montréal (RCM/MCM), the Fédération québécoise de cyclotourisme [now Vélo Québec], the Canadian Cycling Association [now Cycling Canada, which oversees competitive cycling], Sauvons Montréal, Espaces verts, the STOP [Save Tomorrow, Oppose Pollution], the SVP [Société pour vaincre la pollution], and other ecological and cycling organizations. The Alliance des professeurs de Montréal and the Montreal Teachers' Association have both published our manifesto and placed our posters in all the schools where their members teach. The active support of these two organizations is particularly significant because the teachers realize that the majority of cyclists are under ten years old and that the young people, their pupils, are sacrificed to the cult of the automobile.

Faced with a growing number of cyclists, city officials have so far responded with contempt. A few weeks ago, responding to questions from MCM councillors John Gardiner and Bob Keaton regarding bicycle equipment, the director of the traffic department, Jacques Barrière, replied: "Bicycles are not a priority for us right now. If we encouraged bicycles, would we put cars in our pockets?"

It must be gasoline flowing through Mr. Barrière's arteries.

The long-term goal of le Monde à bicyclette is to replace the private automobile with the bicycle for the greatest number [of people] to get to work (in conjunction, of course, with a better adapted and more rational public transport system).

Firstly; we are demanding the conversion of certain north-south and east-west streets into bicycle lanes (a bicycle lane being a paved surface separated from automobiles by a physical barrier). In addition, to complete the bicycle transportation system, we require the development and proper maintenance of a dedicated bicycle lane on the right side of major streets.

The growing popularity of cycling without adequate service facilities has created tension between cyclists and motorists frustrated with the problems of driving in today's traffic jams. Many times, cyclists experience complete disdain for their lives without mentioning their right to ride the streets. That is why we demand an intensive campaign to educate the public about the use of the bicycle, as well as the recognition and enforcement of the rights of cyclists.

Frequent thefts make it unwise to leave your bike unattended. We therefore ask for sturdy and theft-proof parking lots throughout the city. Factories, schools, office buildings, theatres, libraries, and department stores must also set up their bicycle parking facilities. In the United States, coin-operated parking is already widespread. Eight bicycles can occupy the space of an automobile. In Montreal, such parking is only available at two locations at Maison de Radio Canada [CBC Building], and Sir George Williams [now Concordia] University has wardens who watch the bicycles.

It is almost impossible to reach the South Shore [of the St. Lawrence River] by bicycle. The Jacques Cartier Bridge offers a sidewalk but it is insufficient. To remedy this absurd and unfair situation, we are demanding a bicycle lane on all bridges to the South Shore. Sometimes our bikes break down and we find ourselves stranded far from home. Cyclists should be allowed to use the last metro car outside of rush hour.

We would like there to be recreational trails around Montréal and in the countryside. Particularly important would be the development of a track along the river on the South Shore of the St. Lawrence. On [Montreal] island itself we could start immediately with Gouin Blvd and the Lakeshore Road. Given that there is no cross-traffic on these two arteries and little habitation, we propose that the inner half of these two roads become one-way streets for cars and that the outer half be developed into a cycle path. A barrier would be built to separate the two lanes.

Once these measures are adopted, cycling will undoubtedly experience a phenomenal development. It is in this spirit that le Monde à bicyclette is launching its "orange plan" to develop cycling in Montréal. Firstly, the city of Montréal must buy 10,000 bicycles and put them at the disposal, in common ownership, of the population of the city. To make them visible in the dark, the bicycles will be coloured orange. They will be struck with a capital M and will bear the seal of the city.

These bicycles will be kept in municipal warehouses scattered throughout the city. To ensure the protection of these communal properties, a deposit and proof of identification will be required for the bicycle loan. The cost of such a program would be only a fraction of the $350 million wasted on the east-west highway or the $57 million invested in the Olympic velodrome.

Le Monde à bicyclette launches bike week by offering a five-speed CCM "Elite" brand bicycle, provided by the company, to the mayor and members of the executive committee of the City of Montreal, for regular use.

We are confident that these gentlemen will know how to put it to good use. To get around downtown, for inspection visits to the Olympic construction sites, for lunches at the Hélène de Champlain restaurant on Île Sainte-Hélène, to attend shows at Place des Arts, they will fully enjoy it. Each day will see an improvement in their physical condition, when they are freed from their glass and steel cages with a driver and bar they will finally be able to understand their hometown. Soon they will discover the marvelous simplicity and efficiency of their bicycle, and, being healthy and responsible men, they will no longer lose their pedals and will recommend and facilitate the use of the bicycle by as many people as possible.

On Thursday, May 29, a race will take place between a motorist, a public transport user, and a cyclist. The race will start at 5:00 p.m. [at] Place Ville Marie and end at the corner of Saint-Denis and Laurier streets. Everyone is invited to follow this race using the mode of transport of their choice.

Cycling Week will culminate on Saturday, May 31, with the Grand Parade of Cyclists (June 7 in case of rain). The parade will begin around 1:00 p.m. at Jeanne-Mance Park, at the corner of Avenue du Parc and rue Duluth and will take the following route: Duluth to Saint-Urbain, Saint-Urbain to Sherbrooke, west on Sherbrooke to Mackay, Mackay to Sainte-Catherine, Sainte-Catherine to Panet, and up Panet to Lafontaine Park.

Everyone who wants to make Montréal a less alienating city should participate. We specifically address those who experience the oppression of the automobile on a daily basis: the dwellers of the city centre, cyclists, pedestrians, roller skaters and scooter enthusiasts. Disgruntled motorists are [also] welcome. We all have fond memories of those days in April when, after the great storm, there was a rare sense of community as we walked for once in peace and safety.

It is not excluded that other innovative events will be included in the program of the week. Le Monde à bicyclette is a permanent organization that intends to acquire premises and the necessary staff. We plan to self-finance by asking cyclists to join for the sum of five dollars per year. We are also thinking of raising funds from bicycle companies and dealers, which can be expected to benefit immensely from us starting such a program. Our plans for the future also include the creation of bicycle purchasing and maintenance co-operatives, as well as the publication of information for consumers on the respective merits of a particular brand or bicycle dealer.

The renaissance of cycling is an international phenomenon. For the past three years, sales of bicycles have surpassed those of automobiles in the United States, and last year some 14.1 million bicycles were sold compared to 8.8 million cars.

To meet the needs of cycling, several municipalities have built bike paths in the US, following a federal law passed in 1973, $120 million has been allocated for the creation of a national network of cycle paths. Already, some twenty-five states have used this federal money to build 30,000 miles of bike paths. In that country there are currently more than 200,000 miles of bike paths.

Closer to home, in Ottawa, there are now 32 miles of bike paths with more planned.

The case of Grenoble, France, is even more encouraging. A report in the March 26 edition of *Time* magazine illustrates the realism and common sense of our program, and demonstrates "what we can do." *Time* reports that the civil authorities of Grenoble are banning cars from the city centre, replacing them with buses, trams and bicycles. The mayor of Grenoble predicts that the city centre will be served exclusively by public transport from 1980.

Still according to *Time*, "One solution is to separate cyclists from motorists, and Grenoble has rightly allocated $1.2 million to do this. Starting in 1979 there will be six miles of lanes exclusively reserved for bicycles, to be developed along the new urban roads, or reserved for downtown streets. No other European city has gone this far, and no city has ever treated the cycle path network as part of a mass transport system. To begin with, Grenoble set up bike stations at bus stops, where cyclists can switch from their two wheels to the four wheels of the bus."

Because automobile abuse is an international danger that must be fought in all cities, groups like le Monde à bicyclette exist and are springing up all over the world. We are part of this movement, which from Stockholm to Tokyo is starting to mobilize the armies of old common sense. We share ideas and experiences with each other. We are all united behind the slogan: "Cyclists of the world unite! You have nothing to lose but your chains."

The logic and common sense of the cycling movement is obvious. Sooner or later our movement will become an irresistible wave that will overthrow the "Juggernaut."

NE PERDEZ PAS LES PEDALES!

(This last phrase could be literally translated as "don't let your feet off the pedals" or figuratively as "don't lose control.")

MàB and BIXI

In the mid-1970s, MàB called for a fleet of ten thousand collective bicycles in Montreal. In 2009, almost half a century later, the city launched its BIXI program of collective bikes. But even with this late start date, BIXI still became "North America's first large-scale bike sharing system."

The name BIXI combines letters from the words *bicycle* and *taxi*. A sturdy, yet adjustable, step-through (unisex) bicycle design was selected, initially with three gears inside the rear hub. However, the "made in Quebec" bikes are heavy at some 18 kg (40 lb) each. The program, which includes solar-powered, automated docking stations, proved very popular; some thirteen million trips were made on BIXIs in 2024! Many users buy annual subscriptions; a short-term (hourly) rate can also be accessed with a credit card.

Montreal then franchised its system to New York, London, Toronto, and Melbourne, among other cities. Ultimately, legal and financial issues forced Montreal to abandon its sale of the system to other cities, concentrating instead on the Montreal market.

In 2022, Montreal had 11,000 BIXIs (including 2,600 electric ones), slightly exceeding the 10,000 that the MàB had demanded nearly half a century earlier. In 2023, the service was offered for the first time in winter.

Silverman and MàB's Legacy Today

There is no doubt that Silverman and his colleagues profoundly changed Montreal. As evidence, we now have over a thousand kilometres of bike lanes, the Réseau express vélo (REV), bicycle access to the metro and many major bridges, express bus lanes, BIXI, Communauto, outdoor volleyball in city parks, and tree-lined neighbourhoods near downtown. A year after his death, many called for Silverman's name to be preserved in his city. Journalist Josh Freed wrote in *The Gazette* that he could not think of anyone who changed the landscape of Montreal more than Silverman. The book's co-author, Stéphane Desjardins, suggests that Silverman will ultimately shape Montreal more fundamentally than Mayor Drapeau did. Yet Silverman's influence goes beyond Montreal: US-based writer Jeff Mapes credits Silverman with "being the spark of the cycling revolution in Canada." Angela Bischoff, an environmental activist with Clean Air Alliance Ontario, echoes that "Silverman was the granddaddy of the cycling movement in Canada."

Some accolades come from even farther afield: "He was a genuine revolutionary, because he wanted to empower ordinary people. Few people deserve this qualifier, Bob is one of them. He wanted major social changes, not just adjustments to capitalism. He had a perception of the world that was not coloured by commerce. He influenced a lot of people across the United States," says Steve Stollman, a prominent bike advocate in New York, where Silverman frequently visited.

Silverman was also known to bike advocates in Europe: "I spoke a lot with Bob, who seemed to me to have points in common with Jacques Essel, his Parisian counterpart: very leftist and the same anarchist tendency, non-bourgeois way of life, modest income, and identification with the cause," notes Isabelle Lesens, a Paris politician. A cycling activist since the 1980s, in 1994 Lesens instigated opening of the banks of the Seine on Sundays to pedestrians and to cyclists.

Silverman was also a regular contributor to the *Bicycle Network*, a US-based cycling newsletter distributed worldwide. George Bliss, a noted cycling advocate, and bike designer in New York never met Silverman, but nevertheless qualifies him as "the originator of the international cycling movement!" Among his credentials, the first use of the cycling term *critical mass* is attributed to Bliss in 1992. Montréal journalist Josh Freed makes a similar claim that Silverman was the originator of World Bicycle Day.

The Cost of Cars

Industrialized countries—especially in North America—live in a car culture. This culture grew directly out of the postwar "American Way of Life," which Silverman criticized for most of his life.

The car has profoundly changed our lives: it has transformed geography and our way of life to the point of becoming indispensable. It led to the creation suburbs and sustainably transformed cities, the quality of life and the environment for past, current and future generations. A central component of modern comfort, Western-style materialism and individualism, and ambient culture (notably in the cinema, in the media, and literature), the automobile is now a subculture, synonymous with freedom and prosperity. More than a social status, the automobile has established itself as an extension of the human body in the minds of many citizens and decision-makers.

This status has profound implications in the economy and personal finances. The automobile plays a central role in the Canadian economy with some 26.2 million vehicles registered in 2021, according to Statistics Canada.[1] In 2022, just over 135,000 vehicles were sold monthly in Canada and approximately 33,000 in Quebec (Statistics Canada).[2] Some 1.5 million new vehicles were sold domestically in mid-2022 (versus 1.7 million in mid-2021), according to HSBC.[3] Quebec, with its 8.6 million inhabitants, had just less than five million passenger vehicles and light trucks registered in 2021, according to the Quebec Institute of Statistics.[4]

Weight of Industry

The manufacturing of motor vehicles and parts for that industry, along with the auto dealership and parts subsector, accounted for 1.4 percent of the Canadian economy in 2021, according to Statistics Canada.[5] So, for every $1 of goods and services produced by the Canadian economy, 1.4 cents come from the automotive industry.

For more than a century, Canada has been one of the top twelve producers of light vehicles in the world, with the presence of five major manufacturers and more than seven hundred parts suppliers. The contribution of the automotive industry to Canadian GDP was $12.5 billion in 2020.[6]

It is one of the largest industrial sectors in the country, directly employing 117,200 people and indirectly between 400,000 and 500,000 people, including dealer networks, after-sales service, parts, and tire manufacturing, according to various sources. Canada produces approximately 1.4 million vehicles annually, or 10 percent of all vehicles produced in North America.[7]

The Canadian automotive industry represents 16.8 percent of product sales in this country and is the main Canadian export, amounting to $42.9 billion in 2020, 93 percent of which went to the United States. About 20 percent of the trade within Canada, the United States, and Mexico, or $230 billion, is related to the automotive industry. Some parts can therefore cross the Canada–United States–Mexico borders up to eight times before being integrated into a vehicle assembled at a Canadian, American, or Mexican assembly plant.[8]

Canadian motorists are obliged to insure their vehicles. In most Canadian provinces, automobile insurance covers damage to the vehicle, civil liability, and bodily injury. Some provinces have public plans, others semi-public or completely private. For some, including Quebec, the public plan only covers bodily injury.

In reality, the Canadian auto insurance market is gigantic. In 2019, the average auto insurance premium was $675 in Canada, according to the *Groupement des assureurs automobiles* (GAA).[9] Direct written auto insurance premiums totalled

$27.4 billion, according to the Insurance Bureau of Canada (IBC) in 2022.[10] In Quebec alone, direct premiums written by motorists totaled $5.4 billion in 2021, according to the *Autorité des marchés financiers* (AMF).[11]

Popularity

In Quebec, the number of cars is increasing faster than the population. Between 1980 and 2016, the human population aged sixteen and over grew by 41 percent, while the number of passenger vehicles rose by 110 percent for the same period, according to SAAQ figures cited in a study by the Suzuki Foundation.[12] In fact, 100,000 vehicles are added to the roads of Quebec each year (after replacements).[13] Since 2000, the growth rate of the Quebec automobile fleet has therefore been over twice that of the population, again according to the Suzuki Foundation.

The motorization rate in Quebec was therefore 464 vehicles/1,000 people aged sixteen and over in 2017, compared to 413 in 2000, an increase of 12 percent.

In addition, consumers are buying more and more sport utility vehicles (SUVs), which are more fuel-intensive, more polluting and more expensive. In 2021, SUVs represented 39 percent of sales, according to Statistics Canada.[14] SUVs are also more dangerous for cyclists and pedestrians.

Between 1990 and 2019, SUV sales exploded by 284 percent. By 2019, eleven SUVs were sold for every electric vehicle in Quebec.[15] If current sales trends continue, no other models of cars will be sold in 2026 except for SUVs, estimates Professor Pierre-Olivier Pineau, holder of the energy chair at HEC Montréal.

In 2017, 66.4 percent of work trips were made by cars with a single occupant (the driver), 3.3 percent by car with at least one passenger, 22.3 percent by public transport, 5.2 percent on foot, and 2.0 percent by bicycle in the Montreal CMA, according to Statistics Canada. In relative terms, Montreal might be the North American bicycling capital, but in absolute terms, it remains a city of cars.[16]

Consequences

The extensive use of the automobile has consequences (according to various sources):

- Cars and light trucks are responsible for 21.9 percent of Quebec's GHG emissions (Canada is one of the highest per capita emitters of GHG worldwide); transportation is the main source of air pollution in Quebec; air pollution kills 15,300 Canadians and 4,000 Quebecers each year.
- The car contributes to urban sprawl, which leads to the creation of heat islands and the destruction of arable land and ecosystems, particularly wetlands; the development of thoroughfares and parking lots has specifically destroyed many urban, rural, and historic landscapes.

- There were 347 deaths, 1,227 serious injuries, and 26,314 minor injuries on Quebec roads in 2021. The increasing popularity of SUVs increases the risk of serious accident and death for pedestrians and cyclists.
- The costs of medical care related to accidents and loss of productivity were estimated at $917 million in 2010 in Quebec.
- Noise pollution from urban traffic increases the risk of depression.
- The automobile promotes a sedentary lifestyle and obesity, which leads to various diseases including cardiovascular and joint-muscle disorders, diabetes, sleep apnea, and arterial hypertension; the medical costs associated with these pathologies are borne by all taxpayers.
- Cars increase the trade deficit: consumers buy automobiles manufactured outside Quebec and spend more than $6.5 billion annually on petroleum products from outside the province; the combined annual bill for these imports is $20 billion, or 24 percent of Quebec's total imports.
- The costs of traffic congestion were estimated at $3.3 billion in 2013.

Taking into account external costs (not borne by individuals), each dollar spent by a motorist would cost society $2.55. A 2018 Suzuki Foundation study, using data from the Conference Board of Canada, accounted for household and government spending on road infrastructure, as well as externalities. Quebecers therefore pay between $41 billion and $51 billion (2015 dollars) for the privilege of driving their vehicles.[17]

These facts were repeatedly denounced over the years by Silverman at MàB protests, including those at the Montreal Auto Show in the 1970s.

Personal Finance
While housing, transportation, and food are the three largest expenditure items for Canadians, 18.5 percent of total household spending was allocated to transportation, for an average expenditure of $12,737 in 2019. Of this sum, $11,258 represents private transportation, or $5,434 for the purchase or rental of a vehicle and $5,707 on operating costs (i.e. fuel). By comparison, they spent $300 on public transit, according to Statistics Canada.[18] Canada is truly a country of motorists.

According to CAA Quebec, the average annual budget allocated for private car use in 2020 was $11,000 per Quebec household, including registration fees, insurance, tire changes, and fuel. Obviously, the amount varies greatly depending on the vehicle model. For a compact car, fuel costs will average $3,300 per year, compared to $9,000 for an SUV.[19]

However, 7.5 percent of Quebec commuters travel less than one kilometre between their home and work (36 percent travel less than five kilometres). According to figures from the 2016 census compiled by the Montreal Metropolitan Community (CMM in French), 10 percent of commuter motorists in the Montréal agglomeration travelled 1–2.9 km, 30 percent from 3–4.9 km, 40 percent from 5–6.9 km, and 20 percent from 7–9.9 km.[20] Some of these distances can easily be covered on foot or by bicycle, assuming there is a safe bike path or sidewalk.

The use of "transportation cocktails" (combinations of cars / public transport and active transport) would allow savings of 50–75 percent for Quebecers living in the city, according to Equiterre.[21]

It is important to emphasize that a typical car is parked 95 percent of the time, according to various research works, in particular those of Donald Schoup, a Distinguished Research Professor at UCLA.[22] Schoup discovered that in American cities, one thousand square feet are devoted to each car, compared to eight hundred square feet of housing space per person![23]

Few people realize the immense strain that this puts on their household finances: they devote a fifth of their income to an object that is used only 5 percent of the time and that depreciates, on average, by 50 percent after five years.[24]

Are people alienated by car culture? Silverman said so in the 1970s, at the time shocking many people.

Le Jardin du Petit Monde à Bicyclette

In September 2020, the City of Montréal and partners inaugurated Le Jardin du Petit Monde à Bicyclette, a training site where young children can learn how to bike safely. Present for the inauguration was Marianne Giguère, the city councillor responsible for active transport.

"The choice of name, following a call for ideas, is a poetic nod to the group le Monde à bicyclette, which campaigned in the 70s and 80s in favour of urban bicycling," said Giguère in a press release.

Among those also present were Éric Alan Caldwell, the elected official in charge of urban planning and CEO of the STM; Magali Bebronne of Vélo Québec; Marc Lauzon, chief of the local police station 38; a representative of La Société de l'assurance automobile du Québec (SAAQ); and a representative of the Plateau-Mont-Royal Caisse Desjardins (credit union). The setting is in La Fontaine Park, a large municipal park, in the Plateau Mont Royal district. It is also across the street from the Vélo Québec headquarters.

Who Carries the Torch Today?

It has been decades since the MàB shut down, but some groups that carry on work similar to that of MàB include Critical Mass, Cyclo Nord-Sud, Encore du Monde à bicyclette, Vélo fantôme, Vélo Québec, and Vélorution Montréal.

"Never doubt that a small group of thoughtful committed individuals can change the world. In fact, it's the only thing that ever has." Quote attributed to Margaret Mead.

The Authors
John Symon is a long-time avid bicyclist who met Robert Silverman playing volleyball in Jeanne-Mance Park. As a freelance journalist, he was the Quebec correspondent for Toronto-based *Pedal Magazine* for about fifteen years. In the 1990s and 2000s, John authored a series of popular guidebooks about family-friendly places around Montreal and Ottawa. John's bicycling guidebook for Montreal features a preface written by Silverman.

Stéphane Desjardins has been a journalist for forty years, writing a column on personal finance for the *Journal de Montréal*. He is the editor-in-chief of *Coopoint* magazine and the *Journal des Voisins*. He has also directed and collaborated with numerous media. In another life, he was a columnist for *Le Devoir*. He is the author of several personal finance guides and a science fiction novel, *Le Rapporteur*. He was a member of le Monde à bicyclette in the 1980s.

Why We Wrote This Book
While at university in Montreal, I joined a pickup volleyball game in Jeanne-Mance Park. Between games, I began chatting with an older man who introduced himself as "Bob." And so I met "Bicycle Bob" Silverman.

Later, working as a freelance journalist, I wrote much about bicycling news. If it was a story about bike advocacy, Silverman invariably had good insights. I called him often and we became friends.

I became aware that Silverman was much bigger than "Bicycle Bob." He told me of his bookstore, cutting sugarcane with Che Guevara, and shaking hands with Yasser Arafat. It occurred to me that there was an incredible story to tell. Silverman gave his blessing to the project, asking that I describe him honestly "warts and all." Originally, this was supposed to be an "authorized biography," and Silverman did approve some early drafts of the first two chapters, but his dementia and then his passing prevented him from approving anything more.

By tremendous good luck, I stumbled across some key people who had known Silverman at important junctures in his life. I was also lucky to be contacted by Stéphane Desjardins, an accomplished journalist, wanting to collaborate on this work. As a former MàBer, he shared great anecdotes and many keen insights about Silverman.

J. S., March 31, 2023

The idea of writing a biography of Bob Silverman had been on my mind for years. When I learned the sad news of his death, I knew at the same time that another Montréal journalist had been working on this project for a long time. I wanted to meet John and, quickly, I joined this slightly crazy project to describe the extraordinary, romantic, cinematographic journey of this unsung hero of the global cycle. I knew Bob, I campaigned with him and Claire Morissette, who came into

Figure A.1. John Symon (*left*) with Silverman. *Source*: John Symon.

my life when I was a rebellious and already cynical young adult. They have, each in their own way, exerted a positive and constructive influence because their life was completely integrated with their convictions. On a daily basis, Bob and Claire made only slight compromises, while the rest of us succumbed massively to the charms of materialism. They were faithful to their ideals until the end. And they will never have known how much they have transformed society, despite the fact that they are, until now, only a footnote in history textbooks. What injustice! I had the privilege of meeting Bob, of working with him, of sharing certain joys and sorrows. I am a better human being thanks to him and it made sense to participate in this project that John led with zeal and tenacity.

S. D., March 31, 2023

Notes

List of Figures in this Book
1. Yves Boisvert, "Les rêves de son père," *La Presse*, September 12, 2008.

Foreword – A Prophet before His Time
1. *Gazette*, July 21, 1980, p. 3.
2. Lavallée died in 2022; he generously gave of his time with research for this biography.
3. Josh Freed, 1981.
4. Claire Morissette, "À Bicycle Bob," undated (see Annex for the French original).

1. Killed by a Car, Reborn on a Bicycle
1. Robert Silverman, "Family Poems: *To my father on my 50th birthday*," circa 1983.
2. Jacques Benoit, 1981.
3. Richard Burnett, 2022.
4. Porter Sargent, *A Handbook of Private Schools for American Boys and Girls*.
5. Nicolas Bednarz.
6. Gordon Cohen, telephone interview.
7. Pierre Hamel.
8. *Encyclopedia Britannica*, Cold War.
9. Sean Mills, p. 16.
10. Pierre Fortin.
11. Anthony Depalma.
12. Radio-Canada, "René Lévesque, le souverainiste."
13. Valérie Beauchemin.
14. Valérie Beauchemin.
15. Vincent Destouches.
16. Radio Canada, "La Révolution tranquille."
17. Jacques Desjardins.
18. *The Canadian Encyclopedia*, "Bomarc Missile Crisis."
19. Dimitri Roussopoulos.
20. Maria Worton.
21. David Lewis Stein.

2. The Seven Steps Bookstore
1. Henny Lowy.
2. City Lights, Our Story.
3. Henny Lowy, p. 9.
4. Henny Lowy.
5. Henny Lowy.
6. Gurdeep Stephens.
7. Dimitri Roussopoulos, telephone interview.
8. Edith Silverman.
9. "Approaching Marriages," *Canadian Jewish Review*, October 13, 1961.

10. According to comments on one online reference, Dylan's 1962 performance there was not a hit and members of the audience walked out. See: "Seven Steps – The Potpourri" by lavvy. Posted January 2011: http://boppin.com/1995/04/seven-steps-potpourri.html (accessed June 2, 2020).
11. Dominic Tardif.
12. YouTube.com.
13. *Far Out Magazine*.
14. Anna North.
15. Mikal Gilmore, December 2016.
16. Bernard Hallé.
17. Mikal Gilmore, November 2016.
18. Michael Posner, p 183.
19. *Far Out Magazine*.
20. Lowy, *Canadian Jewish Chronicle*, August 12, 1960, p. 9.
21. *The Gazette*, "Person to Person."
22. Elspeth Cameron.
23. Daniel McCabe.
24. Canada's Human Rights History.
25. Max Layton.
26. Daniel McCabe.
27. Suzanne Verdal website, Suzanne Verdal & Leonard Cohen.
28. This Chapters bookstore operated for about twenty years at 1171 Sainte-Catherine Street West before closing in 2015. At the time of writing, the venue had become a lingerie boutique.
29. John Max. The *Maclean's* article by Max has one photo showing Godfrey Stephens doing graffiti on the wall of what is presumably Silverman's very messy apartment; a pensive Roussil is shown in another photo, but Silverman is not seen. Much of the article's text deals with the lifestyle of Montreal beatniks. Stephens recounts later catching a freighter to Europe and visiting with Roussil who was then established in southern France.
30. Nick Auf der Maur, 1981.
31. Max Layton recounts: "Many years later, I owned my own bookstore and found myself in the same situation. Remembering Bob's actions, I also let the shoplifter go free."
32. Henny Lowy, p. 9.
33. *Gazette*, "Bailiff Sales," 1962.
34. Coolopolis.
35. Ann Diamond.

3. Arriving in Castro's Cuba

1. *Gazette*, "Bailiff Sales." May 19, 1962.
2. Sean Mills, p. 15.
3. *Encyclopedia Britannica*, "Cuban Missile Crisis."
4. History.com: "Cuban Missile Crisis."
5. Karen Dubinsky, 2018.
6. Sociable.
7. Karen Dubinsky, 2016.
8. The 1920s saw a bitter power struggle between Leon Trotsky and Joseph Stalin for leadership of the Soviet Union. Stalin won in what could be termed "a victory of opportunism over ideology." Trotsky was banished from the Soviet Union, but wrote a scathing critique of Stalin's regime, *Revolution Betrayed* (1936), which correctly predicted how the Soviet Union would collapse some seven decades later. Trotsky was assassinated in Mexico City in 1940, presumably on Stalin's orders.

4. Back in Montreal, Protesting against the Vietnam War

1. *New York Times*, "Dr. King Leads Chicago Peace Rally," March 26, 1967.
2. John Wilson.
3. David Lewis Stein.
4. Christopher Powell.
5. *Montreal Star*, "Demonstrators Mark Hiroshima Anniversary."

6. Stephen Milder.
7. Robert Silverman, "Do you remember Viet-Nam?"
8. *Encyclopedia Britannica*, "Gulf of Tonkin incident."
9. Christopher W. Powell, p. 62, citing Pierre Berton.
10. CTV Montreal.
11. Éric Clément.
12. Jason Von Meding.
13. Kieran Mulvaney.
14. Rex Weyler.
15. Personal communication with the authors.
16. Jan Steyaert.

5. Meeting His Second Wife at an Israeli Kibbutz
1. The term "kibbutz" is derived from the Hebrew word kvutza, meaning "group." A Kibbutz, typically a communal farm, operates under the premise that all income generated by the Kibbutz and its members goes into a common pool. When first established, it was a revolutionary idea of a voluntary society in which people live in accordance with a specific social contract, based on egalitarian and communal principles in a social and economic framework. The main characteristics of Kibbutz life were established in adherence to collectivism in property alongside a cooperative character in the spheres of education, culture, and social life. With this came the understanding that the Kibbutz member is part of a unit that is larger than just his own family. Excerpted from: www.jewishagency.org/what-exactly-is-a-kibbutz/.
2. K. Vandersypen.
3. An iconic bike store founded by the Laporte family, including Olympic cyclist Joe Laporte, in 1913. In 1973 it was purchased by Simon Roy. La Porte à bicyclette is credited by bike aficionados in Montreal as having pioneered a bicycle specifically for winter use. Today the company is located in St-Jean-sur-Richelieu. Text adapted from https://www.laporteabicyclette.com/a-propos/.
4. Pierre Hamel and François Marcil.
5. S. S. Wilson p. 82.
6. Ivan Illich, p. 16.

6. The Save Montreal Movement
1. *The Gazette*, "History Through Our Eyes: March 19, 1971, the Van Horne mansion."
2. Martin Drouin.
3. J.D. Gravenor.
4. Michel Prescott.
5. Stephen Giesler.
6. Stephen Giesler.
7. Dick Pother.
8. Brian Mckenna.
9. D'Alimonte Michael.
10. Brian Mckenna.
11. Robert Silverman, "Bikesheviks cycling for freedom."
12. Pierre Hamel and Francois Marcil.
13. Benoit Gignac.

7. Le Monde à Bicyclette
1. *Montreal Star*, 1975.
2. Tim Humphreys.
3. *Nanaimo Daily News*, "Environmentalist Promotes Bicycle Power," January 24, 1991.
4. Hamel et al.
5. *Le Jour*, "Le Manifeste de la bicyclette pour une ville plus vivable," 1975.
6. Hamel et al.

8. The First Demonstration
1. Andrew Phillips.

2. Vélo Québec, "Battles of the 70s…Victories of the 80s!," 2017.
3. Robert Silverman, "Twenty Years with le MàB."
4. Stéphane Desjardins, "Claire Morissette a changé la société avec sa bécane," 1995.
5. Robert Silverman, "Twenty Years with le MàB."
6. Stéphane Desjardins, 1995.
7. Stéphane Desjardins, 1995.
8. Daniel Ross.
9. France Lebeau.
10. Stéphane Desjardins, 1995.
11. Monique Laforge, "Claire Morissette, la grande dame du vélo urbain."
12. Robert Silverman, "Cycling Advocate Claire Morissette Passes Away."
13. Jeanne Corriveau, 2020.
14. Tooker Gomberg, "Arrested in Montreal: Sofa, So Good."
15. Josh Freed, "Bicycle Bob, an Urban Guerilla on Wheels," 1981.

9. Storming the Metro
1. *La Presse*, "Décès de Lawrence Hanigan," 2009.
2. Hubert Bauch, "Despite Some Bumps, Transit Boss Riding High."
3. Maurice Chenier. Readers should appreciate that because of long-standing rivalry between the two cities, Montrealers often made Toronto the butt of their jokes.
4. Stéphane Desjardins, 1995.
5. Maurice Chenier.
6. Robert Silverman, "Bikesheviks Cycling for Freedom."
7. *The Gazette*, "6 Cyclists Arrested."
8. Robert Silverman, "A Serious Injustice."
9. Julien Garnier.
10. Julien Garnier, p. 60 (our translation).
11. Julien Garnier, p. 61.
12. Julien Garnier.
13. René Laurent, 1981; *The Gazette*, "Metro: Bikes not Ruled Out," 1981.
14. *The Gazette*, "Bicyclists Will Be Fined if They Ride the Metro," 1981.
15. René Laurent, 1981.
16. *The Gazette*, "A $5 Permit Will Allow You to Lug a Bike onto Métro," June 19, 1982.
17. Vélo Québec, "Battles of the 70s…Victories of the 80s!," 2017.
18. The problem here is apparently objections from the bus drivers about reduced visibility; strangely this does not seem to be a problem anywhere other than Montreal.
19. *La Presse*, "Décès de Lawrence Hanigan," 2009; Irwin Block.

10. The Battle for Bike Lanes
1. René Laurent, "City moving on bicycle lanes," 1975; Robert Silverman, "Cons and Cyclists: The Tale of Cell Block A."
2. *The Gazette*, "Do-It-Yourself Bike Path Results in 2 Arrests," September 12, 1980.
3. *The Gazette*, "Cyclist in Cell Loved View of Bikers' Path," October 28, 1981.

11. Convincing Drapeau to Do the Right Thing
1. Vélo Québec, "Battles of the 70s…Victories of the 80s!," 2017.
2. Copenhagenize Index (website), "The Most Bicycle-Friendly Cities of 2019, #18: Montréal."
3. Radio-Canada, "Le chemin parcouru pour faire de Montréal une ville cyclable," July 24, 2019.
4. *Le Droit*, "Bob Silverman, un enragé de la bicyclette," June 28, 1982. https://numerique.banq.qc.ca/patrimoine/details/52327/4456800.
5. Copenhagenize Index (website), "The Most Bicycle-Friendly Cities of 2019, #18: Montréal."
6. Copenhagenize Index 2019, "About, Methodology."
7. Vélo Québec, June 2021.
8. *Le Soleil*, "Grève, pas grève, à bicyclette… comme à Pékin."
9. Erika Benke.
10. Stéphane Desjardins, "Claire Morissette a changé la société avec sa bécane," 1995.

11. Equiterre.
12. Stéphane Desjardins, "Claire Morissette a changé la société avec sa bécane," 1995.

12. A Brief History of Montreal Bike Paths
1. S. S. Wilson.
2. Montréal, "Mémoires des Montréalais, Montréal ville cyclable, hier et aujourd'hui," January 25, 2017.
3. Some attribute the invention of the car to Frenchman Nicolas-Joseph Cugnot in 1769, although his was a steam-powered model; Englishman Richard Trevithick had his own steam-powered vehicle by 1801. Another possibility is that the car was essentially invented by the Belgian, Étienne Lenoir, when he developed the internal combustion engine in 1860. Other contenders include various French inventors: Amédée Bollé in 1873, Léon Serpollet in 1888, and Armand Peugeot in 1889. German Nikolaus Otto developed the four-stroke engine in 1876 while fellow German Gottlieb Daimler refined internal combustion engine technology for motorcycles and automobiles circa 1883. But it was another German, Karl Benz, who developed the first commercially available automobile in 1886. Siegfried Marcus, a German living in Austria, may have developed a working car circa 1870, but records of his invention were largely destroyed by the Nazis because of his Jewish heritage.
4. Carlton Reid, 2012.
5. Carlton Reid, 2014.
6. David Magil.
7. René Laurent, 1975.
8. Brad Plumer, September 26, 2016.
9. Marie-Michèle Sioui.
10. Trajectoire Québec et la Fondation David Suzuki.

13. One Million Cyclists Trapped on Montreal Island
1. Longueuil (Ville de), 2018.
2. JCCB (Ponts Jacques Cartier Champlain Bridges).
3. Robert Silverman, "Cons and Cyclists: The Tale of Cell Block A."
4. *La Presse*, "Quatre cents cyclistes défient la loi sur le pont Jacques-Cartier," 1975.
5. Robert Silverman, "Bikesheviks Cycling for Freedom," 1980.
6. Robert Silverman, "Bikesheviks Cycling for Freedom," 1980.
7. BAnQ numérique, 1977.
8. Pierre Foglia, July 8, 1977?"
9. Henri Ouellette-Vézina.
10. Robert Silverman, "Bikesheviks Cycling for Freedom," 1980.

14. A Bike-Friendly Mayor Is Elected
1. Michel Prescott.
2. Brian McKenna, p. 328.
3. Stéphane Desjardins was aboard the Montreal's Old Port to Boucherville ferry for its maiden run when the boat became stuck on a sandbank in the middle of the river. It briefly seemed that passengers and crew would need to be evacuated by the Coast Guard. Luckily, the ferry freed itself and continued on its way.
4. Gérard Bérubé.
5. Plume Latraverse (website).
6. *Journal de Montréal*, 2021.
7. Lanken, 1976.
8. Scott, Marian, 2015.
9. Kilpatrick, p. 9.
10. *The Gazette*, "History Through Our Eyes: October 12, 1976, 'Bicycle Bob' Silverman."
11. Longueuil, 2025.
12. Quote by Jacques Desjardins as part of the "Encore du Monde à bicyclette" exhibit at the Maison de la Culture NDG on Botrel Street early 2021.

13. This bridge was constructed for Expo 67 and used by Expo Express train; a bike lane was built in 1993 directly on the path of the Expo Express, linking the Lachine Canal path to Jean Drapeau Park; over 4,000 cyclists use it daily. Source: Habitat 67, p. 11.
14. Robert Silverman, "Twenty years with le MàB," 2000.
15. André Fauteux, p. 9.
16. André Fauteux, p. 9.
17. Robert Silverman, "Twenty years with le MàB," 2000.
18. Maryse Bérubé.
19. John Symon, "Le Monde à Bicyclette Celebrates 40 Years," 2015.
20. Daniel Ross, citing January 1976 MàB newsletter.
21. John Symon's communication with Ministry of Transport officials.

15. Protesting the Auto Show
1. Daniel Ross, citing January 1976 MàB newsletter.
2. *Gazette*, "Car Show Aura Denounced as Appeal to Sex, Power." January 17, 1977.
3. Tom Berry.
4. *Vancouver Sun*.
5. Silverman (1980) in *Open Road*.
6. Agence France-Presse.
7. Silverman (1980) in *Open Road*.
8. Josh Freed.
9. In the late 1980s, Stéphane Desjardins applied for a paid job at le Monde à bicyclette. During the job interview, Silverman asked: "if you won a million dollars, would you keep it?" Desjardins replied that he would give most of it to MàB, a response which pleased Silverman.
10. *Gazette*, "Bert Silverman obituary," February 15, 1993.
11. *Gazette*, "Florence Silverman obituary," March 17, 1987.
12. Daniel C. Cuff.
13. Nora Underwood.

16. The Philadelphia Bicycle Coalition and International Connections
1. Jeff Mapes, 2022.
2. Meghan Bailey.
3. Jeff Mapes, 2011.
4. Jean-François Pronovost.
5. Julia Maskoulis.
6. M. Lalonde.
7. Dane Lanken.
8. CCNR.
9. Gordon Edwards, 2021.
10. Gordon Edwards, 1983.
11. Stuart Anthony Stilitz.
12. *Gazette*, "Group Tours and Nature Programs Make Cycling Educational," July 27, 1985.

17. MàB and Vélo Québec: Allies or Rivals?
1. FQSC.
2. Vélo Québec, "Vélo Québec : de 1967 à aujourd'hui" (n.d.).
3. Robert Silverman, "Twenty years with le MàB."
4. Jacques Desjardins.
5. FQSC.
6. C. Bain.
7. Benoît Gignac.
8. Another non-profit organization, the Fédération québécoise des sports cyclistes (FQSC), oversees competitive cycling in Quebec.
9. Florence Ferraris.
10. Suzanne Lareau.
11. Bernard Hallé.

12. Stéphane Desjardins, 2017.
13. Michel Labrecque.
14. Vélo Québec, "Battles of the 70s...Victories of the 80s!" *Public Engagement, The History of Cycling*, April 1, 2017.
15. Reid, 2015.
16. Jeff Mapes, 2011.
17. Michel Labrecque was also CEO of VQ from 1985–2000. He went on to serve as CEO of the STM from 2009 to 2013.
18. Vélo Québec, "Battles of the 70s...Victories of the 80s!," 2017.
19. Vélo Québec, "Battles of the 70s...Victories of the 80s!," 2017.
20. Vélo Québec, "Battles of the 70s...Victories of the 80s!," 2017.
21. Josh Freed, 1981.
22. *La Presse*, November 29, 1985.
23. Government of Canada, 2022.

18. Participatory Volleyball, Good Volleyball is like Good Sex

1. Brian Johnson, 1974.
2. Brian Johnson, 1974.
3. Michael Posner, p. 183.
4. *The Gazette*, "Terrence Regan obituary," May 22, 2021.
5. Johnson, 1974.
6. Auf der Maur, 1981.
7. This congregation of nuns played a key role in the founding of Montreal's first hospital, Hôtel-Dieu de Montréal in 1642.
8. Angela Bischoff.
9. Brian Johnson, 1974.

19. The Handbook of How to Run a Vélorution

1. Eric Norden.
2. *Encyclopedia Britannica*, "Community Organizing."
3. Sanford D. Horwitt.
4. Sanford D. Horwitt.
5. Michael Patrick Leahy and Gina Loudon, *Rules for Conservative Radicals*.
6. Excerpt from *Rules for Radicals*, by Saul Alinsky.
7. Merriam-Webster Online Dictionary, "Anarchy."
8. Sara Bonisteel.
9. United Nations.
10. Robert Silverman, telephone interviews.
11. *Radio-Canada*, "Le journal *Le Jour*, une présence éphémère dans le paysage médiatique," December 1, 2021.
12. The Cyclists' Manifesto is reproduced in the Annex.
13. Robert Silverman, telephone interviews.
14. F. Lebeau.
15. Robert Silverman, "Spreading the Vélorution," 2000.
16. Michel Labrecque.
17. Jean-François Pronovost, Facebook post.
18. Michel Labrecque.

20. Vietnam and Cuba

1. Marc Doré, 1989; Josh Freed, 1988.
2. Spencer Tucker; William Scheck.
3. Johs Freed, 1988.
4. Phuong Nguyen.
5. BNP Paribas.
6. Marc Doré.
7. Josh Freed, 1977.

8. Charles Churchill et al.
9. University of Florida.
10. Ivan Illich, 1974.
11. Manuel Franco.
12. Bill Weinberg.
13. Bill Weinberg.
14. Peter McQueen.
15. Ronn Pineo.

21. Silverman and Politics
1. Alex Tyrrell.
2. Michael William.
3. Terrence Regan.
4. Henri Richard, also a Stanley Cup-winning hockey player, was the younger brother of Maurice Richard, referred to earlier in this book. While Richard owned the bar, it appears there was little contact between him and Silverman.
5. When Silverman gave a copy of Maurice Brinton's book *The Irrational in Politics* to Morissette, he included this inscription: "À mon amie Claire, Je donne ce livre original à mon amie Claire, écologiste, botaniste, anarchiste, androgyne, Vélorutionnaire et révolutionnaire, douée, conviviable et inoubliable, pour qu'elle aiguise plus sa conscience critique et qu'elle approfondie ses connaissances des êtres humains. Bob."
6. Robert Silverman, "Official Le MàB Position on Helmet Law."
7. Robert Silverman, "The Case Against Helmet Laws."
8. Hillman, April 11, 1992.
9. Jane Jacobs.
10. Robert Silverman, telephone interview.
11. Dane Lanken,
12. Bradford Snell.
13. Bradford Snell.
14. Pierre Hamel.
15. *Gazette*, "Car Show Aura Denounced as Appeal to Sex, Power," January 17, 1977.
16. Daniel Rufiange.
17. Daniel Rufiange.
18. Johns Hopkins Medicine.
19. Johns Hopkins Medicine.
20. Robert Silverman, "On reaching 60."
21. Ray Gottlieb, telephone interview.
22. Ray Gottlieb.
23. J. A. Rawstron.
24. Janet Goodrich.
25. Josh Freed, 1981.
26. Gordon Edwards.
27. Robert Silverman, "On reaching 60."
28. Some branches of Judaism do subscribe to reincarnation.
29. Mind Journal.
30. Chinese Zodiac.
31. Google Books, "Review of *Revolution for the Hell of It: The Book That Earned Abbie Hoffman a Five-Year Prison Term at the Chicago Conspiracy Trial*, by Abbie Hoffman."
32. Abbie Hoffman.
33. Google Books, "Review of *Revolution for the Hell of It: The Book That Earned Abbie Hoffman a Five-Year Prison Term at the Chicago Conspiracy Trial*, by Abbie Hoffman."
34. *Encyclopaedia Universalis*.
35. John Symon, 2015.
36. Josh Freed, 1988.
37. Tom Vallance.
38. Kathryn Watson.

39. Jacques Desjardins.
40. Abraham Weizfeld.
41. Montreal has seen many riots throughout its history. The city also served briefly as the capital of Canada until Tory rioters burned down the Parliament buildings in 1849.
42. Silverman seemed unaware of the Abbie Hoffman comparison.
43. From Morissette's poem: "He gives the villains their pill, Of paradox, of ridicule."
44. Andy Riga.
45. Michel Camus.
46. Zvi Leve.

22. Milton Park Days
1. Martin Bérubé.
2. Lucia Kowaluk.
3. Lucia Kowaluk.
4. Susan Schwartz.
5. Valérie Beaulieu.
6. Stéphane Desjardins, 1995.
7. Fédération de l'habitation coopérative du Québec, https://fhcq.coop/en/cooperatives/milton-parc
8. Elizabeth Kaegi.
9. Robert Silverman, *Must the Treatment Be Toxic?*
10. Elizabeth Kaegi.
11. Elizabeth Kaegi.
12. L. Harris.
13. Days of the Year.
14. Nawrocki.
15. Bischoff.
16. Robert Silverman, *Oxygen Park Opens*.
17. Jeanne Corriveau, 2014.
18. Depave Paradise.

24. Déménagement à Val-David
1. Musée national des beaux-arts du Québec.
2. Robert Silverman, "Pourquoi je m'installe à Val-David."
3. Galerie de L'âme.
4. Galerie de L'âme.
5. Alternative Information & Development Centre.
6. "The mission of the local community services centre (CLSC) is to provide, to the population of its territory, frontline common health and social services, as well as preventive, curative, rehabilitative and/or reintegration services and carry out public health activities," according to the Quebec Health Ministry: www.msss.gouv.qc.ca/en/reseau/etablissements-de-sante-et-de-services-sociaux/.

25. Nearing the Finish Line
1. Carlton Reid.
2. R. Wutzke.

26. Epilogue and Homages
1. Matt Hansen.
2. Jean-François Nadeau.
3. Coralie Laplante.
4. Coralie Laplante.
5. Ville de Montréal, 2022.
6. Richard Wutzke.
7. David Birnbaum.

Annex
1. Statistique Canada, 2023.

2. Statistique Canada, 2022.
3. HSBC, 2022.
4. ISQ, 2022.
5. Basé sur des valeurs en dollars de 2012 en chaîne de Fischer.
6. Innovation, Sciences et Développement économique Canada, 2021.
7. HSBC, 2022.
8. Association canadienne des constructeurs de véhicules (CVMA), 2017.
9. Groupement des assureurs automobiles, 2020
10. BAC, 2020.
11. Autorité des marchés financiers.
12. Jérôme Laviolette, 2020.
13. Stéphane Blais, 2022.
14. Nicolas Bérubé, 2022.
15. Baril, Hélène, 2021.
16. Jérôme Laviolette, 2020.
17. Jérôme Laviolette, 2020.
18. Statistique Canada, 2023.
19. Alice Mariette, 2020.
20. CMM, 2018.
21. Sarah V. Doyon and Christian Savard, 2022.
22. Donald Schoup.
23. Dayna Evans, 2021.
24. Guide de l'auto, 2021.

Bibliography

ACCV (CVMA). "Faits importants – Données sur l'industrie automobile du Canada." December 19 2017, [Online]. [www.cvma.ca/wp-content/uploads/2018/01/Website-WP-Important-Facts-Pdf-Dec-19-2017-FR.pdf].

ACCV (CVMA). "Faits importants - L'industrie automobile canadienne: force motrice pour l'emploi, les investissements et l'innovation." 2021, [Online]. [www.cvma.ca/fr/lindustrie/faits/].

Agence France-Presse. "Les routes tuent 1,35 million de personnes à travers le monde." *Radio-Canada*, December 7, 2018, https://ici.radio-canada.ca/nouvelle/1140413/oms-organisation-mondiale-sante-accident-route-mort-monde.

Alinsky, Saul. *Rules for Radicals: A Pragmatic Primer for Realistic Radicals*, Knopf Doubleday, New York, 1997.

Al Jazeera. "France Drops Arafat Poisoning Investigation." September 3, 2015, www.aljazeera.com/news/2015/9/3/france-drops-arafat-poisoning-investigation.

Alternative Information & Development Centre (AIDC). "7 Che Guevara quotes." October 9, 2017, https://aidc.org.za/7-che-guevara-quotes/.

Art Public Montréal. "Girafes, 1966, Robert Roussil." https://artpublicmontreal.ca/oeuvre/girafes/, accessed April 2, 2020.

Association of Vision Educators. "About the Bates Method." https://www.naturalvisionteachers.org/about-william-bates.e230.

Atkinson, Cathryn. "Obituary - Irving Layton." *The Guardian*, January 23, 2006, https://www.theguardian.com/news/2006/jan/23/guardianobituaries.booksobituaries, accessed March 28, 2020

Auf der Maur, Nick. "Bicycle Bob, 47, Peddles Freedom." *The Gazette*, April 1, 1981. http://robert-silverman.net/47peddlesfreedom.htm.

Bailey, Meghan. *Bicycling Publications in University Archives*. Healey Library at UMass Boston, 2017. https://blogs.umb.edu/archives/tag/bicycle-network/.

Bain, C. "Cyclists Load Bikes Aboard Metro." *Montreal Star*, June 28, 1979.

Balilty, Oded. "AP PHOTOS: Israel's Separation Barrier, 20 Years On." *Associated Press*, June 27, 2022. https://apnews.com/article/politics-middle-east-jerusalem-israel-west-bank-2ce5d9956b729ad6169c880d00068977.

BAnQ numérique. "Bob Silverman, un enragé de la bicyclette." *Le Droit*, June 28, 1982, https://numerique.banq.qc.ca/patrimoine/details/52327/4456800.

BAnQ numérique. "Un des trottoirs du pont sera réparé temporairement samedi." *Le Devoir*, April 22, 1977, https://numerique.banq.qc.ca/patrimoine/details/52327/2775632.

Baril, Hélène. "La voiture est en voie de disparition au Québec." *La Presse*, January 29, 2021, https://www.lapresse.ca/affaires/economie/2021-01-29/rapport-etat-de-l-energie-2021/la-voiture-est-en-voie-de-disparition-au-quebec.php.

Basheer, Shamnad. "Leonard Cohen: Of Love, Light and Copyright." *Wire*, November 16, 2016, https://thewire.in/culture/leonard-cohen-of-love-light-and-copyright.

Bauch, Hubert. "Despite Some Bumps, Transit Boss Riding High." *Gazette*, June 17, 1986.

Beauchemin, Valérie. "McGill University Quota, 1924–1950." translated by Helge Dascher. *Museum of Jewish Montreal*, accessed March 29, 2020, http://imjm.ca/location/1565.

Beaulieu, Valérie. *Hommage à Phillis Lambert (sic) - Melissa del Pinto*, Art Public Montréal, 2019, https://artpublicmontreal.ca/en/oeuvre/hommage-a-phillis-lambert/.

Bednarz, Nicolas. "Le boulevard Décarie avant l'avènement de l'autoroute." *Archives Montréal*, April 18, 2019, https://archivesdemontreal.com/2019/04/18/le-boulevard-decarie-avant-lavenement-de-lautoroute/.

Béland, Gabriel. "Bicycle Bob rêve encore." *La Presse*, July 2, 2017, accessed May 7, 2020, https://plus.lapresse.ca/screens/d1d54dae-dd57-4e84-a8d4-b5f37bd045ed%7Ca5Y4BVFIhMJy.html?fbclid=IwAR1YhYx4j6AqjsZ7lLfeai23B52-A2UL6rPp4E-M8gPYmowRRBmGdcSW5PY.

Béland, Gabriel. "Robert Silverman, cycliste militant « Il a tout gagné »." *La Presse*, February 27, 2022, https://www.lapresse.ca/actualites/2022-02-27/robert-silverman-cycliste-militant/il-a-tout-gagne.php?fbclid=IwAR0EDJp2qTfKGUtyv2-PB4WXmo9CKrloavbqOgSd7FSUYszqBeuc42lVZso.

Benke, Erika. "The Cycle-Mad City in Finland That Doesn't Stop for Snow." (video) BBC, January 21, 2022, https://www.bbc.com/news/av/world-europe-64354089.

Benoit, Jacques. "Le vélo vaincra, dit Bob Silverman." *La Presse*, October 13, 1981.

Bernard, Pablo. "Naissance et évolution de la lutte cyclo-militante à Montréal et à Paris (1972–2004)." Histoire. 2015. dumas-01445326 Université De Versailles Saint-Quentin-En-Yvelines, Mémoire de Maitrise en Histoire contemporaine https://dumas.ccsd.cnrs.fr/dumas-01445326/document.

Berry, Tom. *Le monde à bicyclette* (documentary film), Montreal, 1977, www.youtube.com/watch?v=O6Rbg9Xs-CA.

Bérubé, Gérard. "Perspectives—Le Québec en récession." *Le Devoir*, December 11, 2008, www.ledevoir.com/opinion/chroniques/222685/perspectives-le-quebec-en-recession.

Bérubé, Martin. "La saga de La Cité." 5 juillet 2021, Propos Montréal, https://proposmontreal.com/index.php/la-saga-de-la-cite/.

Bérubé, Maryse. "[Le 'chaînon manquant' de la piste cyclable est maintenant réalisé] vers la Rive-Sud promise, à bicyclette…" *La Presse*, June 26, 1990.

Bérubé, Nicolas. "Le nombre de véhicules est en hausse au Canada." *La Presse+*, December 12, 2022, https://plus.lapresse.ca/screens/3ed1f68d-814f-4397-b19f-4d09fbf26936_7C__0.html?utm_content=email&utm_source=lpp&utm_medium=referral&utm_campaign=internal+share.

Bianco, Martha J. "Kennedy, 60 Minutes, and Roger Rabbit: Understanding Conspiracy-Theory Explanations of The Decline of Urban Mss Transit." Portland State University, November 17, 1998, http://marthabianco.com/kennedy_rogerrabbit.pdf, accessed February 9, 2021.

Bikes not Bombs (website). "Who We Are, Our Mission." https://bikesnotbombs.org/mission-and-model/.
Bilan Québec. "Déclaration controversée du président du Canadien National, Donald Gordon;" Université de Sherbrooke, https://perspective.usherbrooke.ca/bilan/quebec/evenements/20920, accessed March 29, 2020.
Birnbaum, David. "MNA D'Arcy McGee's address to Quebec's National Assembly." Facebook, March 15, 2022, www.facebook.com/watch/?v=964653574064738.
Blais, Stéphane. "Rapport: Québec doit plafonner le parc automobile et s'attaquer à l'auto solo." Les Affaires, June 8, 2022, https://www.lesaffaires.com/secteurs-d-activite/automobile/rapport-quebec-doit-plafonner-le-parc-automobile-et-s-attaquer-a-l-auto-solo/633733.
Bliss, Laura. "If Bicycles Took up as Much Space as Cars." Bloomberg, October 9, 2014, www.bloomberg.com/news/articles/2014-10-09/if-bicycles-took-up-as-much-space-as-cars.
Block, Irwin. "Councillor Weathered Many Transit Strikes." The Gazette, November 5, 2009.
BNP Paribas. Vietnam : Le consommateur, Mai 2024, www.tradesolutions.bnpparibas.com/fr/importer-exporter/vietnam/consommateur.
Bordeleau, Stéphane. «La Ville de Montréal promet 200 km de pistes cyclables de plus d'ici 2027.» Radio Canada, November 1, 2022, https://ici.radio-canada.ca/nouvelle/1929469/plan-pistes-cyclables-montreal-vision-velo-200-km.
Boisvert, Yves. "Les rêves de son père." La Presse, September 12, 2008, www.lapresse.ca/debats/chroniques/yves-boisvert/200809/12/01-21112-les-reves-de-son-pere.php.
Bonisteel, Sara. "Fake Blood." October 15, 2013, https://www.epicurious.com/recipes/food/views/fake-blood-51199810.
Bourgoin, Jean-Maxime. "L'histoire entre les cyclistes et le pont Jacques-Cartier." Journal de Montréal, August 25, 2015, www.journaldemontreal.com/2015/08/25/lhistoire-entre-les-cyclistes-et-le-pont-jacques-cartier.
Bouthillier, Guy. "Camillien Houde et la conscription maudite." Le Devoir, August 5, 2015, www.ledevoir.com/opinion/idees/446735/camillien-houde-et-la-conscription-maudite.
Boyko, John. "Manifeste de Regina." L'Encyclopédie Canadienne, 2 septembre 2021, [Online]. [https://www.thecanadianencyclopedia.ca/fr/article/manifeste-de-regina-1933].
Brosseau-Pouliot, Vincent. "Québec pédale moins vite que nous." la Presse, June 4, 2023: www.lapresse.ca/contexte/editoriaux/2023-06-04/quebec-pedale-moins-vite-que-nous.php.
Brouillard, Marc-André. À vélo vers une ville nouvelle. Editions les 400 Coups, Montréal, 2022.
Bulletin de Liaison de Communauto. "Hommage à Claire Morissette." L'écho-mobile vol. XV, no. 2 (June 2009), www.communauto.com/abonnes/echo-mobile_v15no2.pdf.
Bureau d'assurance du Canada (BAC). Assurances de dommages au Canada 2023, https://a-us.storyblok.com/f/1003207/x/abac0276bf/2023-ibc-fact-book-fr.pdf.
Bumbaru, Dinu. "50 ans de la démolition de la maison Van Horne: mesurer les progrès et les défis du patrimoine de la métropole." September 7, 2023, https://blog.heritagemontreal.org/50-ans-de-la-demolition-de-la-maison-van-horne-mesurer-les-progres-et-les-defis-du-patrimoine-de-la-metropole/, accessed September 4, 2023.
Burnett, Richard. "If It Glitters, It's Montréal's Golden Square Mile." Mtl Blog, September 2, 2022, www.mtl.org/en/experience/golden-square-mile.

Cameron, Elspeth. "Layton, Irving Peter." *Canadian Encyclopedia*. Edmonton: Hurtig, 1988, pp. 1190–1191. https://www.thecanadianencyclopedia.ca/en/article/irving-layton, accessed March 29, 2021.

Camfield, David. "The history and politics of the Communist Party of Canada: an overview." Briarpatch Magazine, July 29, 2020; https://briarpatchmagazine.com/articles/view/the-history-and-politics-communist-party-of-canada, accessed April 23, 2020.

Canada's Human Rights History. "Frank Scott." https://historyofrights.ca/encyclopaedia/biographies/frank-reginald-scott/, accessed March 29, 2020.

Canadian Automotive Industry. "About the Industry." *Innovation, Science and Economic Development Canada*, July 7, 2021, https://ised-isde.canada.ca/site/canadian-automotive-industry/en.

Canadian Elections Database. 1984 Federal Election - Laurier; http://canadianelectionsdatabase.ca/PHASE5/?p=0&type=election&ID=609, accessed March 5, 2021.

Canadian Encyclopedia. "Bomarc Missile Crisis." www.thecanadianencyclopedia.ca/en/article/bomarc-missile-crisis, accessed March 30, 2021.

Canadian Encyclopedia. "Camille Laurin (Obituary)." www.thecanadianencyclopedia.ca/en/article/camille-laurin-obituary.

Canadian Jewish Review. "Approaching Marriages." October 13, 1961, https://newspapers.lib.sfu.ca/mcc-cjr-4413/page-3.

Castaneda, Jorge G. "Che Guevara." Suhrkamp Editor, Berlin, 1998.

Castonguay, Alain. "Hausse de 10,3 % des primes directes souscrites en dommages au Québec en 2023," Portail de l'assurance, 25 juin 2024, https://portail-assurance.ca/article/hausse-de-103-des-primes-directes-souscrites-en-dommages-au-quebec-en-2023/,

CBC (Canadian Broadcasting Corporation). Radio Noon with host Ann Lagacé-Dowson. "Can Bikes and Cars Co-Exist?" Interview with Robert Silverman and John Symon, 2007.

CCNR (Canadian Coalition for Nuclear Responsibility). "My Mommy said there's something in the air that could kill me." advertisement, Gazette, May 12, 1979.

Chenier, Maurice. "We Will Consider Bikes on Metro Says MUTCM Boss." Gazette, May 12, 1978.

Churchill, Charles, and Bruce Petschek. *Vélorution: One City's Solution to the Automobile*. (film) 1996.

City of Melbourne, Cycling Issues Paper. 2005, Space efficiencies of car, tram, bike and walking as cited by ResearchGate (website): https://www.researchgate.net/figure/Space-efficiencies-of-car-tram-bike-and-walking_fig5_232847647.

City Lights Bookstore (website). "Our Story, a Short History of City Lights." https://citylights.com/our-story/a-short-history-of-city-lights/.

City Lights Bookstore (website). Obituary notice for co-founder Lawrence Ferlinghetti (1919–2021), http://citylights.com/, accessed February 28, 2021.

Clément, Éric. "Dans Give Peace a Chance, Charlebois entend sa voix." *La Presse*, April 13, 2019, https://www.lapresse.ca/arts/musique/2019-04-13/dans-give-peace-a-chance-charlebois-entend-sa-voix.

Cléroux, Benoît. "Le métro de Montréal, 35 ans déjà." Hurtubise HMH, Montréal, 2001.

Colville-Andersen, Mikael. "Copenhagenize: The Definitive Guide to Global Bicycle Urbanism." Island Press, Washington, 2018.

Communauté métropolitaine de Montréal (CMM). Déplacements domicile-travail dans le Grand Montréal: Faible progression du transport durable depuis 2001, Perspective du Grand Montréal, février 2018. https://cmm.qc.ca/communiques/deplacements-domicile-travail-dans-le-grand-montreal-faible-progression-du-transport-durable-depuis-2001/.

Communauto. "Augmentation importante de la flotte Communauto après un record d'utilisation en 2021." March 24, 2022, https://communauto.com/augmentation-importante-de-la-flotte-communauto/.

Communauto. "Qui sommes-nous?" https://communauto.com/a-propos/.

The Conversation. Le puissant message du manifeste d'Octobre 1979, https://theconversation.com/le-puissant-message-du-manifeste-doctobre-1970-147426.

Coolopolis. "From the Rainbow to Darwin's, Montreal Bars from the 1970s." http://coolopolis.blogspot.com/2017/05/from-rainbow-to-darwins-montreal-bars.html, accessed March 29, 2020.

Copenhagenize. "Bicycle Map of Montreal 1897." www.copenhagenize.com/2013/10/bicycle-map-of-montreal-1897.html, accessed June 4, 2020.

Copenhagenize Index 2019. "About, Methodology." https://copenhagenizeindex.eu/about/methodology, accessed June 4, 2020.

Copenhagenize Index (website). "The Most Bicycle-Friendly Cities of 2019, #18: Montréal." https://copenhagenizeindex.eu/cities/montreal, accessed June 4, 2020.

Corriveau, Jeanne. "Le parc Oxygène rasé pour faire place aux condos." *Le Devoir*, June 27, 2014, www.ledevoir.com/politique/montreal/411995/destruction-d-un-parc-au-centre-ville.

Corriveau, Jeanne. "La piste cyclable du pont Jacques-Cartier sera déneigée." *Le Devoir*, November 8, 2019, www.ledevoir.com/societe/transports-urbanisme/566511/la-piste-cyclable-du-pont-jacques-cartier-sera-deneigee-pour-25-personnes.

Corriveau, Jeanne. "Montréal compterait un million de cyclistes." *Le Devoir*, July 5, 2016, www.ledevoir.com/politique/montreal/474795/montreal-compterait-un-million-de-cyclistes, accessed July 19, 2020.

Cosner Gallery artist biographies. "Guy Montpetit." https://www.galeriecosner.com/en/artists/1182-guy-montpetit.html.

Critical Mass. https://archive.ph/20120529190357/http://www.telegraph.co.uk/travel/729324/London-How-cyclists-around-the-world-put-a-spoke-in-the-motorist's-wheel.html, accessed April 25, 2020.

CTV Montreal. "50 Years of Giving Peace a Chance, as Queen Elizabeth Hotel Celebrates Anniversary of Lennon, Ono's Bed-In." May 23, 2019, https://montreal.ctvnews.ca/50-years-of-giving-peace-a-chance-as-queen-elizabeth-hotel-celebrates-anniversary-of-lennon-ono-s-bed-in-1.4434482.

Cuff, Daniel C. "New President Chosen at Deprenyl of Toronto," *New York Times*, May 4, 1990.

The Cyclists' Vehicle. "Newsletter of the Edmonton Bicycle Commuters." Spring 1990, https://static1.squarespace.com/static/5adabc778ab7228340d6ofdc/t/5bf8b6978985839163a afe9d/1543026340588/EBC-Newsletter-Spring-1990.pdf.

Cyclo Nord-Sud. "Mission." https://cyclonordsud.org/en/about-us/, accessed July 18, 2020.

Days of The Year. "World Car Free Day," [Online]. [www.daysoftheyear.com/days/world-car-free-day/], 2025.

Depalma, Anthony. "Pierre Vallieres, 60, Angry Voice of Quebec Separatism, Dies." *New York Times*, December 26, 1998, www.nytimes.com/1998/12/26/world/pierre-vallieres-60-angry-voice-of-quebec-separatism-dies.html.

Depave Paradise. "GCC Celebrates 10 Years of Depave Paradise," [online]. [https://depaveparadise.ca/gcc-celebrates-10-years-of-depave-paradise/], 2025.

Desjardins, Stéphane. "Claire Morissette a changé la société avec sa bécane." *Vélo Mag*, Summer 1995.

Desjardins, Stéphane. "Le Vélo prend sa place au Québec." *Vélo Mag*, Hors Série 2017.

Desjardins, Stéphane. «Les infrastructures cyclables ailleurs dans le monde,» Vélo Mag, January 19 2019, [Online]. [https://www.velomag.com/actualites/reportage/infrastructures-cyclables-monde/#:ffi:text=Xiamen, Chine,-Xiamen compte 1&text=Elle est située dans la,m de largeur, 30000 lampadaires].

Destouches, Vincent. "Fécondité: pourquoi le Québec a besoin de vous." *Actualité*, April 29, 2016, https://lactualite.com/societe/fecondite-pourquoi-le-quebec-a-besoin-de-vous.

Diamond, Ann. "How I (Finally) Met Leonard Cohen." (n.d.) GEIST, www.geist.com/fact/essays/how-i-finally-met-leonard-cohen/, accessed April 1, 2020.

Dieul, Nathalie. "Les prophéties de « Bicycle Bob » pour l'avenir du vélo à Montréal." *Epoch Times*, January 19, 2016, https://www-eu.epochtimes.fr/les-propheties-de-bicycle-bob-pour-lavenir-du-velo-a-montreal-10206.html, accessed July 27, 2020.

Doré, Marc. "Que le Vietnam se le tienne pour dit, Silverman arrive." *La Presse*, February 26, 1989, https://numerique.banq.qc.ca/patrimoine/details/52327/2261564?docsearchtext=silverman.

Doyon, Sarah V., and Christian Savard. "S'affranchir de la deuxième voiture." *La Presse*, August 19, 2022, www.lapresse.ca/debats/opinions/2022-08-19/s-affranchir-de-la-deuxieme-voiture.php.

Drouin, Martin. "Van Horne Mansion (1870–1973)." *Encyclopedia of French Cultural Heritage in North America*, www.ameriquefrancaise.org/en/article-459/Van_Horne_Mansion_(1870-1973):_a_Demolition_That_Changed_the_History_of_Heritage_Preservation.html.

Dubinsky, Karen. "Cuba and the Making of a United States Left." *Black Perspectives*, September 14, 2018, www.aaihs.org/cuba-and-the-making-of-a-united-states-left/.

Dubinsky, Karen. "Leonard Cohen—'The Last Tourist in Havana.'" *CBC News*, November 16, 2016, www.cbc.ca/news/opinion/cohen-in-havana-1.3852156.

Duchesne, André. "Leonard Cohen: ses femmes, ses muses." *La Presse*, Novembre 12, 2016, https://www.lapresse.ca/arts/musique/201611/12/01-5040633-leonard-cohen-ses-femmes-ses-muses.php, accessed March 29, 2021.

Echohungry.com. "Energy efficiency in transport"; https://ecohungry.com/energy-efficiency-in-transportation/, accessed April 27, 2020.

Eckermann, Eric. "World History of the Automobile." Society of Automotive Engineers, Warrendale (PA), 2001.

Edmonton Elections. Past Election Results, https://www.edmonton.ca/city_government/municipal_elections/past-results, accessed June 6, 2020.

Edwards, Gordon. "Canada's Nuclear Industry and the Myth of the Peaceful Atom." CCNR, 1983, https://www.ccnr.org/myth_1.html.

Emploi et Développement social Canada. "Assurance-Emploi," https://www.canada.ca/fr/emploi-developpement-social/programmes/assurance-emploi.html, 2024.

Encyclopedia Britannica. "Cold War." www.britannica.com/event/Cold-War, accessed March 21, 2020.

Encyclopedia Britannica. "Cuban Missile Crisis." https://www.britannica.com/event/Cuban-missile-crisis, accessed April 15, 2020.

Encyclopedia Britannica. "Gulf of Tonkin Incident." www.britannica.com/event/Gulf-of-Tonkin-incident, accessed April 15, 2020.

Encyclopaedia Universalis. Don Quichotte, https://www.universalis.fr/encyclopedie/don-quichotte/, accessed april 15, 2024.

ENS de Lyon. "Suburbs, Ressources de géographie pour les enseignants Eduscol." October 2021, suburbs / suburbanisation http://geoconfluences.ens-lyon.fr/glossaire/suburbs-suburbanisation.

Equiterre. "Cocktail Transport." November 2009, www.equiterre.org/fr/ressources/fiche-cocktail-transport.

European Cyclists' Federation. "Cycling Modal Share." https://ecf.com/cycling-data/cycling-modal-share, accessed November 21, 2021.

Evans, Dayna. "Free Parking Is Killing Cities." *Bloomberg BusinessWeek*, August 31, 2021, www.bloomberg.com/news/features/2021-08-31/why-free-parking-is-bad-according-to-one-ucla-professor?leadSource=uverify wall.

Fauteux, André. "Red Tape Is Stalling Plans for a Bike Link." *Gazette*, September 8, 1988.

FEAROF. "The Ultimate List of Phobias and Fears." www.fearof.net/fear-of-money-phobia-chrometophobia-or-chrematophobia/, accessed March 29, 2020.

Fédération de l'habitation Coopérative du Québec. Our Coop - Milton Park, [onlilne]. [https://fhcq.coop/en/cooperatives/milton-parc], 2025.

Ferraris, Florence. "Du Rêve à l'Action." Vélo Mag, Special Edition, 2017.

Fitterman, Lisa. "Activist Robert Silverman Helped Claim Space for Bicycles on Montreal's Streets." *Globe And Mail*, March 11, 2022, www.theglobeandmail.com/canada/article-activist-robert-silverman-helped-claim-space-for-bicycles-on-montreals/?fbclid=IwAR2Kvb94zV6Ps8gtjVH9TkVnicahQAmPPKmj-46FUpsEWplhenFLu1_EX4A.

Foglia, Pierre. "Avez-vous votre plaque?" *La Presse*, July 8, 1977, https://diffusion.banq.qc.ca/pdfjs-1.6.210-dist_banq/web/viewer.html?file=//diffusion.banq.qc.ca/pdfjs-1.6.210-dist_banq/web/pdf.php/jrv77tjjMPdzAdYajq328g.pdf#page=1.

Foglia, Pierre. "La révolution de Silverman, Pierre." *La Presse*, July 2, 1977, https://diffusion.banq.qc.ca/pdfjs-1.6.210-dist_banq/web/viewer.html?file=//diffusion.banq.qc.ca/pdfjs-1.6.210-dist_banq/web/pdf.php/18LxeKfOkFDeoppRvRg24A.pdf#page=1.

Foglia, Pierre. "Promenade pour grand père." *La Presse*, July 21, 1977, http://numerique.banq.qc.ca/patrimoine/details/52327/2610302, accessed July 16, 2020.

Fortier, Marco. «La piste cyclable de tous les dangers sur le pont Jacques-Cartie,» *Le Devoir*, November 22 2024, [Online]. [https://www.ledevoir.com/societe/transports-urbanisme/824149/piste-cyclable-tous-dangers-pont-jacques-cartier].

Fortin, Pierre. "Nègres blancs, métaphore juste en son temps." *Le Devoir* (lettres), July 8, 2020, www.ledevoir.com/opinion/lettres/581946/negres-blancs-metaphore-juste-en-son-temps.

Fotheringham, William. "Tour de France Could Be Staged this Summer without Any Spectators." *The Guardian*, March 26, 2020, www.theguardian.com/sport/2020/mar/26/tour-de-france-could-be-staged-this-summer-without-any-spectators, accessed April 28, 2020.

FQSC (Fédération québécoise des sports cyclistes). "Temple de la Renommée: 'Gabriel Lupien, bâtisseur.'" 2018, https://fqsc.net/temple-de-la-renommee/pierre-gendron-1.

Francis, Diane. "Les gens d'affaires de Toronto redoutent le pire de Bob Rae," *Le Soleil*, November 3 1990.

Franco, Manuel. "Health Consequences of Cuba's Special Period." *Canadian Medical Association Journal* vol. 179, no. 3 (July 29, 2008): 257, https://pmc.ncbi.nlm.nih.gov/articles/PMC2474886/#:ffi:text=During%20this%20period%2C%20Cubans%20essentially,25%25%20of%20their%20body%20weight.

Freed, Josh. "Bicycle Bob, an Urban Guerilla on Wheels." *The Gazette*, June 6, 1981.

Freed, Josh. "Cyclomaniacs Rejoice! Bikelandia Is Open for Business." *The Gazette* (Montreal), June 8, 2014, https://montrealgazette.com/opinion/josh-freed-cyclomaniacs-rejoice-bikelandia-is-open-for-business/.

Freed, Josh. "Montreal's cycling culture sure beats the car-nage in T.O." *The Gazette* (Montréal), November 15, 2014, https://montrealgazette.com/news/local-news/josh-freed-montreals-cycling-culture-sure-beats-the-car-nage-in-t-o.

Freed, Josh. "Ten Speeds Si…in Cuba." *Montreal Star*, April 21, 1977.

Freed, Josh. "Watch Out Vietnam, Say-Dap Bob's Coming." *The Gazette*, September 24, 1988.

Galerie de l'Âme. "About." https://galeriedelame.wixsite.com/galeriedelame/about, accessed November 4, 2021.

Garnier, Julien. "Métro, quartiers, ville : étude de quelques dimensions de l'expérience quotidienne de montréal au travers du concept foucaldien de pouvoir," présentée comme exigence partielle du doctorat en sociologie de l'Université du Québec à Montréal, 2006, https://archipel.uqam.ca/8582/1/D3025.pdf, accessed May 29, 2020.

Gazette, The. "6 Cyclists Arrested." August 30, 1979.

Gazette, The. "A $5 Permit Will Allow You to Lug a Bike onto Métro." June 19, 1982.

Gazette, The. "Bailiff Sales." May 19, 1962.

Gazette, The. "Bert Silverman Obituary." February 15, 1993.

Gazette, The. "Bicyclists Will Be Fined if They Ride the Metro." August 27, 1981.

Gazette, The. "Cyclists Wear the Wings but the Mayor Takes Flight." July 21, 1980.

Gazette, The. "Cyclists Block Papineau Bridge." May 22, 1976.

Gazette, The. "Cyclist in Cell Loved View of Bikers' Path." October 28, 1981, www.newspapers.com/image/421970409/?terms=sILVERMAN&match=1, accessed May 24, 2021.

Gazette, The. "Do-It-Yourself Bike Path Results in 2 Arrests." September 12, 1980, Page? https://www.newspapers.com/image/421805546/?terms=Monde%20a%20bicyclette&match=1.

Gazette, The. "Florence Silverman Obituary." March 17, 1987.

Gazette, The. "Group Tours and Nature Programs Make Cycling Educational." July 27, 1985.

Gazette, The. "History through Our Eyes: October 12, 1976, 'Bicycle Bob' Silverman." October 12, 2019. https://montrealgazette.com/news/local-news/history-through-our-eyes/history-through-our-eyes-oct-12-1976-bicycle-bob-silverman.

Gazette, The. "History through Our Eyes: March 19, 1971, the Van Horne Mansion." March 19, 2019, https://montrealgazette.com/news/local-news/history-through-our-eyes/history-through-our-eyes-march-19-1971-the-van-horne-mansion.

Gazette, The. "Let Cyclists onto Metro." (editorial) August 24, 1979.

Gazette, The. "Metro: Bikes not Ruled Out." August 28, 1981.

Gazette, The, "Person to Person" (events calendar), November 9, 1960.

Gazette, The. "Terrence Regan Obituary." May 22, 2021, https://montrealgazette.remembering.ca/obituary/terrence-regan-1082418630.

Gignac, Benoit. "Faire Flèche de Tout Bois." *Vélo Mag*, Special Edition, 2017.

Giesler, Stephen. "You Have to Be a Bit of a Fruitcake…" *The Gazette*, August 19, 1976.

Gilmore, Mikal. "Leonard Cohen: Remembering the Life and Legacy of the Poet of Brokenness." *Rolling Stone*, November 30, 2016, www.rollingstone.com/music/music-features/leonard-cohen-remembering-the-life-and-legacy-of-the-poet-of-brokenness-192994/.

Gilmore, Mikal. "Why Bob Dylan Is a Literary Genius: Ahead of Nobel Prize Ceremony, We Explore how Dylan Wrote not Just Songs or Poetry, but History." *Rolling Stone*, December 9, 2016, www.rollingstone.com/music/music-features/why-bob-dylan-is-a-literary-genius-105108/.

Gittell, Ross. Encyclopedia Britannica, "Community organizing," britannica.com, May 17 2016, [Online]. [https://www.britannica.com/topic/community-organizing].

Gnarowski, Michael. "Louis Dudek." June 15, 2015, The Canadian Encyclopedia, https://www.thecanadianencyclopedia.ca/en/article/louis-dudek, accessed April 2, 2020.

Georgetown Universities. "2000 Toronto municipal election." Political Database of the Americas, Electoral systems and Data: https://pdba.georgetown.edu/Elecdata/Canada/mun00.html, accessed October 11, 2020.

Gomberg, Tooker. "It Is Time to Bury the Car." *Greenspiration*, 1999, http://greenspiration.org/it-is-time-to-bury-the-car/.

Gomberg, Tooker. "Arrested in Montreal: Sofa, So Good." *Greenspiration*, http://greenspiration.org/arrested-in-montreal-sofa-so-good/, accessed September 5, 2021.

Goodrich, Janet. *Natural Vision Improvement*. Ten Speed Press, Berkeley, California, 1995.

Google Books. "Review of *Revolution for the Hell of It: The Book That Earned Abbie Hoffman a Five-Year Prison Term at the Chicago Conspiracy Trial*, by Abbie Hoffman." Google Books, accessed June 15, 2021, https://books.google.ca/books/about/Revolution_for_the_Hell_of_It.html?id=CR4fRd8j5IkC&source=kp_book_description&redir_esc=y.

Gottlieb, Ray. "More About Ray, Vision for a Better World, Syntonic Optometry." https://raygottlieb.com/, accessed April 15, 2022.

Gottlieb, Ray. Telephone Interview. April 15, 2022.

Government of Canada. Assurance-emploi, D'Emploi et Développement social Canada: www.canada.ca/fr/emploi-developpement-social/programmes/assurance-emploi.html, accessed April 14, 2022.

Government of Canada. "Medical assistance in dying: Overview"; https://www.canada.ca/en/health-canada/services/health-services-benefits/medical-assistance-dying.html, accessed November. 21, 2021.

Gravenor, J. D. "Rubens, Rembrandt, Velasquez—Up in Flames on Sherbrooke Street." *Coolopolis*. April 3, 2008, http://coolopolis.blogspot.com/2008/04/van-horne-fire-of-1933.html.

Greenspiration. "Bio: Tooker Gomberg." http://greenspiration.org/tooker/bio-tooker-gomberg/, accessed October 11, 2021.

Grenon, Hector. "Camillien Houde." Stanké, Montréal, 1979.

Groupement des assureurs automobiles. "Statistiques annuelles, un portrait de la l'assurance auto." Octobre 21, 2020, https://gaa.qc.ca/fr/professionnels-de-l-assurance/nouvelles/2020/statistiques-annuelles-un-portrait-de-l-assurance-auto/.

Guevara, Che. "Guerrilla Warfare." Monthly Review Press, New York, 1961.

Guide de l'auto. "Les véhicules âgés de 5 ans qui ont le mieux conservé leur valeur." November 9, 2021, https://www.guideautoweb.com/articles/62045/les-vehicules-ages-de-5-ans-qui-ont-le-mieux-conserve-leur-valeur/.

Habitat 67. Tropiques nord condominiums, «La Cité du Havre, Un trésor négligé,» Mémoire déposé devant l'Office de consultation publique de Montréal, September, 2019. https://www.habitat67.com/wp-content/uploads/2019/10/Cite-du-Havre-Un-tresor-neglige23.pdf.

Hamel, Pierre, and Françoix Marcil. (Interview with Silverman for the Vélo Québec magazine *Cyclo-Nouvelles* [circa 1978]). Translation by Ann Rajan (courtesy of Encore du Monde à bicyclette).

Hanley, Steve. "Calculating the True Cost of a Society Based on Automobiles." *CleanTechnica*, February 13, 2020, https://cleantechnica.com/2020/02/13/calculating-the-true-cost-of-a-society-based-on-automobiles/.

Hansen, Matt. "Montreal's 'Bicycle Bob,' a Cycling Activist for 50 Years, Dies at 88." *Canadian Cycling Magazine*, February 23, 2022, https://cyclingmagazine.ca/sections/news/montreals-bicycle-bob-a-cycling-activist-for-50-years-dies-at-88/.

Harris, L. "Park-Pine Interchange Must Go, Cyclists Say." *Gazette*, January 16, 1990.

Henken, Ted. *Cuba: A Global Studies Handbook*, Bloomsbury Academic, London, 2008.

Hillman, Mayer. "Cycling and Health," *British Medical Journal*, 11 April 1992, pp. 986–87 [Online]. https://www.ncbi.nlm.nih.gov/pmc/articles/PMC1882282/pdf/bmj00068-0066f.pdf.

Hinkson, Kamila. "4 Venues Built for the 1976 Montreal Olympics: Games Left Montreal with a Number of New Buildings, and a Billion-Dollar Debt." *CBC News*, July 24, 2016, www.cbc.ca/news/canada/montreal/montreal-olympics-venues-stadium-cost-1.3679041, accessed June 28, 2020.

History.com, "Cuban Missile Crisis." January 4, 2010, https://www.history.com/topics/cold-war/cuban-missile-crisis.

History.com, "Vietnam War Protests." February 22, 2010, www.history.com/topics/vietnam-war/vietnam-war-protests, accessed September 11, 2021.

Hoffman, Abbie. "Review of *The Rise and Fall of Counterculture's Jester*, by Marty Jezer." *Los Angeles Times*, January 13, 1993, https://www.latimes.com/archives/la-xpm-1993-01-13-vw-1114-story.html.

Hoffman, Abbie. "Steal This Book." Pirate Editions / Grove Press, New York, 1971.
Hook, Sidney. "Bolshevik Coup Lacked Popular Support." (letter to *The New York Times*), August 1, 1988, www.nytimes.com/1988/08/20/opinion/l-bolshevik-coup-lacked-popular-support-478688.html, accessed May 15, 2020.
Horwitt, Sanford D., "Let Them Call Me Rebel: Saul Alinsky, His Life and Legacy." Penguin Random House, New York, 1989.
Hotel Nacional de Cuba. "Hotel Overview"; https://hotelnacionaldecuba.com/about-the-hotel-nacional-de-cuba/, accessed April 15, 2020.
HSBC. "2022 Sector Snapshot: Canadian Automotive." August 23, 2022, www.business.hsbc.ca/en-ca/insights/innovation-and-transformation/2022-sector-snapshot-canadian-automotive.
Humphreys, Tim. "Bliss Can Be a Bicycle." *Montreal Star*, May 20, 1975.
Illich, Ivan. *Energy and Equity*. Harper & Row, New York, 1974.
Independent Jewish Voices Canada. "About." https://www.ijvcanada.org/about-ijv/.
Institut de la statistique du Québec (ISQ). "Nombre de véhicules en circulation selon le type d'utilisation, le type de véhicule et l'âge du véhicule, Québec et les régions administratives." Banque de données des s officielles du Québec, 2022, https://bdso.gouv.qc.ca/pls/ken/ken213_afich_tabl.page_tabl?p_iden_tran=&p_lang=1&p_m_o=SAAQ&p_id_raprt=3372#tri_age=1&tri_tertr=0.
IBC (Insurance Bureau of Canada). «Assurances de dommages au Canada 2023,» Bureau d'assurance du Canada, 2023, [Online]. [https://a-us.storyblok.com/f/1003207/x/abac0276bf/2023-ibc-fact-book-fr.pdf].
Jack, Douglas. Telephone Interview. June 18, 2020.
Jacobs, Jane. *Dark Age Ahead*, Random House, New York, 2004.
JCCBI (Ponts Jacques Cartier Champlain Bridges). "History of the Toll at Jacques Cartier Bridge." https://jacquescartierchamplain.ca/community-heritage/structures-and-projects/jacques-cartier-bridge/peage/?lang=en, accessed October 15, 2021.
Johnson, Brian. "Teachers Occupy Language Schools in Contract Battle." *Gazette*, January 22, 1974.
Johns Hopkins Medicine. "Age-Related Macular Degeneration (AMD)." https://www.hopkinsmedicine.org/health/conditions-and-diseases/agerelated-macular-degeneration-amd.
Le Jour. "Le Manifeste de la bicyclette pour une ville plus vivable." May 26, 1975, p. 13.
Journal de Montréal. "Montréal retour sur l'image: un monde pour la bicyclette." April 3, 2021, www.journaldemontreal.com/2021/04/03/montreal-retour-sur-limage-un-monde-pour-la-bicyclette.
Journet, Paul. "Éloge de la Sobriété." *La Presse*, February 25, 2023, https://plus.lapresse.ca/screens/3d4ccad5-4067-46de-9071-9b3548d5248d__7C___0.html?utm_content=email&utm_source=lpp&utm_medium=referral&utm_campaign=internal+share.
Kaegi, Elizabeth. "Unconventional Therapies for Cancer: 6. 714-X." *Canadian Medical Association Journal* vol. 158, no. 12 (June 16, 1998): 1621–24, www.cmaj.ca/content/cmaj/158/12/1621.full.pdf.
Kempton, Richard. "Provo: Amsterdam's Anarchist Revolt." Autonomedia, New York, 2007.
Kilpatrick, Julia. "Bike Path Named in Honour of Cycling Activist." *The Gazette*, August 25, 2008.

Kowaluk, Lucia, and Carolle Piché-Burton. "Communauté Milton-Parc; How We Did It and How It Works Now." Communauté Milton-Parc, 2012: https://bibliographies.uqam.ca/bhm/bibliographie/EZALGX4J, accessed February 7, 2021.

Laforge, Monique. "Claire Morissette, la grande dame du vélo urbain." *Mémoires des Montréalais* (series) : a site of the Centre d'histoire de Montréal, November 15, 2017, https://ville.montreal.qc.ca/memoiresdesmontrealais/claire-morissette-la-grande-dame-du-velo-urbain, accessed August 30, 2020.

Laforge, Monique. «Montréal ville cyclable, hier et aujourd'hui,» *Mémoires des Montréalais* (series): a site of the Centre d'histoire de Montréal, January 25, 2017: https://ville.montreal.qc.ca/memoiresdesmontrealais/montreal-ville-cyclable-hier-et-aujourdhui.

Laforge, Monique. "Robert Silverman, quand la « cyclofrustration » mène à l'action." November 15, 2017, *Centre des mémoires montréalaises*, https://ville.montreal.qc.ca/memoiresdesmontrealais/robert-silverman-quand-la-cyclofrustration-mene-laction.

Laing, G., and Celine Cooper. "Royal Commission on Bilingualism and Biculturalism." *Canadian Encyclopedia*, 2019, www.thecanadianencyclopedia.ca/en/article/royal-commission-on-bilingualism-and-biculturalism.

Lalonde, M. "Bike Stands Get Boot," *The Gazette*, June 16, 1998.

Lanken, Dane. "Cyclist Sets His Sights on All Those Culprit Cars." *The Gazette*, October 12, 1976.

Laplante, Coralie. "Achalandage sur le REV Saint-Denis : Des cyclistes se rassemblent pour célébrer." *La Presse*, October 23, 2021, https://www.lapresse.ca/actualites/grand-montreal/2021-10-23/achalandage-sur-le-rev-saint-denis/des-cyclistes-se-rassemblent-pour-celebrer.php.

Laramée, François. "À vélo sur le pont Jacques-Cartier, même en hiver." *La Relève*, September 9, 2020, www.lareleve.qc.ca/2020/09/09/a-velo-sur-le-pont-jacques-cartier-meme-en-hiver/.

Latraverse, Plume. "La piste cyclable." (song) https://genius.com/Plume-latraverse-la-piste-cyclable-lyrics.

Laurent, René. "Bicycles Ban on Subway will Stay, says Hanigan." *The Gazette*, August 26, 1981.

Laurent, René. "City moving on bicycle lanes." *The Gazette*, September 4, 1975.

Laviolette, Jérôme. L'état de l'automobile au Québec: constats, tendances et conséquences, Fondation Suzuki - Jalon Montréal, October 2020 https://fr.davidsuzuki.org/wp-content/uploads/sites/3/2020/10/Rapport_Fondation-David-Suzuki-Final-Part1-Dependance-auto-10.2020.pdf.

Lavoie, Jonathan. "Y a-t-il vraiment plus de kilomètres d'autoroute à Québec qu'ailleurs?" *Radio-Canada*, December 27, 2018, https://ici.radio-canada.ca/nouvelle/1143950/kilometres-autoroutes-quebec-troisieme-lien.

Lavy, "Seven Steps – The Potpourri," [Online]. [http://boppin.com/1995/04/seven-steps-potpourri.html], January 2011.

Layton, Max. Telephone Interview. March 2020.

Leahy, Michael Patrick, and Gina Loudon. *Rules for Conservative Radicals: Lessons from Saul Alinsky, the Tea Party Movement, and the Apostle Paul in the Age of Collaborative Technologies*, C-Rad Press, Nashville, January 2009.

Lefebvre-Ropars, G. et al. "Caractérisation du partage de la voirie à Montréal : Note de recherche." Polytechnique Montréal, 2021, 15 pages, https://share.polymtl.ca/alfresco/service/api/path/content;cm:content/workspace/SpacesStore/Company%20Home/Sites/chaire-de-recherche-mobilit-web/documentLibrary/publications/Notes%20de%20recherche/note_recherche_partage_voirie_mtl_2021.pdf?guest=true.

Les Années RCM (Montreal Citizens' Movement). Un site de documentation sur le Rassemblement des citoyens et citoyennes de Montréal et sur la Ville de Montréal sous l'administration du maire Jean Doré: https://lesanneesrcm.ca/, accessed Sept 4, 2021.

Longueuil. "1969: Des histoires et des archives."©2025: https://archives.longueuil.quebec/1969.

Longueuil, Ville de (website). "Plan directeur des déplacements cyclables." May 2018, https://investir.longueuil.quebec/sites/default/files/contenu/fichiers/plan%20directeur%20d%C3%A9placements%20cyclables.pdf.

Lowy, Henry. "Seven Steps Bookstore." *Canadian Jewish Chronicle*, August 12, 1960, p. 9, https://news.google.com/newspapers?nid=883&dat=19600812&id=ge9OAAAAIBAJ&sjid=ZUwDAAAAIBAJ&pg=3209,3237373&hl=en, accessed March 4, 2020.

MacLennan, Hugh. *Two Solitudes*. McGill-Queen's University Press, Kingston and Montreal, June 2018.

McCabe, Daniel. "Remembering Leonard." *McGill News Alumni Magazine*, November 2016, https://mcgillnews.mcgill.ca/s/1762/news/interior.aspx?sid=1762&gid=2&pgid=1599#:ffi:text=%E2%80%9CI%20taught%20him%20how%20to,talents%20%E2%80%93%20the%20McGill%20Debating%20Union.

McKenna, Brian, and Susan Purcell. *Drapeau*. Clarke, Irwin & Co., 1980.

McNicoll, Arion. "British Inventors Claim World's First Flying Bicycle." *CNN*, June 20, 2013, www.cnn.com/2013/06/20/tech/innovation/worlds-first-flying-bicycle/index.html, accessed April 27, 2020.

Magil, David. "Bicycle Touring Routes Proposed for City." *Gazette*, May 31, 1972, www.newspapers.com/image/421158522/, accessed May 23, 2021.

Mapes, Jeff. Email Correspondence. September 27 and October 13, 2022.

Mapes, Jeff. "Trailblazers on Two Wheels: How Bicycle Advocates Defined North American Cycling Culture since 1970." *Momentum Magazine/Tyee Magazine*, July 8, 2011, https://thetyee.ca/Life/2011/07/08/BicycleTrailblazers/.

Margolis, Jason. "Cyclists Accuse Toronto Mayor Ford of 'War on Bikes.'" *BBC*, May 3, 2012, www.bbc.com/news/magazine-17914504, accessed May 28, 2021.

Mariette, Alice. "Possédez-une auto, combien ça coûte?" *Protégez-Vous*, August 12, 2020, www.protegez-vous.ca/nouvelles/automobile/cout-utilisation-auto-connaitre.

Martin, Jean-Guy. "Le Monde à bicyclette ne recule devant aucune méthode." *Journal de Montréal*, April 21, 1981.

Martin, Stéphanie. "Privilégier l'automobile coûte très cher à la société." *Journal de Montréal*, May 1, 2017, www.journaldequebec.com/2017/05/01/privilegier-lautomobile-coute-tres-cher-a-la-societe.

Maskoulis, Julia. "Bicycle Brigade Storms City Hall with Vision of Ban on Automobile." *Gazette*, August 7, 1975.

Max, John. "The Last Bohemia." *Macleans*, April 22, 1961, https://archive.macleans.ca/issue/19610422#!amp;&pid=24.

Layton, Max (website). http://www.maxlayton.com/tabid/211/Default.aspx"www.maxlayton.com/tabid/211/Default.aspx, accessed March 30, 2020.

Mayo Clinic. "Diseases and Conditions, Cataracts." September 28, 2023, www.mayoclinic.org/diseases-conditions/cataracts/symptoms-causes/syc-20353790.

MEM. Centre des mémoires montréalaises, Jacques Cartier Bridge, "Le pont Jacques-Cartier." February 12, 2016; https://ville.montreal.qc.ca/memoiresdesmontrealais/le-pont-jacques-cartier, accessed July 16, 2020.

McClelland, Norman. "Encyclopedia of Reincarnation and Karma." MacFarland & Company, Jefferson (NC), 2010.

Merriam-Webster Online Dictionary. "Manifesto." https://www.merriam-webster.com/dictionary/manifesto.

Merriam-Webster Online Dictionary. "Presbyopia." www.merriam-webster.com/dictionary/presbyopia, accessed August 29, 2020.

Merriam-Webster Online Dictionary. "Anarchy." https://www.merriam-webster.com/dictionary/anarchist, accessed January 23, 2021

Middle East Policy Council. "Who Killed Yasser Arafat." https://mepc.org/commentary/who-killed-yasser-arafat, accessed May 22, 2021.

Milder, Stephen. "Global Environmental Movements Petra Kelly and the Transnational Roots of Green Politics." *Arcadia* no.8 (2013) Arcadia Collection, https://www.environmentandsociety.org/arcadia/petra-kelly-and-transnational-roots-green-politics.

Mills, Sean. *Contester l'Empire*. Hurtubise, Montreal, 2011 (translation of *The Empire Within*. McGill-Queens, 2010).

Mind Journal. "How Souls Choose Their Parents and Families before Birth." https://themindsjournal.com/souls-choose-parents-families/, accessed December 18, 2020.

Montreal Star. "Bicycle Movement." April 10, 1975.

Montreal Star. "Civic Rites Planned for Houde." September 12, 1958.

Montreal Star. "Demonstrators Mark Hiroshima Anniversary." August 7, 1964.

Montreal Star. Potpourri ad, June 27 1962, p 26.

Montréal (City of). "Bicycle Map in 1897," Centre des mémoires montréalaises, Encyclopédie du MEM, 1897 [Online]. [https://ville.montreal.qc.ca/memoiresdesmontrealais/en/files/bicycle-map-1897].

Montréal (City of). "Le pont Jacques-Cartier," Centre des mémoires montréalaises, February 12, 2016, [Online]. [https://ville.montreal.qc.ca/memoiresdesmontrealais/le-pont-jacques-cartier]

Montréal (City of). "Les Religieuses Hospitalières de Saint-Joseph de Montréal," *Le Site Officiel du Mont-Royal*, [Online]. [https://ville.montreal.qc.ca/siteofficieldumontroyal/religieuses-hospitalieres-saint-joseph-montreal].

Montréal (City of). "Le REV : un réseau express vélo," May 3 2024, [Online]. [https://montreal.ca/en/articles/rev-express-bike-network-4666].

Montréal (City of). "Piste cyclable Claire-Morissette - La sécurité une priorité," Cabinet de la mairesse et du comité exécutif, September 4 2019, [Online]. [https://www.newswire.ca/fr/news-releases/piste-cyclable-claire-morissette-la-securite-une-priorite-826764920.html].

Montréal (City of). Vélo et pistes cyclables." https://montreal.ca/sujets/velo-et-pistes-cyclables, accessed December 5, 2022.

Morissette, Claire. "A Bicycle Bob" (poem reproduced with permission from her family).
Morissette, Claire. *Deux roues, un avenir*. Montreal: Les éditions Écosociété, collection Retrouvailles, 2009.
Mulvaney, Kieran. "A Brief History of Amchitka and the Bomb." *Greenpeace*, 2007, www.greenpeace.org/usa/a-brief-history-of-amchitka-and-the-bomb/, accessed December 14, 2021.
Musée National des Beaux-Arts du Québec. "Paul-Émile Borduas," [Online]. [https://collections.mnbaq.org/fr/artiste/600000485], 2025.
Nadeau, Jean-François. "L'urgence du vélo." *Le Devoir*, July 25, 2022, www.ledevoir.com/opinion/chroniques/737589/l-urgence-du-velo.
Nanaimo Daily News. "Cycling in New Direction." (editorial reprinted from *The Gazette*), May 28, 2002, p. 6.
Nanaimo Daily News. "Environmentalist Promotes Bicycle Power." January 24, 1991, p. 24.
New York Times. "Dr. King Leads Chicago Peace Rally." March 26, 1967, p. 44, www.nytimes.com/1967/03/26/archives/dr-king-leads-chicago-peace-rally.html.
New York Times archive. Death of Henry H. Bliss; "Fatally Hurt by Automobile"; https://timesmachine.nytimes.com/timesmachine/1899/09/14/102413700.pdf, accessed March 19, 2021.
Nguyen, Phuong. "Vietnam's VinFast Ships First Electric Vehicles to U.S. Customers." *Reuters*, November 25, 2022, www.reuters.com/business/autos-transportation/vietnams-vinfast-ships-first-electric-vehicles-us-customers-2022-11-25/.
Noakes, Taylor C. "How Bicycle Bob 'Vélorutionized' cycling culture in Montreal." *CultMtl* (blog), April 20, 2022, https://cultmtl.com/2022/04/how-robert-bicycle-bob-silverman-Vélorutionized-cycling-culture-in-montreal/?fbclid=IwAR2f1wuihf7yuTI3a1Yq6p1-NV7lYSZx6pIr899gOb9yGJE4gGn5LIfA7xU.
Norden, Eric. "Playboy Interview with Saul Alinsky. A Candid Conversation with the Feisty Radical Organizer," *Playboy*, March 1972, https://scrapsfromtheloft.com/movies/saul-alinsky-playboy-interview-1972/#google_vignette.
North, Anna. "Why Bob Dylan Shouldn't Have Gotten a Nobel." *New York Times*, October 13, 2016, www.nytimes.com/2016/10/13/opinion/why-bob-dylan-shouldnt-have-gotten-a-nobel.html, accessed March 26, 2021.
North, David. "Trotsky's Analysis of the Soviet Union Has Been Vindicated by History." *International Committee of the Fourth International (ICFI)*, World Socialist website, October 1991, www.wsws.org/en/special/library/fi-19-1/23.html, accessed March 31, 2021.
Ouellette-Vézina, Henri. "En route vers un record?" *La Presse*, October 21, 2022, www.lapresse.ca/actualites/grand-montreal/2022-10-21/achalandage-cycliste-sur-le-pont-jacques-cartier/en-route-vers-un-record.php.
Peck, Nick. "Viva la Vélorution! Bringing Back the Bike, "(online posting) www.robert-silverman.net/backthebike.htm, accessed August 4, 2020.
Phillips, Andrew. "Group Peddles Health Lure in New Cycle of Publicity." *Gazette*, May 27, 1975.
Pineo, Ronn. "Cuban Public Healthcare: A Model of Success for Developing Nations." *Sage Journals* vol. 35, no. 1 (March 4, 2019), https://journals.sagepub.com/doi/full/10.1177/0169796X19826731.

Posner, Michael. *Leonard Cohen, Untold Stories: The Early Years.* Simon & Schuster, Toronto, 2020.

Pother, Dick. "Commuter's Guide to Buying a Bike." *Philadelphia Enquirer,* February 24, 1974, p. 93.

Powell, Christopher W. "Vietnam: It's Our War Too:'The Antiwar Movement in Canada: 1963-1975.'" (dissertation) University of New Brunswick, September 2010.

La Presse. "Hanigan blanchi." November 29, 1985.

La Presse. "Décès de Lawrence Hanigan." November 4, 2009, www.lapresse.ca/actualites/quebec-canada/national/200911/04/01-918482-deces-de-lawrence-hanigan.php, accessed May 8, 2020.

La Presse. "Quatre cents cyclistes défient la loi sur le pont Jacques-Cartier." June 9, 1975, http://numerique.banq.qc.ca/patrimoine/details/52327/2604521.

Pronovost, Jean-François. Facebook posting after Silverman's demise, February 21, 2022, https://www.facebook.com/jeanfrancois.pronovost.1.

Radio-Canada. "Il y a 60 ans, l'émeute du Forum." https://ici.radio-canada.ca/nouvelle/711666/emeute-forum-maurice-richard-hockey, accessed March 29, 2020.

Radio-Canada. "La Cour suprême dit oui à l'aide médicale à mourir." February 6, 2015, https://ici.radio-canada.ca/nouvelle/705653/suicide-cour-supreme-aide-mourir-province-loi.

Radio-Canada. "La Révolution tranquille, 50 ans après." September 7, 2009, https://ici.radio-canada.ca/ohdio/premiere/grandes-series/239/larevolutiontranquille50ansapres.

Radio-Canada. "Le chemin parcouru pour faire de Montréal une ville cyclable." (includes a 1975 video interview with Silverman), July 24, 2019, https://ici.radio-canada.ca/nouvelle/1234742/velo-bicyclette-montreal-securite-militantisme-piste-cyclable-archives.

Radio-Canada, Ohdio. "Le journal Le Jour, une présence éphémère dans le paysage médiatique." December 1, 2021, https://ici.radio-canada.ca/ohdio/premiere/emissions/aujourd-hui-l-histoire/segments/entrevue/382270/journal-le-jour-parti-quebecois-independance.

Radio-Canada. "Michel Labrecque à la tête de la RIO." February 19, 2014, https://ici.radio-canada.ca/nouvelle/654614/michel-labrecque-rio-pdg, accessed June 30, 2020.

Radio-Canada. "René Lévesque, le souverainiste." October 31, 2017, https://ici.radio-canada.ca/nouvelle/1064349/rene-levesque-souverainiste-archives.

Radio-Canada. "Un Tour de l'Île en imperméable." June 2, 2019, https://ici.radio-canada.ca/nouvelle/1173166/montreal-velo-tour-ile-2019, accessed October 10, 2020.

Rawstron, J. A., et al. "A Systematic Review of the Applicability and Efficacy of Eye Exercises." *Journal of Pediatric Ophthalmology and Strabismus* 42, no.2 (2005): 82–88.

Reid, Carlton. *Bike Boom: The Unexpected Resurgence of Cycling,* Island Press, Washington, DC, 2017.

Reid, Carlton. *Roads Were Not Built for Cars: How cyclists Were the First to Push for Good Roads and Became the Pioneers of Motoring.* Island Press, Washington, DC, 2014.

Reid, Carlton. "The Demise and Rebirth of Cycling in Britain." *The Guardian,* March 10, 2015, www.theguardian.com/environment/bike-blog/2015/mar/10/the-demise-and-rebirth-of-cyling-in-britain, accessed June 30, 2020.

Reid, Carlton. "How a Book Dedication Saved This Bicycle Advocate's Life." February 2017, www.bikeboom.info/life/.
Reid, Carlton. "World's First Filling Station Was a drugstore: Roads Were not Built for Cars." 2012:,https://roadswerenotbuiltforcars.com/berthabenz/.
Replogle, Michael A. *Bicycles and Public Transportation: New Links to Suburban Transit Markets*. Bicycle Federation, Washington DC, 1983.
Rexford, Gammell, McBain. "The History of the High School of Montreal." Old Boys' Association of the High School of Montreal, 1950?, 310 p.; BAnQ Numérique: https://numerique.banq.qc.ca/patrimoine/details/52327/2873646, accessed August 12, 2020
Riga, Andy. "Pioneer Recalls Uphill Battle for Cyclists." *The Gazette*, April 15, 2016, www.pressreader.com/canada/montreal-gazette/20160415/281522225255304, accessed June 1, 2020 (includes video).
Ro, Christine. "How Cycling Clothing Opened Doors for Women: Advances in Biking Gear Had an Impact on Advances in Gender Equality. An Object Lesson." *The Atlantic*, April 15, 2018, www.theatlantic.com/technology/archive/2018/04/how-cycling-clothing-opened-doors-for-women/558017/.
Robert, Mario, "Les débuts de l'automobile à Montréal." Chronique Montréalité no 48 : Archives Montréal, November 2, 2015: https://archivesdemontreal.com/2015/11/02/chronique-montrealite-no-48-les-debuts-de-lautomobile-a-montreal/.
Robitaille, Antoine. "Montréal—Un parti anti-automobile." *Le Devoir*, June 30, 2004, https://www.ledevoir.com/politique/regions/58026/montreal-un-parti-anti-automobile?.
Roussopoulos, Dimitri. "Facebook, About." June 28, 2011, www.facebook.com/profile.php?id=211900712178380&paipv=0&eav=AfZvX8Aari2CBFtPEHzqa2QR16V2CvhfD9n8tMyWHuQWnezz8bE_WBgkAJUctgzL9WQ&_rdr.
Rowe, Daniel. "The Champlain Bridge Bike and Pedestrian Path Has Opened." *CTV News*, December 22, 2019, https://montreal.ctvnews.ca/the-champlain-bridge-bike-and-pedestrian-path-has-opened-1.4740807, accessed July 16, 2020.
Rosen, Judy. "The Bicycle as a Vehicle of Protest." *New Yorker*, June 10, 2020, www.newyorker.com/culture/cultural-comment/the-bicycle-as-a-vehicle-of-protest?utm_source=pocket-newtab, accessed June 11, 2020.
Ross, Daniel. "'Vive la Vélorution!': Le Monde à Bicyclette and the Origins of Cycling Advocacy in Montreal." *Canadian Countercultures and the Environment*. Edited by Colin M. Coates. University of Calgary Press, 2016, https://prism.ucalgary.ca/bitstream/handle/1880/51091/CanadianCountercultures_2016_chapter06.pdf;jsessionid=FE5EA903307BFA419EED8F204BE15894?sequence=8.
Rufiange, Daniel. "Just Under 150,000 People Visited the 2023 Auto Show." *Auto.com*, updated February 2, 2023, https://www.auto123.com/en/news/montreal-auto-show-2023-future/70027/.
Sargent Porter. *A Handbook of Private Schools for American Boys and Girls*, 1935. As cited in "Clark Preparatory School." Internet Archive, accessed 29 July 2021, https://archive.org/stream/in.ernet.dli.2015.177995/2015.177995.A-Handbook-Of-Private-Schools-For-American-Boys-And-Girls-An-Annual-Survey_djvu.txt.
Scheck, William. "During the Struggle between $6 Million Aircraft and $15 Bicycles along the Ho Chi Minh Trail, the Bicycles Won." *Vietnam* 13, no. 5 (Feb 2001): 14, 60.

Schwartz, Susan. "Milton Park Mural Pays Homage to Visionary Architect Phyllis Lambert." *Gazette*, October 08, 2019, https://montrealgazette.com/news/local-news/milton-park-mural-pays-homage-to-visionary-architect-phyllis-lambert.

Schmolka, Vicki. Telephone Interview. March 30, 2020.

Schoup, Donald. "The High Cost of Free Parking." *Journal of Planning Education and Research*, January 2005, www.researchgate.net/publication/235359731_The_High_Cost_of_Free_Parking.

Scott, Marian. "'Bicycle Bob' Silverman, a Father of Montreal's Vélorution, Dies at 88." *The Gazette*, February 21, 2022, https://montrealgazette.com/news/local-news/robert-bicycle-bob-silverman-dead-at-87?fbclid=IwAR0EDJp2qTfKGUtyv2-PB4WXm09CKrloavbqOgSd7FSUYszqBeuc42lVZso.

Scott, Marian. "Obituary: Former City Councillor John Gardiner Remembered as Bridge-Builder." *Gazette*, September 22, 2015, https://montrealgazette.com/news/local-news/john-gardiner-city-politician-1944-2015-2.

Shawwnf. "Bob Dylan –Finjan Club, 1962," *YouTube*, 2017, [En ligne]. [www.youtube.com/watch?v=H-tSdW85VQI].

Shlaim, Avi. "It's Now Clear: The Oslo Peace Accords Were Wrecked by Netanyahu's Bad Faith." *The Guardian*, September 12, 2013, www.theguardian.com/commentisfree/2013/sep/12/oslo-israel-reneged-colonial-palestine.

Silverman, Edith. "Letters to the Editor." *Gazette*, May 9, 1962, p. 8.

Silverman, Robert. "A Serious Injustice." (letter) *Gazette*, August 24, 1979, p. 9.

Silverman, Robert. "My Life, Poems—English Poems." 2000, https://robert-silverman.net/poems/index.html.

Silverman, Robert. "Bikesheviks Cycling for Freedom." *Open Road* no. 11 (Summer 1980), http://openroadnewsjournal.org/?fbclid=IwAR0ifsyUovIklbF0hZYSG1L7TSQM7M_YdfvLcVkM4fW4-xyvJ_maQwzvlas, accessed February 1, 2021.

Silverman, Robert. "Cons and Cyclists: The Tale of Cell Block A." originally published in the *McGill Daily*, November 26, 1981, republished in 2000 on www.robert-silverman.net/.

Silverman, Robert. "Cycling Advocate Claire Morissette Passes Away." *Pedal Magazine*, July 26, 2007, https://pedalmag.com/cycling-advocate-claire-morissette-passes-away/.

Silverman, Robert. "Do you remember Viet-Nam?" (blog) originally published in the *Le Monde à Bicyclette Journal*, Autumn 1985, https://www.robert-silverman.net.

Silverman, Robert. "Jews Speak Out against the Occupation." Robert Silverman English texts, (blog post) 2000, https://www.robert-silverman.net.

Silverman, Robert, "Robert's Impressions of 1997 Cuba Bike Trip," (undated blog post): https://robert-silverman.net/cubatrip.htm.

Silverman, Robert. "Must the Treatment Be Toxic? Quebec Doctors Take Naessens to Trial." 2020 (blog) https://robert-silverman.net/treatmentoxic.htm.

Silverman, Robert. "Official Le MàB Position on Helmet Law; Public Hearings on Proposed Changes to the Highway Code, Quebec City," Robert Silverman Homepage, 2000, https://robert-silverman.net/.

Silverman, Robert. "On Reaching 60." Robert Silverman Homepage, 2000, https://robert-silverman.net/.

Silverman, Robert. "Oxygen Park Opens." (blog) 2000, https://robert-silverman.net/treatmentoxic.htm.

Silverman, Robert. "Poèmes à Claire Morissette." Robert Silverman Homepage, Poèmes français, 2000, https://robert-silverman.net/poems/index.html, accessed July 19, 2020.

Silverman, Robert. "Pourquoi je m'installe à Val-David." *Journal Ski se Dit*, September 2004 p. 3.

Silverman, Robert. "Spreading the Vélorution." 2000, www.robert-silverman.net/.

Silverman, Robert. Telephone Interviews. 2015 to 2021.

Silverman, Robert. "The Case against Helmet Laws." *Gazette*, February 14, 2000, p. 19.

Silverman, Robert. "Twenty Years with le MàB." Robert Silverman Homepage, 2000, http://robert-silverman.net/20ans.htm.

Sioui, Marie-Michèle. "La mort de Mathilde Blais choque les Montréalais." *La Presse*, April 29, 2014, www.lapresse.ca/actualites/justice-et-affaires-criminelles/faits-divers/201404/29/01-4761910-la-mort-de-mathilde-blais-choque-les-montrealais.php.

Snell, Bradford. "Statement of Bradford C. Snell before the United States Senate Subcommittee on Antitrust and Monopoly." Hearings on the Ground Transportation Industries in Connection with S1167. SCRTD Library, Washington, DC, February 26, 1974.

Sociable. "That Time Fidel Castro Appointed Che Guevara Head of Cuba's Natl. Bank." August 13, 2016, https://sociable.co/web/fidel-castro-appointed-che-guevara-bank/.

Le Soleil. "Grève, pas grève, à bicyclette... comme à Pékin." January 21, 1982, p.A3, https://numerique.banq.qc.ca/patrimoine/details/52327/2730610.

Statistics Canada. "Vehicle Registrations, 2023." Automotive statistics, October 10, 2024, https://www150.statcan.gc.ca/n1/daily-quotidien/241021/dq241021c-fra.htm#.

Statistics Canada. "Ventes de véhicules automobile neufs, tableau 20-10-0001-01." December 13, 2022, https://www150.statcan.gc.ca/t1/tbl1/fr/tv.action?pid=2010000101&pickMembers[0]=1.6&pickMembers[1]=2.1&pickMembers[2]=3.1&pickMembers[3]=5.1&cubeTimeFrame.startMonth=06&cubeTimeFrame.startYear=2022&cubeTimeFrame.endMonth=10&cubeTimeFrame.endYear=2022&referencePeriods=20220601,20221001.

Statistics Canada. "Household spending, Canada, regions and provinces, 2021." October 18, 2023, https://www150.statcan.gc.ca/t1/tbl1/fr/tv.action?pid=1110022201.

Stein, David Lewis. "The Peaceniks Go to La Macaza." *Macleans*, August 8, 1964, p 10, https://archive.macleans.ca/article/1964/8/8/the-peaceniks-go-to-la-macaza.

Stephens, Gurdeep. "Wood Storms, Wild Canvas: The Art of Godfrey Stephens," D.I.E., Winnipeg, 2014, 144 p.

Steyaert, Jan. "1961 Jane Jacobs, Urban visionary." History of Social Work, 2009, https://historyofsocialwork.org/eng/details.php?cps=18&canon_id=145.

STM. "Les 132 policiers de la Section métro du SPVM entrent en fonction," Société de transport de Montréal (STM), June 18 2007, [Online]. [https://www.stm.info/fr/presse/communiques/2007/les-132-policiers-de-la-section-metro-du-spvm-entrent-en-fonction].

Symon, John. "The Adventures of 'Bicycle Bob' Silverman on Quebec's Route Verte." *Pedal Magazine*, September 25, 2009, https://pedalmag.com/the-adventures-of-bicycle-bob-silverman-on-quebecs-route-verte/.

Symon, John. "Le Monde à Bicyclette Celebrates 40 Years." *Pedal Magazine*, May 29, 2015, https://pedalmag.com/le-monde-a-bicyclette-celebrates.

Symon, John. "Montreal's Bicycle Bob Silverman of Le Monde à Bicyclette Celebrates 80th This Weekend." *Pedal Magazine*, November 23, 2013, https://pedalmag.com/montreals-bicycle-bob-silverman-of-le-monde-a-bicyclette-celebrate-80th-this-weekend/.

Symon, John. "Montreal Election—How Cycling Was Affected by the Outcome." *Pedal Magazine*, November 2, 2009, https://pedalmag.com/montreal-election-how-cycling-was-affected-by-the-outcome.

Symon, John. "Where Is Mercier Bridge Bikepath?" *Montreal Times*, July 23, 2016.

Tardif, Dominic. "Quand Bob Dylan jouait à Montréal devant dix personnes." *La Presse*, October 28, 2023, https://www.lapresse.ca/arts/musique/2023-10-28/quand-bob-dylan-jouait-a-montreal-devant-dix-personnes.php#:ffi:text=Le%2028%20ojuin%201962%2C%20Bob,devant%20une%20dizaine%20de%20personnes.

Taylor, Charles. "Snow Job: Canada, the United States, and Vietnam (1954–1973)," House of Anansi Press, Toronto, 1974, 209 p.

Taysom, Joe. "How Bob Dylan Influenced The Beatles' Songwriting." *Far Out Magazine* (late 2020), https://faroutmagazine.co.uk/how-bob-dylan-influenced-the-beatles-lennon-mccartney/, accessed March 26, 2021.

The Telegraph. "London: How cyclists around the world put a spoke in the motorist's wheel, December 16 2003, [Online]. [https://archive.ph/20120529190357/http://www.telegraph.co.uk/travel/729324/London-How-cyclists-around-the-world-put-a-spoke-in-the-motorist's-wheel.html].

Thomas, Lee. "Bob Dylan's Favourite Leonard Cohen Songs," *Far Out Magazine*, 19 March 2021, [Online]. [https://faroutmagazine.co.uk/bob-dylan-favourite-leonard-cohen-songs-and-his-greatest-genius]

Trajectoire Québec et la Fondation David Suzuki. "Évolution des coûts du système de transport par automobile au Québec, Montréal, Canada." 2017, https://fr.davidsuzuki.org/wp-content/uploads/sites/3/2018/01/%C3%89tude_%C3%89volutionCo%C3%BBtsSyst%C3%A8meTransportQC_FINALE.pdf.

Trotsky, Leon and Max Eastman. *The Revolution Betrayed*. Dover Publications, New York, first published 1937.

Tucker, Spencer. *Encyclopedia of the Vietnam War: A Political, Social and Military History*. Oxford University Press, 2000, 175–77.

Tyrrell, Alex. Facebook messenger communications with the PVQ leader concerning Silverman's role in the 2014 Quebec elections, September 11, 2021.

Underwood, Nora. "Enthusiasm's Pitfalls." *Macleans*, October 5, 1992, p S7 https://archive.macleans.ca/article/1992/10/5/enthusiasms-pitfalls.

United Nations. "Secretary-General's Message for 2021: World Bicycle Day, 3 June." www.un.org/en/observances/bicycle-day, accessed Jan 9, 2022.

University of Florida. *Bicicleta china (Chinese bicycle) – June 1995*, Cuban Studies, 2024, https://cubanstudies.history.ufl.edu/special-period-in-a-time-of-peace/bicicleta-china-chinese-bicycle-june-1995/.

United States Government, . "U.S Consulate General in Montreal: History of the Consulate." https://ca.usembassy.gov/u-s-montreal-consulate/, accessed September 12, 2020.

Vallance, Tom. "Lamont Johnson: Emmy-winning film and television director." *Independant*, December 27, 2010; https://www.independent.co.uk/news/obituaries/

lamont-johnson-emmywinning-film-and-television-director-2169717.html, accessed Nov 15, 2021

Vancouver Sun. "Protestors Hate Autos." January 17, 1977, p. 26.

Vandersypen, K. "Provo Movement (1960s Anarchism)." University of Michigan, 2003, https://deepblue.lib.umich.edu/bitstream/handle/2027.42/144576/provo.html.

Vélo Québec. "Battles of the 70s...Victories of the 80s!" Public Engagement, The History Of Cycling, April 1, 2017, www.velo.qc.ca/en/the-history-of-cycling/battles-of-the-70s-victories-of-the-80s/, accessed June 30, 2020.

Vélo Québec. "Cycling in Québec in 2020." June 2021, p .21, www.velo.qc.ca/wp-content/uploads/2021/06/vq-edv2020-en.pdf.

Vélo Québec. "Vélo Québec : de 1967 à aujourd'hui." (undated), https://www.velo.qc.ca/a-propos/histoire-de-velo-quebec/, accessed June 30, 2020.

Vélo Québec. "Voies cyclable du Grand Montréal (2022 map)." www.velo.qc.ca/en/toolkits/greater-montreal-bikeway-map.

Verdal, Suzanne (website). "Suzanne Verdal & Leonard Cohen." www.suzanneverdal.com/category/suzanne-verdal/.

Von Meding, Jason. "How U.S. Chemical Warfare in Vietnam Unleashed an Enduring Disaster." *Phys.Org*, October 4, 2017, https://theconversation.com/agent-orange-exposed-how-u-s-chemical-warfare-in-vietnam-unleashed-a-slow-moving-disaster-84572.

Warren, Jean-Philippe. Conscription Crisis of 1944, "Guerre et paix chez les Canadiens français du Québec et les Franco-Américains au temps de la Crise de la Conscription"; Histoire, Économie & Société, April 2017, pp 72-86; https://www.cairn.info/revue-histoire-economie-et-societe-2017-4-page-72.htm, accessed March 24, 2021.

Warren, Jean-Philippe. «Le puissant message du Manifeste d'Octobre 70,» The Conversation, October 5 2020, [Online]. [https://theconversation.com/le-puissant-message-du-manifeste-doctobre-1970-147426].

Watson, Kathryn. "Medically Reviewed by LEGG, Timothy J.: 'Is Rebirthing Therapy Safe and Effective?'" *Healthline*, June 11, 2019, www.healthline.com/health/rebirthing#technique, accessed February 19, 2021,

Weinberg, Bill. "Cuba Verde: As the Long-Isolated Caribbean Nation Opens up to Global Markets, Will Its Low-Carbon Ecological Adaptations Endure?" *Earth Island Journal*, Autumn 2017, www.earthisland.org/journal/index.php/magazine/entry/cuba_verde/, accessed September 4, 2021.

Weyler, Rex. "Irving and Dorothy Stowe: Mentors to a Movement." *Greenpeace*, August 7, 2021, https://www.greenpeace.org/international/story/48966/irving-dorothy-stowe-greenpeace-history-founders-mentors/.

Wheels.ca. "Jack Layton Saw the Future and It Was on a Bicycle." *Toronto Star Newspapers Limited and Metroland Media Group Ltd*, August 26, 2011, www.wheels.ca/news/jack-layton-saw-the-future-and-it-was-on-a-bicycle.

William, Michael. "Montreal Anarchist Candidates Off and Running." *Fifth State Collective*, #345, Winter 1995, https://www.fifthestate.org/archive/345-winter-1995/getting-nowhere-fast, accessed March 5, 2021.

Wilson, John. "Toronto Conference Exposes Canada's Role in Vietnam." *Socialist History Project*, 1966, www.socialisthistory.ca/Docs/1961-/Vietnam/YSF-Antiwar-65-68.htm, accessed March 29, 2021.

Wilson, Kea. "'An Epic Mistake': Donald Shoup Reflects on America's Parking Failure." November 19, 2021, https://usa.streetsblog.org/2021/11/19/an-epic-mistake-donald-shoup-reflects-on-americas-parking-failure-and-his-hopes-for-the-future/.

Wilson, S. S. "Bicycle Technology." *Scientific American* vol. 228, no. 3 (March 1973): 81–91, www.scientificamerican.com/article/bicycle-technology/.

Worton, Maria. "Interview: Keeping up with the Guerilla-Bicyclist of Montreal." *Montreal Serai* Article 7, 2003, https://montrealserai.com/_archives/2003_Volume_16/16_4/Article_7.htm, accessed March 30, 2021.

Wutzke, R. "Eulogy for Robert." Facebook post, March 16, 2022.

Bob's Best Books (supplementary bibliography)

In addition to the documentation listed in the bibliography, here are authors and titles that were not necessarily used in the preparation of this manuscript but nonetheless influential in shaping Silverman's ideology.

Alinsky, Saul. *Rules for Radicals*, Vintage Books, a Division of Random House, Inc./New York, 1971.

Anand, Margo. *The Art of Sexual Ecstasy*. Los Angeles: Jeremy Archer Press, 1989.

Bates, William. *The Cure of Imperfect Sight by Treatment without Glasses*. Black & White, New York, 1920.

Behrman, Daniel. *The Man Who Loved Bicycles: The Memoirs of an Autophobe*. HarperCollins, New York, 1973.

Biehl, Janet, and Murray Bookchin. *The Murray Bookchin Reader*. Black Rose Books, Montréal, 1999.

Bird, Christopher. *The Life and Trials of Gaston Naessens: The Galileo of the Microscope*. Les presses de l'université de la Personne, St. Lambert, Quebec, 1990.

Bird, Christopher. *The Persecution and Trial of Gaston Naessens*. H.J. Kramer, Tiburon, Calif, 1991.

Boothroyd, Sarah. "Spraypaint Slingers, Celebration and a Tidal Wave of Outrage (Montreal, Canada)." in *Critical Mass: Bicycling's Defiant Celebration*, edited by Chris Carlson. Edinburgh, Scotland: AK Press, 2002.

Brinton, Maurice. *Authoritarian Conditioning, Sexual Repression and the Irrational in Politics*. Solidarity, London, 1970.

Buel, Ronald. *Dead End: The Automobile in Mass Transportation*. Prentice-Hall, Englewood Cliffs, N.J, 1972.

Furness, Zack. *One Less Car: Bicycling and the Politics of Automobility*. Philadelphia: Temple University Press, 2010.

Gehl, Jan and Gemzøe, Lars. *Public Spaces, Public Life*. Copenhagen: The Danish Architectural Press, 2004.

Goodrich, Carina. *The Practical Guide to Natural Vision Improvement*. The Janet Goodrich Method, Maleny, Queensland, 2010.

Huxley, Aldous. *The Art of Seeing: An Adventure in Re-education*. Harper & Brothers, New York, 1942.

Illich, Ivan. *Deschooling Society*. Harper & Row, New York, 1971.
Illich, Ivan. *Tools for Conviviality*. Harper & Row, New York, 1973.
Jacobs, Jane. *Death and Life of Great American Cities*, Random House, New York City, 1961.
Kavner, Richard S. and Lorraine Dusky. *Total Vision*. New York: A & W Visual Library, 1978.
Mendelsohn, Robert S. *Confessions of a Medical Heretic*. Contemporary Books, Chicago, 1979.
Rodinson, Maxime. *Israël, fait colonial?* Les Temps modernes, Paris, 1967 (in English, published as *Israel: A Colonial-Settler State?* Monad Press, New York, 1973).
Rothschild, Emma. *Paradise Lost: The Decline of the Auto-Industrial Age*. Vintage Books, New York, 1974.
Schneider, Kenneth. *Autokind Vs. Mankind: An Analysis of Tyranny, a Proposal for Rebellion, a Plan for Reconstruction*. iUniverse, Bloomington, Indiana, 2001.
Scholl, Lisette. *Visionetics*. HarperCollins Canada, 1979.
Smith, Robert. *A Social History of the Bicycle, Its Early Life and Times in America*. American Heritage Press, New York, 1972.
Tucker, Spencer. *The Encyclopedia of the Vietnam War: A Political, Social, and Military History*. Spencer C. Tucker Editor, Buffalo, 2000.
Walker, Peter. "Dies-In and Political Bravery; How Mass Cycling Happens," appearing in *How Cycling Can Save the World*, Penguin Random House, London, 2017
Watson, Roderick, and Martin Gray. *The Penguin Book of the Bicycle*. Penguin Books, London, 1978.

Silverman considered Che Guevara, Ho Chi Minh, and Ivan Illich to be his heroes. He also enjoyed the work of the following journalists: Tariq Ali, Julian Assange, Phyllis Bennis, William Blum, Max Blumenthal, Andrew Cockburn, Patrick Cockburn, Daniel Ellsberg, Norman Finkelstein, Ray Gottlieb, Chris Hedges, Richard Moser, Gaston Naessens, John Pilger, Vijay Prashad, Paul Street, and Mike Whitney.

We conducted interviews with the following individuals. In some cases, we also collected their comments about Silverman on social media:
Angela Bischoff
George Bliss
Alain Brunet
Michel Camus
Gordon Cohen
Gerard Dab
Hedy Dab
Jacques Desjardins
Yvon Dinel
Pryor Dodge
Debby Dowlin
John Dowlin
Anne Lagacé Dowson
Gordon Edwards
Peter Feldstein
Michael Fish

Josh Freed
Marianne Giguère
Ray Gottlieb
Bernard Hallé
Douglas Jack
Anna Louise Fontaine
Charles Komanoff
Michel Labrecque
Suzanne Lareau
Diane Larsen
André Lavallée
Max Layton
Marie-Josée Legault
Raymond Lemieux
Isabelle Lesens
Zvi Leve
Peter McQueen
Jeff Mapes
Serge Mongeau
Guy Montpetit
Christian Morissette
David Murray
Norman Nawrocki
Alex Norris
Nick Peck
Michel Prescott
Jean-François Pronovost
Terrence Regan
Carlton Reid
Dimitri Roussopoulos
Sheindl Rothman
Vicki Schmolka
Robert Silverman
Godfrey Stephens
Stollman Steven
Armand Vaillancourt
Scott Weinstein
Abraham Weizfeld
Richard Wutzke

Duo
A New Imprint Dedicated to Literary Works and Ideas

Duo presents works of fiction and non-fiction, in French and in English, as well as in Indigenous languages, from established writers and emerging talents. It is one of the imprints of Les Presses de l'Université d'Ottawa / University of Ottawa Press (PUO-UOP).

Other Literary Titles Published by the University of Ottawa Press

Works of Fiction

Abla Farhoud, *Happiness Has a Slippery Tail*, translated from French by Judith Weisz Woodsworth, 2025.

Jean-Louis Grosmaire, *Mouvance et espérance*, 2025.

Yolande Bastarache, *Détresse et nostalgie*, 2024.

Robert Major, *Éloge de la procrastination et autres facéties*, 2022.

Michel Picard, *Kilis*, 2021.

Jean-Louis Grosmaire, *Acadissima*, 2021. Prix France-Acadie.

Yolande Bastarache, *Mon village, la côte*, 2021.

Maurice Henrie, *Odette*, 2020.

Michel Picard, *Memoriam*, 2020.

Camilla Grudova, *L'alphabet des poupées*, translated from English by Véronique Lessard et Marc Charron, 2020.

Maurice Henrie, *La maison aux lilas*, 2019.

Andrew F. Sullivan, *Tout vient à mourir*, translated from English by Marc-André Clément, 2017.

Literary Non-fiction

Pierre Calvé, *Le français grandeur nature : portrait et défense d'une langue vivante*, 2025.

Nicole V. Champeau, *Pointe Maligne, retrouvée par les textes : présence française dans le Haut Saint-Laurent* (tome II), 2023.

Robert Major, *Identité, appartenances : un parcours franco-ontarien*, 2023.

Maurice Henrie, *La tête haute*. 2022. Prix du livre d'Ottawa.

Robert Major, *Témiscamingue : châtiments, miracles, et autres propos du concierge de l'évêché*, 2021.

Robert Major, *Carnets du rang 5 : fragments d'un enracinement, fragments d'un parcours*, 2021.

Robert Major, *Mes conversations avec Claude*, 2019.

Biographies and Memoirs

Monique Aubry-Frize, *Une femme en ingénierie : mémoires d'une pionnière*, translated from English by Suzanne Aubry, 2024.

Roy MacGregor, *L'étoile du nord : le mystère éternel de Tom Thomson et de la femme qui l'aimait*, translated from English by Benoit Léger, 2023.

Fred Langan, *Elle a osé réussir : biographie de l'honorable Marie-P. Charette-Poulin / She Dared to Succeed: A Biography of the Honourable Marie-P. Charette-Poulin*, 2023.

Michel Bastarache and Antoine Trépanier, *What I Wish I Had Told My Children*, translated from French by Julie Da Silva, 2023.

Stéphane Desjardins, *La famille Fermanian : l'histoire du cinéma Pine de Sainte-Adèle*, 2022.

Michel Bastarache and Antoine Trépanier, *Michel Bastarache : ce que je voudrais dire à mes enfants*, 2019.

Discover Duo and all works of fiction and literary non-fiction here:
www.editionsduo.ca

For a complete list of titles published by the University Ottawa Press, please visit:
www.Press.uOttawa.ca

www.ingramcontent.com/pod-product-compliance
Lightning Source LLC
Chambersburg PA
CBHW051050230426
43666CB00012B/2632